MW00903691

a Primer for

ASCENSION

Lessons Learned on the
Path of Enlightenment

Pierre Richard Dubois

———

A Primer for Ascension

www.iammonad.com

———

ISBN-13: 978-1491027288
ISBN-10: 1491027282

Printed in the USA

Table of Contents

Prologue

The world is changing rapidly. In order for humanity to survive, we have to adapt to a new set of circumstances: melting polar ice caps; frequent earthquakes causing catastrophic tsunamis; extreme weather patterns like typhoons, cyclones, hurricanes, and frankenstorms. One can debate whether cyclical global warming is the cause or whether humanity is responsible for these atmospheric changes. What is irrefutable is that we have to adapt to survive. The apathy and laissez-faire attitude formerly displayed by world leaders is now changing into one of concern. It is as if the planet and the environment in which we exist are shifting into a different gear, requiring us to evolve, grow, and mature at an accelerated pace, whether we want it or not. At the rate that things are going, maintaining the status quo is suicidal. We have to acclimate ourselves to live by different principles and adopt new, sustainable values that acknowledge the interdependence of all things. We have to be educated about the interconnection that exists between everything. We have to broaden our understanding and widen our perspective individually and collectively, if we are to continue living.

The ancients predicted that in our lifetime, the planet would be transitioning into an evolution of human consciousness heralding the beginning of a golden age. The great shift is upon us. The hour is late and the time for subtlety is over. The examination of the sustainability of all aspects of our existence on this blue world and the application of the needed corrections will advance our evolution into a higher state of awareness. What is this highest form of human existence? It is known as self-realization, individuation, ascension, or enlightenment. What you call it is not important. It is simply a state of higher awareness that men and women before us achieved after years of self-development, effort, practice, and the following of a spiritual practice, leading them into a blessed field were the perception of pain and suffering ended. Moreover in that expanded state, they experienced the interconnectedness of all, which brought with it profound wisdom and understanding, insightful leadership, and governance.

Ascension is mastery of the physical, emotional, mental, and spiritual bodies. There are many books written on the topic, and the majority of them focus on the mastery of the spiritual or energy body, which is 25% of the total process. Following an ascension process without the mastery of the physical, emotional, and mental bodies will stunt your growth and lead you into a path that is filled with dangerous turns and turmoil. In this volume, I will bring into focus the issues facing the seeker relating to the mastery of the physical, emotional, and mental bodies. I will outline this process while sighting personal examples to illustrate the growth of wisdom, maturity, and the expansion of consciousness in a manner that is relatable.

Simply reading this book will not cause you to ascend, for ascension is not a mental or intellectual phenomenon; rather it is a workship that is attained by the transmutation and transformation of your daily life. If you are trying to ascend and your personal life is in chaos, you are not integrating what you are learning. The abstract, intellectual, and arcane knowledge has to be demonstrated in your daily living by the mastery and control of all aspects of your life. Knowledge without application is perverse. This is where the rubber meets the road—anything short of that is untrue and a waste of time.

The topics herein will bring into focus the achievements, pitfalls, landmarks, and signposts that you need to watch for, but that other teachers are not talking about. All the subtleties and nuances will be discussed with complete candor and honesty. My teacher Dr. Joshua David Stone told me long ago: "Pierre, you can only keep what you willing to give away." It is the most profound thing I have ever heard to date. Since I want to keep everything, I will tell you everything. I will teach you how to stand shoulder to shoulder with me, and if in the process you ascend, then God wins. This is the age when men and women become Gods and Goddesses.

This book is dedicated to my students, who are my greatest teachers. Without my interpersonal exchanges with them and my continual desire to mentor them into future planetary leaders, I would not be the being that I am today. This book is written for them as an act of love, guidance, and as a spiritual sieve for all.

Pierre Richard Dubois

Chapter One

Prelude to Ascension

*One does not become enlightened by imagining figures of light,
but by making the darkness conscious.*

– Carl Jung

W e are living in an extraordinary time. At no other moment in history have there been such public acceptance, openness, and tolerance of personal growth, alternative spiritual practices, and consciousness mechanics. A quick look at your local bookstore, or a search on Google or Amazon, will reveal how popular these topics are and how many teachers and authors have penned books and manuals on the topics. This was not always the case. In our recent history, these topics were taboo and punishable by death. So many of our predecessors were decapitated, quartered, tarred, feathered, hung, or burned for holding what were considered heretical or alternative views and beliefs from the predominant religious institutions. We take for granted that we can talk to our friends about our precognitive dreams or our intuitive, psychic, or clairsentient abilities. Any open mention of these abilities would have caused someone to call you a witch, and that is all that it would have taken for a religious authority to descend on you. During those times, seekers of higher truth were forced underground. The teachings were given to few who not only risked their lives to get the information, but received it through secret orders with special initiations. Oaths and promises had to be made so that the safety of the whole group and, more importantly, the succession of the teachings would be assured. This is not to say that the entire planet is open to these alternative concepts today. There are plenty of communities, cities, states, and countries where narrow-mindedness, intolerance, and bigotries are law. How many book burnings have you witnessed in the news lately? But for most of us in the West, we have arrived at a time of great acceptance and tolerance. Hurray for openness and disclosure.

However, a closer look at books written on the topic of ascension and enlightenment mechanics will reveal that not all of them are created equal. Some stand out as great works of profound insight, intuitive clarity, and true wisdom while the majority are just mediocre works that muddle the topic and confuse the seeker. Just because I speak French does not qualify me to teach French. Moreover, many of these authors may be great psychics and channels and may even channel entities that speak about the ascension process, but these facts do not qualify them to know what ascension is or how to teach it. These authors may mean well, but the process and mechanics that they are teaching are often more complicated than a cosmic game of twisters. You have to fast, meditate, receive light-code activations, reactivate your 48 strands of DNA, clear yourself, increase your energy body, connect to your power animal, etc.

What is Ascension?

I was talking to a friend about a popular ascension mechanism, and she remarked: "This is too complicated to be true. The Universe is simple and elegant. That level of complication was made by man." The truth is that ascension is not a climb, an arduous task, or an effort. It is a letting go and a surrendering. It is the letting go of all desire to control or to be God's assistant. It is the realization that everything that you need is already here if you let go and allow the Universal Light substance that permeates the entire Universe to wash over you. This is a natural process to which humanity is inching closer and closer. Every time you listen to your higher self and do what is good and selfless, you move closer to it. Every time you share and give to others the blessings that you have, you move a notch closer. Every time you allow your consciousness to expand, by going outside of your comfort zone, you get nearer to it. Given enough time, all seven billion people on the planet would eventually get there. It is the next step on the evolutionary ladder—a progression in which we as a species have evolved from Homo habilis to Homo erectus and now from Homo erectus into Homo luminous beings.

Evolution of Self-Awareness

If it is a natural process, then why not let humanity evolve at its own pace? We have nothing to worry about. All the ascension mechanics and teachings are not needed. That line of thinking would be valid if time and the choices that we as a species have made were on our side. In 2009 at a Wesak celebration in Hancock, NY, I channeled Gaia and she said something that shocked me: "You are not trying to save me. It is you as a species that is going extinct. Gaia will live. By the choices that you have made, you are in the process of making the planet hostile to your own survival. If you cease to exist, Gaia will continue to be. And after several million years, life will be regenerated, but you will not be here. For that not to happen, you need to radically change your priorities and make different choices."

This startling revelation reminded me that the planet is alive and evolving according to its own schedule. It is the Gaia principle: the fact that every eco system is intricately linked and that the flutter of a butterfly on one side of the planet can cause a hurricane on the opposite side. This interconnectedness is a form of awareness and intelligence that is unlike ours, and it creates a super-sentient form of existence. By extension, the sun and planets of our solar system must exist in a similar interconnected relationship to the other planets within our solar system, and therefore they must be sentient. Moreover, the Milky Way Galaxy also must have a superconsciousness that regulates the interconnectedness of the more than 200 billion solar systems that are in it. Therefore it must be sentient, too.

These realizations support the Mayan Elders' prediction of an imminent alignment of the earth with the sun and the galactic core, which will herald a radical shift in consciousness. The superconsciousness that is Gaia is evolving within the superconsciousness that is the solar system, and both of them are evolving within the giant collective consciousness that is the Milky Way Galaxy. They are all scheduled to align, evolve, and shift dimensions and awareness. If one species is not ready, out of the millions of species that exist on earth, it is not going to make a major difference or hold back the evolutionary time frame. In other words, the earth is evolving with or without us. But what will happen to humanity if we are not ready? There are numerous theories. Here is the most prevalent belief: those inhabitants of the planet who are not evolving in consciousness will be left in a 3-D reality while the rest of the earth and those humans who are ready will move into the fourth or even fifth dimensions. That sounds fair and great. But here's the question that no one is asking: to those humans moving up the evolutionary ladder, what would that look like to them. Would they wake up one morning and find that half of the population of the earth is not here? Right now, I do not know with certainty the answers to this question.

The Rescue Plan

What is clear is that if we want to help humanity, avoid this potential catastrophe, and redeem this world, something radical has to take place. As it turns out, the Galactic Regent Council, which is the giant collective that oversees the evolution and governance of the Milky Way Galaxy, foresaw this predicament. As a result, they asked long ago for volunteers. Galactic, angelic, elohim, and starseed beings were asked to volunteer for a rescue mission—to shed their powers, descend, and incarnate in human form, sharing the DNA makeup of the rest of humanity. This plan asks for 144,000-plus beings to descend and incarnate as human beings. As Lord Melchizedek said in a channeled message, "And there will be 144,000 elected ones who will become the gates and pillars for the New Jerusalem." At the appointed time, they are to become the critical mass who would ascend and broadcast the ascension frequencies through their DNA to the rest of the planet. Since they would become the critical mass, the "100th-monkey" effect would take place, and 7 billion people would ascend by osmosis. Many Holy Scriptures and prophecies, including the Bible, talk about the 144,000 who would be marked by a special seal on their forehead and play a critical role in the establishment of the New Jerusalem or future earth. In Revelation, chapters 7 and 14, we learn that there would be 12,000 from each of the 12 tribes of Israel, which can be interpreted as a code name for the 12 original root species and races created in the 15th dimension in the Lyra Galaxy—the cradle of all life in the Universe. So, 12,000 volunteers from each of those 12 starseed races will compose this collective.

Here is how this plan will work. The superconsciousness that is the earth, Gaia, has 156 chakra points in a similar manner that humans have chakras. Robert Coon in his extraordinary book *Earth Chakras* reveals the geometric centers and the theme for each of the earth chakras. For the ease of explaining this, let us consider the earth chakra in my grid in the New York area, whose center is in Niagara Falls. For the plan to work, at each earth chakra location, a minimum of 12 volunteers need to stand up in spiritual rectitude to initiate a spin that will bore an opening or gate into the heavens. They will become the gates and pillars for their circle of influence. Suppose that the 12 for the New York area stand up and the opening is created. Our local earth chakra will expand to a radius of 777 miles, redeeming every life-form in that radius. Suppose now that the 12 volunteers north of us in Canada do the same. The earth chakra there will expand 777 miles as well, with the two chakra radiuses overlapping each other, edge to center. If the same happens to the south, east, and west, all the radiuses will overlap each other, edge to center. This process is to happen at 156 locations around the earth, and when this occurs, the entire planet will become the living "flower of life." Through these 156 tunnels and open gates, a call will be sent to the heavens, asking for the activation of the redemption plan of the earth. Light from Source will cascade and descend through these open gates and plunge into the core of the planet; the prana seed of the planet will absorb the light, re-ignite, and explode outward; and the fifth dimension will be here.

Sharing the details and particulars about how to do this is one of my life purposes. I train potential volunteers on how to stand in rectitude in their specific grid locations around the world. But truth be said, this ideal model is not the reality on the ground. Instead, the more accurate scenario would be that vast distances would separate the rescued areas as the 12 stand in disconnected locations, like 12 in New York, 12 in South America, 12 in Indonesia, etc. Discrete area by discrete area will be rescued, and for a while, the planet will be like Swiss cheese with pockets of redeemed zones while others will still be struggling behind.

The Descent of the Rescuers

These volunteers play a critical role in this rescue plan. We have already established above that they were exhaulted spiritual, angelic and starseed beings who are now on earth for probably the first time. For this collective, the descent into a physical vessel and body requires great sacrifices. It is the constriction and entombment into a physical embodiment of a Being of Light that is by nature vast and infinite. All the powers, abilities, knowledge, wisdom, and multi-dimensionality must be dropped and let go. And so these volunteers fragment, shed, and hide parts of themselves in things—in crystals, objects, trees, temples, locations around the planet, in other dimensions, and even inside other human beings who agreed to serve as a kind of safe haven for them. After incarnation and in due time, they will pilgrimage back to these places or people and gather the hidden fragments back in order to reassemble themselves. At every stage of the descent and fragmentation, they are losing cohesiveness, memories, and integrity of their former estate. They incarnate as humans with all the failings and vulnerabilities of humanity, but with some key differences. They know within their core that they are strangers on earth and that they came here to rescue this world.

What that rescue looks like and how to do it is elusive, but the inner knowing is ever present with them. At a pre-appointed time, they will begin to feel compelled to journey to specific locations and retrieve the hidden fragments. One can spot them in a crowd easily. They are the ones who look lost and ill at ease because this is probably their first or second incarnation on earth. They are trying to figure out how and why earthlings behave in such a strange manner, for, from their memories or inner knowings, things are not fragmented. It is not easy for them to come from such elevated stock and witness in physical embodiment the chaos and level of fragmentation that humanity has chosen to experience. This often creates great emotional pain and suffering for them. To the rest of humanity, they appear to be over sensitive and emotional or even having a depressive disposition. But all of it comes from an inner knowing that what humanity thinks is normal is actually abnormal to the way the Universe operates.

Since all sentient life-forms in the Universe have free choice, these beings took oaths and made promises to take part in this rescue. Yet while in embodiment, they can choose to do something else. Everyone has the right to change their mind and renegotiate contracts and agreements. If this were to happen, the number of volunteers would diminish below the threshold of 144, 000, the exact number needed for the plan to work. Therefore, a number far greater than 144,000 volunteered in order to give the plan a fighting chance, as was understood and foreseen by the Galactic Regent Council. In my training of the 144,000, I have seen beings, recognized by me as part of this collective, begin the training and walk away. Without judgment, I wished them luck and I continued to radiate the necessary frequencies to attract other volunteers.

Accelerated Ascension Explained

Before going on a trip, you would try to find a map to plan your itinerary and figure out your route. If I were to go on a drive, I would use Google Maps to find the destination or input the address in a GPS system. If we are embarking on an accelerated training of the 144,000-member collective for the ascension process, what does accelerated ascension look like and how do we get there?

Accelerated ascension is about mastery. It is the mastery of the physical, emotional, mental, and spiritual bodies.

— **Physical mastery** is control and grounding into the physical reality. Far too many lightworkers are ungrounded and have survival and grounding issues. They are so focused on light, spiritual vision, and inspiration that they are not connected to the needs of the body. You should be able to pay your bills and meet your financial obligations. Furthermore, you have to take care of your vessel. Your body is the temple that your soul animates. Make sure that the temple is healthy and beautiful. Are you eating a healthy diet? Are you exercising? Are you taking all the needed vitamins? Additionally, any diseases and health conditions with which you are saddled are nothing more than disconnections from Light. Restore the connection to Source and the conditions disappear. Finally, our DNA was manipulated and altered in a time so distant that none of us remember that we have been robbed, violated, and dumbed down. In our original estate, we had 12 stands of DNA. Now we stand with 2 physical strands and 10 shadow strands. The restoration and reconstruction of our DNA is an essential key to the process and is such a vast topic that I am writing a separate book about it. Suffice it to say that in 2008, I was able to bring to the planet a DNA reconstruction process that will regrow all 12 stands of DNA.

— **Emotional mastery** is the control of the emotional or desire body. The vast majority of humans live in their emotional bodies. To those going through an emotional reaction, what they feel is real. Yet emotions are nothing more than the release of hormones from the hypothalamus into the blood stream, causing your entire cellular structure to change and alter, causing you to feel and experience the world via the specific mood of this chemical flow. It is nothing more than a self-released biochemical flow that alters your mood and colors your experience.

As powerful, convincing, and riveting as our emotions are, they are not actuality. They are holograms that interpret your experience. They simply give value, character, and color and qualify how we internalize what is happening around us. Here is the amazing thing: these values, colors, and qualifiers are perceived and not real. One can change the values and colors if one alters one's reaction to the event. As long as we allow the status quo to continue, we are on autopilot. Those qualifiers, interpretations, and colors are purely subjective and can be completely controlled to allow us to experience life without being automatically triggered. It is the mastery and reprogramming of the negative ego and contents of the subconscious mind that will lead you to this blessed field.

Few schools teach this because the teachers themselves are completely reactive. This is however where the rubber meets the road. Doing this work will accelerate your ascension process faster than anything I know, but few attempt it, for it is unsexy, unglamorous, and painful. Nothing is more frightening than the darkness that lurks within. It means that you have to stop blaming the world and take responsibility for everything that happens to you. Take a look at your life. Any lack that you are experiencing is your creation. It is the reprogramming and ascension of the shadow of your subconscious mind into the Light that will catapult the seeker forward. This is the "work" to which all ascended masters often refer. It is far easier to focus on the glamour, energy, and lightwork of the ascension process, than to transmute the lead of our reactive system into the gold of a proactive consciousness. In truth, energy work is only a small percentage of the totality of the process.

— **Mental mastery** is the control of the mind. Thoughts are things and are the creators of reality. Thoughts create the structure that energy and reality follow. If your emotional body is causing you to feel victimized, fearful, and fragmented, change your thoughts and your emotional body will follow. Simple enough, but some may argue: "I've tried that and it doesn't seem to work for me." The flaw in this statement is the strength of your intention. The average person on earth intends and un-intends three to five times per minute. This is due to the fact that most people have many contradictory programs and voices in the subconscious mind, telling them the opposite of what they are trying to alter and change. Reprogram the multitude of negative programs that exist in the subconscious mind by bringing them into an ascended place, and nothing will fight and contradict the intention that you put forth. The subconscious mind was created for the purpose of helping us create and manifest whatever intentions we hold. If you have a fragmented consciousness and psyche with various programs each having different intentions and purposes, you have a formula for a manifestation device that will not function. Reprogram the negative aspects of your subconscious mind, and you will have reassembled your psyche; and when your thoughts command, the Universe will obey. This is simply because your subconscious mind is connected to the subconscious mind of every living thing into what Carl Jung termed "the collective unconscious." By extension, that network connects all sentient life forms in the Universe.

— **Spiritual mastery** is expansion of your God concept. You will only grow and evolve to the level of the highest God concept that you hold. In time past, man believed that forces of nature were gods. This evolved into the pantheon of gods and goddesses. Pharaoh Akhenaton was the first to propose the concept of a monotheistic god as a force that was everywhere, whose symbol was the sun. Today, many realize that when they are calling upon God, they are activating a morphogenic field that is dual and bipolar by nature. In the name of God, men have done good and bad things; thus the energy field that any God concept generates has a negative and positive aspect to it.

If you are to transcend this, you must go to Source and zero point outside of time and space where neutrality exists. This is about goal setting; the highest spiritual concept that you hold will determine where you go. Make sure that your God concept—the ascended companies that you keep or your guides—is of the highest level possible. Otherwise, you are clipping your own wings. Lowering goals to emulate and become a being with the known negative aspects of a lower spiritual level is to limit the height of your own ascension.

Initiating the Ascension Process

The ascension process cannot be initiated by reading books. It is not a mental activity or intellectual curiosity. To begin the process, one has to send a visceral and emotional call into the Heavens that you want to merge back with your highest God concept, as if you want ascension as much as you need oxygen. The Universe will orchestrate the means for it to happen. So many seekers and students spend time reading books and being intellectually stimulated by the topic, but they never send an emotional call to the higher realms. It is the difference between reading about a sport and going out and playing the sport. Many say that they want ascension, but really what they seek is the demonstration of power, psychic abilities and gifts, being loved, being important or listened to. Examine your motives. Why do you want to ascend? Please understand that ascension is a merger back with God. It is the path of return to the point from which you descended. All the other stuff is just icing on the cake. You may start on your ascension path with all kinds of motives and reasons, but as long as you are working on your negative ego, these will be transmuted into a consuming desire to blend with the essence of Divinity and to serve by showing others how to achieve your level of bliss.

Negative Ego Reprogramming

The safe way to initiate this process is to first work on all the negative ego programs that reside in the subconscious mind. Self-awareness—the "I" or the "Chooser"—must be in charge at all times of all programs that the subconscious mind is running. All internal negativity that attempts to hijack self-awareness must be reprogrammed into a positive experience. When one begins this process, it is easy to be overwhelmed by the long lists of programs and areas of the subconscious mind that need work. I remember feeling that there was not enough time in the day for me to address this effectively. I was critical of what I was doing and was feeling unworthy.

It took a year to realize that this feeling was also a negative ego program. A journey of one thousand steps starts with the first step. Do not worry about the many other negative programs that may be in your future. Do the best that you can do in the now. When you are done, move to the next issue. Many of the programs are interrelated. Some programs are subprograms of others. One by one they will be transmuted into their higher aspects. You are doing the work of a lion tamer walking into a cage filled with wild beasts; one crack of your whip will bring them to order, and at your command, they will jump through the hoop of fire. In your journey, if you happen on a school that is not teaching the mastery of the emotional body and the reprogramming of the negative ego, run! This is not a safe path.

Having done this work over a period of time, you will get to a point where a large portion of your subconscious mind will have been reorganized. This will lead you to the first step of ascension. This began for me as waves of euphoria and ecstatic bliss shooting through my head during meditation. Then, these moments of bliss began to occur during my daily activities: at the supermarket, walking down the street, at work, etc. Over a few months' time, I became aware that my energy grid was outside of my body. My field was increasing and was a distance away from me. My grid was wide and I could sense anything in that field. An additional realization came with this expansion. I knew with every fiber of my being that I could extend my peace and serenity around anyone, banishing their pain and suffering, if I had their permission. I cannot over emphasize the permission part of this statement. You are not allowed to interfere or comingle your energy with any other life-form without their permission. Everyone has free will and has the right to choose their path and destiny. With great power comes great responsibility. That powerful energy increase is the first step of ascension, and it brings with it the ability to manifest and perform what appears to the rest of humanity to be miracles. But the fact is that it is so easy, it is like blinking your eyes.

The First Step of Ascension: Power Increase

There are reasons why you have to do the negative ego work first. The increase in your energy field can be reached without the negative ego work. There are yoga, breath work, energetic me-chanics and even twilight masters that will bring you to that first level of ascension and leave you there at your peril. If your energy field increases without doing the negative ego work, the entire contents of your subconscious mind will become just as big as your field. At that point, the genies will be out of the bottle. You will have to wrestle and try to tame them in the real world. More significant is the fact that you can now manifest. Your thoughts now create. And when you are hijacked by a negative ego program, you can hurt yourself and others.

I have been on the spiritual path since I was 11 years old, and I have witnessed many who had achieved that level of energy increase without any negative ego work. These teachers and healers are always surrounded by a large crowd. The public is so gullible and is so often attracted to demonstrations of power. These healers put on a great show. They touch anyone in the crowd of devotees, and people fall to the floor. But none of that impresses me. I grew up in Haiti, and I have seen too many dark shamans who demonstrated abilities too fantastic to mention. Yet they were hurting people on a continual basis.

Many well-intended individuals, teachers, and healers get to this energy increase without malice. They simply did not know any better. What you do after you get to that crossroad will determine who you are and what path you will follow. My first approach to this energy increase was not without hiccups. Although I had diligently worked on my negative ego, there were three flaws that I had identified as negative ego programs. But I decided they were part of my character and did not want to get rid of them, for I felt that they were essential parts of me. So over the weeks that followed this energy increase, I began to notice that when these negative ego programs took over my self-awareness, their immediately manifested effects were in front of me in five to ten minutes. Since the last thing I wanted was to hurt others, I began this editing process, stalking them, and telling them every time they surfaced that they were not allowed.

What you resist persists, and I was now doing this 24 hours a day, 7 days a week, even in my sleep. The pressure became unbearable for me, and one evening, I prayed and told God that I was not ready for the gift and to take that cup away from me. In the morning, my energy grid was back to the edge of my physical body. It took me three more years of work to reprogram these three negative programs and to safely restart the energy increase again. Most teachers and healers who approach this level of energy increase without doing the negative ego work, who are packing auditoriums and lecture halls because they can demonstrate seeming miracles, will not give it up so easily even if they know they should. This is how a well-intended soul slips into grey and dark paths.

The Second Step of Ascension: Unconditional Love

The second step of ascension is a vast increase in your capacity to love and a realization that there is no separation or distance between you and any life-form. This part of the process for me was easy. My heart space expanded. When I was working in an office setting, there were days when the love that I felt was bursting out of my chest. So I would walk out of my office and hug everyone for a good two to three minutes each, pouring my love into them. I would let them know I much I loved them and how much God and Divinity adored them. This kind of action comes from a complete knowing that everyone in my increased energy grid is an aspect of me. Therefore, I should be more loving, compassionate, patient, caring, and kind to me. This is beyond empathy. However, most empaths are seeking information from others in order to gain something. It is like being a psychic spy. They gather the information and retreat back into their shell with that knowledge, which is drastically different from the expression of unconditional love. It is the knowledge that everyone around you is a cell in your body. I am not separated from them. I cannot retreat. I am them and they are me. These aspects of you may be at various levels of growth and evolution, but you love them and hold space that in time they too will get to the serenity and profound peace that you are enjoying. You may not like or approve of their behaviors, but you love them nonetheless. Everyone will eventually get it. The time frame for this to happen is not in your control.

Every sentient life-form is on its own journey, and whatever choice they make is the right choice for them to learn and evolve. All you can do is hold space, and if they come to you for coaching or counseling, you can listen in a way that is hard to describe in words. Because of your vast increase in love and compassion toward that aspect of you, you can hear and see details they may be hiding from themselves or not consciously perceive. And if you choose to share your insight, you will appear to them as having great wisdom and psychic abilities. It is not a miracle; it is simply the result of work that you have done and the demonstration of spiritual laws. In fact, anyone can get there who puts in the time and the effort to do what you did.

The Third Step of Ascension: Wisdom

The third step of ascension is the acquisition of wisdom, and wisdom is knowledge rightly used. In truth, this is something I don't know how to teach. Let me explain. Once you reach the second stage of ascension, you will have access to a vast amount of information about the individuals in your circle of influence. Not all data, truths, and information should be shared. There are sins of omission and sins of commission. For instance, what do you do if you are counseling someone and you happen to gather that they are blocking an abusive memory, and further that this memory is responsible for their current out-of-control behavior? Their psyche has blocked the memory because they are not ready to retrieve it. If you tell them about this, you will shatter them into pieces. This will earn you negative karma, and you will have to spend a lot of time trying to restore them to stability. Wisdom comes from knowing when to speak. Timing is everything. This cannot be taught for there is no protocol or set of criteria that will confirm that it is all right to tell the whole truth. You have to perceive and discern that information. What is usually helpful is for me to ask: Is this knowledge in their highest and best interest? Is this truth going to help or hurt them? Everyone is on their own journey and therefore different. The only teacher is time and experience, which are needed to develop the maturity to discern if a person or a group is ready to hear the whole true.

Sometimes in counseling, a client will ask me to tell them the whole truth, but I know that they are not ready to hear it. Instead, I will tell them a version of the information that matches their present psychic health. I have had clients and students in that exact situation to which I have revealed partial information for years, and when I get confirmation that their psyche is ready, I call them for a meeting and tell them the whole truth. I once had a young man in my classes for a few years, displaying a destructive, addictive behavior. For the time of our relationship, I tried my best on multiple occasions to give him hints and clues to the true nature of the problem. I knew he was not ready. But one day that perception changed, and I told him that we needed to talk. At the meeting, I told him the whole truth and gave him a protocol to alter the addictive behavior. Since the session was emotional, I texted him two days later to find out how he was doing. He replied that for the first time since childhood he had spent 48 hours without displaying the behavior. What happened next shocked me. Upon reading this, I began to weep uncontrollably for 10 minutes. I asked Spirit for guidance and realized that I had been waiting two lifetimes to tell him this.

William Gray in *The Ladder of Lights* states: "We should never confuse wisdom with knowledge. The essential difference is that wisdom acts rightly because it proceeds from Eternal Good alone." If you have the ultimate good of your students and clients in mind, you will know when and when not to speak. That level of maturity comes with time and experience. No one can acquire wisdom without making mistakes. The mistakes, you will have to live with. But over time, you will mature and begin to sense when the moment is appropriate for you to have a conversation with someone in your care that will reveal blind spots to them. Take care that you also present them with a means to overcome and reprogram the negative ego behavior. To point out the problem without a solution is cruel. Help them heal.

Through this entire process, you will alter and change in ways that may surprise you and those around you. As you expand your consciousness and step out of your comfort zone, you will embrace parts of yourself that were dormant and heal and transmute what were sick. The more whole you become, the more friends and family members will have a hard time relating to you. The energy of the codependent person that they knew is no longer there. You may lose friends or become distanced from them, for you no longer are vibrating at their level. Do not despair; the planet has seven billion people on it. Make new friends with people who are now at your higher frequency. Additionally, old behaviors will no longer resonate with you. I have walked down streets filled with people, where I walked numerous times in the past, but somehow it seemed foreign to me now. It was as if I were a tourist visiting a new city. This came from a consciousness that was changing so rapidly, it felt like some part of my humanity was leaving me.

Beyond Ascension

These three stages of planetary ascension involve the power increase, the expansion of the heart space, and the acquisition of wisdom. It is the burning of the three-fold flames of power, love, and wisdom in perfect harmony, which will secure you a place at the dinner table of the Ascended. Beyond planetary ascension, the initiate will have to choose among several evolutionary paths that will determine the direction of his future growth and continual ascension. Master Djwhal Khul through Alice Bailey describes some of those choices in *Initiation, Human and Solar*, but they are not the complete list by any means. More information is currently available, as humanity is now ready for more extensive paths for growth. Below is a list that I have compiled so far, but I suspect that more choices may be revealed as we collectively continue to open ourselves to more possibilities:

1.   The Path of Service:

This is a path that keeps the earthly ascended link to the spiritual hierarchy and the spiritual government of the planet. It is a pledge of service toward the evolution and group expansion of the planet under the guidance of the members of the spiritual hierarchy. It is not the most popular choice, but it is the most well-known among ascension students.

2.   The Path of Magnetism:

This path is for those who are attracted to the wielding of electrical and magnetic forces. This is the path of control of the formative intentions, structures, and energies that hold matter, density, and vibration in place.

This is done by collective agreements on the astral and etheric planes that bring them into manifestation. Students with a fifth-ray Monad typically follow this path.

3.   The Path of Training for Planetary Logoi:

This path is followed by those who will eventually take up the work of the seven planetary Logoi often referred to as the Buddhas of Activities. After mastering the mysteries of the physical body, one can now become the soul or chakra of something bigger, like a planet. It is a very specialized training, and it takes a student with aptitude for sound and color vibration to be selected for this training. The seven Logoi of this planet have a group of assistants whom they are training for this work.

4.   The Path of Sirius:

Very little is known about this path except that the bulk of humanity goes through this way. It is through the mystery of our relationship with the seven stars of the Pleiades that evolution of our planet and our solar system is hidden. It is a major ascension gate for earthlings.

5.   The Ray Path:

This path is taken by the man to whom the law of vibration is of profound importance. This path involves very complex mathematics and geometry that cannot be understood by the 3-D brain. One evolves along the line of the ray, and this growth takes one to all kingdoms, intricacies, and aspects of that ray. This journey continues all over the solar system and into the sun and eventually into the cosmic root of the rays.

6.   The Path of our Logos:

From a cosmic level, the Universal Logos, Lord Melchizedek, is developing his inner vision, and supporting this effort are very high initiates who help focus the third eye of the cosmos. This path is for certain masters who, here and there, have qualified to replace the original members of this group, who in turn have decided to return into Source as we revolve around the cosmic center. This is a path not often navigated.

7.   The Path of Absolute Son-ship:

This is a path for disciples who are called "the sons of the Master." It is a path for working out the karma of our solar system under the guidance of our solar Logos and the Logos above them as well as through the Sons of the Logos, who are special initiates who know their wishes, desires, and wants.

8.   The Path of the Bodhisattva:

This is the path of total compassion as the enlightened being chooses to remain behind to shepherd every soul on the planet who is still in bondage. It takes a Being of great sensitivity and strength to make this sacrifice, for the pull to move into higher levels of ascension is great. Choosing to remain behind implies that one understands that every soul on the planet is a cell in one body. If one cell ascends and the others do not, the body is not whole.

9.   The Path of Rehabilitation:

This is a special class of trained, dimensional Elohim and Angelic Beings, who rehabilitate the fallen beings who are ready to rejoin the original theme and purpose of creation. The focus of their work is to teach and remind these fallen ones how to digest and take Light directly from Source, rather than parasitically violating other life-forms. They select certain ascended beings as apprentices and assistants and teach them how to do the same.

10.   The Path of the Saviors:

Duality is a pendulum swing that creates perpetual motion. This fluctuation generates imbalances that can bring planets, worlds, and solar systems into perilous conditions that are out of alignment with the divine plan and the evolution of the Universe. In order to restore the divine purpose, a collective of Beings is dedicated to rescuing worlds. They take in apprentices and show them how to help in this noble purpose. These rescues are not accomplished by the effort of one savior, but with the teamwork of an entire collective.

11.   The Path of Understanding:

The Universe, as a sentient Being, is trying to evolve and learn, and this group of Ascended Ones is dedicated to the expansion of knowledge and understanding. Given free will and the various permutations of factors that free choice can create, there is an endless sea of possibilities from which one can learn. This collective seeks and holds the lessons, knowledge, and understanding that these permutations yield.

12.   The Path of Neutrality:

It is a road that is navigated by Beings who choose to hold the energy of neutral space and zero point that exists outside of time and space. These beings are by proxy the representatives of Source in dimensional reality. They carry with them the seed to resolve all imbalanced forces, resulting in the equilibrium of all things. The scalar inverts are allowed to be brought together and cancel each other out in a safe and non-explosive manner. These Beings dissolve conflicts by creating a space that eliminates polarity and duality and supports authenticity.

Initiating the Process

First, you have to send a call to the heavens that you desire to merge back with God more than anything else in the world. You can't fake this, for it is the purity of this desire that will initiate the ascension process and ignite the ascension flame, which will align everything around you to facilitate this process. The "how-tos" are written and coded in your DNA. A pure desire puts the key in the ignition. I cannot do this for you. This is your responsibility.

The safe way to proceed from there is to work on reprogramming the negative ego. This can appear to be a minefield that few may want to approach. Although we are all unique, having specific negative ego issues related to our interaction with our environment and our past life, there are however some basic and core key issues that, if addressed, will lead you into the first stage of ascension. For the remainder of this primer, I will explore these topics from the point of view of someone who has walked the path and traversed that territory. As much as possible, I will illustrate with personal examples. I will give you clues and tools to reprogram these issues. Let us start at the beginning: our descent into matter.

Chapter 2

The Nature of the
Negative Ego

It is better to travel well than to arrive.

– Lord Buddha

According to the Kabbalah, in the beginning there existed only Light, which was imbued with an infinite "Desire to Give." It was everywhere, and nothing existed outside of it. That Desire to Give did not have the ability to be reflected back to itself, for nothing else was present to acknowledge its existence. To become self-aware, it emptied a space from itself and manifested an infinite "Desire to Receive." And for a while, the Desire to Give and the Desire to Receive blended in a perfect spiritual marriage, where every need of the Desire to Receive was instantaneously fulfilled by the Desire to Give.

The Bread of Shame

For reasons that can only be understood as an evolution of unity into duality, over time the Desire to Receive evolved a desire to give but could not fulfill that want, for the Desire to Give, which was the only other being in existence, was not equipped to receive. On the other hand, the Desire to Give wanted nothing more than to satisfy all the needs of the Desire to Receive, but on this one wish, it could not, for the Giver was not equipped to receive. This evolution of wanting to give something back to the "hand that feeds you" is a need or program that the Kabbalists call: "the bread of shame." Let me explain by an example: When babies are born, every few hours they cry and want to be fed or comforted by the caregiver's hands. But at some point, when they begin to eat solid food, they refuse to be fed and want to feed themselves, even if it means putting food all over their face and clothes.

This illustrates a cornerstone program that humanity shares: the need to earn what is given to us. This unfulfilled need of the Desire to Receive became a real dilemma, causing a spiritual crisis to ensue, and the Receiver made a decision that explains our raison d-être. The Desire to Receive, like a child saying "no" to the hands of the caregiver trying to feed him, refused the Light.

This was an unprecedented act, which caused the Desire to Receive that was infinite to now shrink to the size of the head of a pencil. And for the first time, the Desire to Receive experienced edgings and boundaries, a specific physical limit to where it began and ended. This created separation and fragmentation from the Desire to Give and was the first expression of will that the "id" or precursor to the "ego" ever made.

The Creation of Our Universe

The emptiness that followed was too great, and the Desire to Receive called back the Desire to Give. The Desire to Give knew, given the current situation, that returning everything back to the way it was would not solve or remove the bread of shame program. So it devised a means for this to happen. As soon as the Light of the Giver touched the Desire to Receive, there was a giant spiritual detonation and explosion that emanated from the Receiver, which was a point as small as the head of a pencil. The Desire to Receive fragmented and exploded into multiplicity, with time, space, heat, subatomic particles, cosmic radiation, and gases all expelling at incomprehensible speeds. These were the building blocks for the creation of our Universe, which, once cooled down, precipitated life that eventually incarnated as humanity. The Light arranged an arena or matrix to help fulfill that basic program or need–the removal of the bread of shame–by giving the Receiver the opportunity to give and receive between fragments of itself, thus earning and accepting back the Light of Giver.

For this to work, it had to be a real effort on the part of the Receiver. It had to be a true challenge and a difficult thing for the Receiver to overcome. For this reason, the Giver manifested a resisting force designed to test the Receiver and help it remove the bread of shame program. In the Kabbalah, the code name for this force is satan *(pronounced sa-'tan)*.

In a nutshell, this is what occurred and how our Universe and everything in it came to be. But in this birthing process, what may seem like a few steps or moves holds a treasure trove of understanding and wisdom. Let us zoom in and focus on the details. The refusal of the Light by the Desire to Receive and the contraction that followed was the first act of free will. It created fragmentation and separation, and for the first time, there were boundaries and edgings. What was everywhere was now as small as a pencil head, limited by dimensions. Space, although minute and infinitesimally small, was coming into play. This pencil-head point had incomprehensible mass, pressure, density, and more importantly, self-awareness. This self-awareness was the first-recorded expression of the ego or the I, the Chooser, realizing itself and its boundaries, with the awareness that who and what it was ended at the edges of the diameter of the pencil head. The Receiver realized that it was separated from the infinite and boundless expanse of the Giver, so much so that the emptiness was excruciatingly painful, and it called out to the Giver and said: "Please come back. I need you. I made a mistake." But the Giver knew that even if it blended back with the Receiver, it would not solve anything. The original lack that created this crisis would still be present. It could fulfill all the desires of the Receiver except for the removal of the bread of shame program, for it was not equipped to receive. In its infinite wisdom, it devised a plan to fragment the Receiver into multiplicity and placed it into an arena, hologram, and matrix comprised of time, space, and dimensional existence so that fragmented self-awareness would learn to give and receive from itself, and more importantly, remove the bread of shame program in the process.

First Manifestation of the Ego

Additionally, the contraction of the Receiver created not only self-awareness, but a curious effect called the ego, which is a realization of separation. And the two are mutually inclusive; without the ego there is no self-awareness and vice versa. This fact cannot be overly emphasized. There are many who teach ascension mechanisms who are trying to eliminate the ego. It cannot be done, for self-awareness would end. It is important to note that as one moves to higher and higher levels of ascension, self-awareness leads into group awareness, the realization that there is no separation. Ego is then replaced by group consciousness. Furthermore, the moment the fragmentation of the Receiver occurred, it brought into existence duality and its by-products. Whenever unity fragments in two, opposite forces are created. Light and dark, day and night, positive and negative, and good and bad are but a few examples. As one descends the dimensional scale from unity to duality and into multiplicity, the scalar invert or opposite of everything is manifested to balance both sides of the equation. But polarities are always separated by space, for if they were brought together, they would short-circuit and annihilate each other. Therefore, polarity and multiplicity can only exist in dimensional space.

Negative Ego in Dimensional Existence

This descent from zero point into infinite divisions of singularity is the de-volution and creation of all things; but it also holds the path of evolution and ascension, for it is a two-way street. It illustrates the in- and out-breath of Brahma. In the beginning God exhaled, and in the end, it will inhale. This descent fragmented the ego, further separating it into opposites. The positive aspect is the sense that "I am" and am therefore different and separated from everyone else around me. While the negative aspect is the illusion that not only "I am," but since I appear to be separated from everyone, I will serve my personal agenda and move against everyone and everything else that is around me so that I flourish and survive. Since the Universe is also evolving and trying to realize itself, the negative ego or bread of shame program permeates everything and exists in all dimensions of reality. It is the MS DOS or basic operating system for everything that exists. Even the Ascended Beings in all dimensions of space have an aspect of negative ego that they must bring into alignment with Divine purpose. All Ascended Beings in the planetary spiritual hierarchy have negative ego issues with which they are dealing. They simply are better at it than we are. After all, this is what mastery is all about. They are on top of it 24 hours a day, seven days a week.

Furthermore, a means to remove the bread of shame was created. The Giver manifested a program or energy system that resists and blocks our acceptance and realization of the blessings of the Light from the Giver, accentuating the separation and fragmentation. In the Kabbalah, its code name is satan *(pronounced sa-'tan)*. Not the being with the red tail and pitchfork, but a force created by an energy system to make it difficult for us to connect back to the Light. It is not an internal component, but an external force that creates real challenges that we have to overcome to earn back the Light and thus remove the bread of shame. If the negative ego is the motor, this force is the fuel. It powers the negative ego system, thus making it even more difficult for us to realize that separation is an illusion. This energy can be summarized by one word: fear.

Fear as Our Teacher

As Receivers, all the blessings of Heaven are ours. The Light of the Giver, Aur, is 80% of the contents of the Universe. We are swimming in it. Every wish that we have should be fulfilled instantaneously by the Giver, but the bread of shame is stopping our acceptance of this, and the resisting force is giving us an opportunity to work through the shame and realize the blessings of the Light. It is a real test by an evolving intelligence that makes it almost impossible for us to earn the Light. That effort could manifest as years of perceived pain and suffering, a physical handicap, a pilgrimage, years of spiritual practice, an ascension plan, or overcoming karmic life challenges. Whatever form it takes once we overcome it, our vessel expands and we allow in the blessings of the Light. Thus, as human beings, we find ourselves to be players in a drama, trying to remove fear programming from our negative ego so that we can earn back the Light. In the end, the fear is giving us an opportunity to expand our vessel and merge back with the Light and is therefore our greatest teacher.

Three Aspects of the Mind

Understand, it is not the ego that we are trying to reprogram. It is the negative aspect of it, fueled by the energy of fear and separation, which we are trying to reorganize into ascended programs, patterns, and behaviors. The positive aspect of the ego, we keep as is. It should be noted that we also have three aspects of the mind that work together in a dynamic way to help us to that end:

The superconscious mind is the aspect of our mind that connects us to God, Spirit, our higher self, our Mighty I am Presence, the Angels, and the Masters. It is where intuition and guidance drops in from Spirit.

The conscious mind is where self-realization exists. It is the I, the Chooser, the conscious being, and the seat of self-awareness. And finally, there is the subconscious mind, which is a vast and intelligent machine that was created to do only one thing: manifest. The subconscious mind operates like a computer. It doesn't have morality and doesn't understand right from wrong. Just as you can Google how to solve global warming and get thousands of returns, you can also search how to create a car bomb and get an equal number of results.

The subconscious mind manifests any program that is in it—good or bad. It has no preference or understanding of moral value of the content. It simply manifests and loops whatever program is running to make sure that the purpose of the program is fulfilled. Furthermore, the subconscious mind is relentless in its ability to repeat and loop contents. It is responsible for the body's autonomous functions, such as breathing, cell reproduction, and the growth of our skin and hair. If most of us had to think about these functions, we would forget. But the subconscious mind does this 24 hours a day, seven days a week, even while we sleep, and it will use that same drive and tenacity to manifest any content. Finally, my subconscious mind and that of everyone on the planet—and for that matter, in the Universe—are connected by a vast network coined by Carl Jung, the Swiss psychoanalyst, as the collective unconscious. Remember, separation is an illusion. Now because of this, I can gather and share information and data to and from anyone on the planet and the Universe. Thus all psychic or extrasensory phenomena as well as all creative impulses are funneled through the subconscious mind.

Ideally, we should receive inspiration from the superconscious mind. Then, the conscious mind, the ego, the I, the Chooser would assimilate the intuitive content and decide on its merit, and if it warrants it, the ego would command the subconscious mind to manifest it. For the vast majority of individuals living on the planet, this is not what happens. Instead of the subconscious mind serving and supporting the ego, it rules, controls, and dominates it completely. Fueled by the illusion of fear and separation, the autonomous, fragmented psychic contents and programs buried in the subconscious mind continually loop around, hijacking self-awareness and manifesting reactive and preprogrammed behavior. In this case, there is no expression of free will or, much less, of self-mastery, only externalization of the programmed reactive behavior. How many times do we hear people speaking after the fact about their behavior, saying: "I don't know what came over me"? What actually came over you is that self-awareness was hijacked, and you went on autopilot. This hijacking is not a single event, but continual and repeated assaults that will not stop until the program is resolved or brought into equilibrium.

All unbalanced forces in the Universe will eventually be brought into balance and equilibrium, which is the in-breath of Brahma. Yet what we have examined so far is the reactive system of one program thrown in with multiple programs and patterns of behavior that exist in the subconscious mind. You can get a clear picture of the subconscious chaos that influences the average human being. It is a wonder that we are able to achieve a semblance of normalcy.

The Inception of the Subconscious Mind

How did the subconscious programs get created in the first place? For the answer, we have to look at early childhood development. Although most of us have genetic predispositions and characteristics that are innate in us, the bulk of our reactive system gets created when we are children and are most open and vulnerable. A child's will, personal power, and volition is weak and underdeveloped, and given the right conditions, it can be influenced. Children get domesticated by the caregivers as to the appropriate behavior needed for survival and socialization. The caregiver means no harm and may think that he/she is parenting appropriately but may instead be passing on inherited programs and belief systems that are harmful. The sins of the fathers are passed on to the sons. In infancy, our parents are like gods and goddesses to us, and we want to please them; through behavior modification and repetition, we eventually agree to the patterns and wanted behaviors. Comments like "good girl" or "don't touch that" go a long way to bend the child's weak will-center.

The Creation of Subconscious Programs

Anything with which we agree that is repeated for 21 days drops down below the mental threshold into the subconscious mind, and once there, it becomes law. It may take one day to learn something new, but it takes 21 days for it to become a habit. Remember that the first time you tried to ride a bicycle, you had to learn to pedal continuously, look in front of you and not down, and maintain equilibrium, all at the same time. It took multiple trials and repetitions, but now the moment you get on the bicycle, you no longer have to consciously think about the various steps. You just get on the bicycle, and the subconscious muscle memory takes over without any conscious awareness. After enough repetition, the behavior drops down into the subconscious mind, and a program is created that turns on automatically the moment you start riding. In the case of riding a bicycle, this is a good thing, but if this is a learned emotional reaction that disempowers you, there is a problem.

All subconscious programs are autonomous and independent fragments and behave like splinter psyches. Every time an external event or situation matches any part of the program, it will trigger it, causing it to take over conscious awareness as you go on autopilot. Furthermore, programs will loop ad infinitum, trying to capture the attention of self-awareness for manifestation; after all, this is what they were created for. Unless you do something to delete and reprogram, this content will never stop running. One has to be careful as to how the deletion and reprogramming happens. If I tell you NOT to think of a pink elephant in your mind's eye, you will see a pink elephant. What needs to happen is that the elephant gets transformed into something else, like a butterfly.

Environmental Influences on the Creation of Subconscious Programs

If this were not enough, the domestication process does not end with the family unit. The school system does its part in forcing you into agreements and instills a series of programs. Then, the church and religion do their part in dropping some good programs—but also a lot of negative fear programs—into this manifestation engine called the subconscious mind. Next, the village, the nation, mass media, and television all do their part in populating the subconscious mind with programs. At the end of this process, you have a human being who is filled with programs and reactions triggered by external events, with conscious awareness neither participating nor having any say in the matter. It makes you wonder how anyone can have an original idea or thought or in fact make a free choice. I will go so far as to say that unless you learn to reprogram your subconscious mind, you are sleepwalking and have no access to free will or choice.

Subconscious Programs Hijacking Other Subconscious Programs

When you add to this equation the fact that these multitudes of programs are fighting for the attention and control of conscious awareness, you now begin to understand how imperative the reorganization of consciousness is. Without the Chooser in charge of the show, all of the subconscious voices will assault, bombard, and hijack conscious awareness to fulfill their original purpose. Keep in mind that any program may attack other programs. One program may say, "A woman can do anything that a man can do," while a second may say, "Good girls don't have premarital sex," so that when a woman has premarital sex, she becomes ill. The two programs clash with each other and cause a short circuit. Or one program may say, "People always take advantage of me," and another may say, "I am going to make sure that if anyone hurts me, I hurt them back." So when events trigger the first program, the second one soon follows. One program may say, "I am a victim," while another may say, "I am going to defend myself against all external attacks," both of them cohabitating in the same psyche. When one is activated, the other causes a short circuit to occur, creating illness, pain, or discomfort in the body.

In the end, there is no conscious control over anything, for when the reactive system of these internal programs is triggered by external events, it can cause secondary and tertiary psychological and emotional reactions to take place. Unless you make a conscious effort to create internal and psychological peace, you will forever be tormented by a multitude of independent elements of the psyche seeking manifestation.

Taking Responsibility for the Reprogramming Work

The totality of all these negative ego programs compose the reactive system, which is activated by the fear-fueled perception of events that cause man to go on autopilot and lose control of his emotional reactions. On the surface, an individual may live a good life, having been a good spouse, parent, grandparent, neighbor, and friend, and yet add nothing to the expansion, mastery, and growth of his consciousness. One can pray and ask God, Spirit, the Masters, and the Angels for help, which they are happy to provide, but they will not reprogram the negative ego for us. This is our job. Special meditation, activation, channeling, and connection to stargates will not remove our habitual way of reacting. You may intellectually become wiser, but you will not be able to stop your reactive system unless you do the grunt work that is needed to reprogram the negative ego. There are no shortcuts and no one can bypass this.

To the average man, saying that he has a negative ego is science fiction, for he is completely and totally identified with its subconscious emotional contents. I would however propose that, at times, we have glimpses that we are reacting, but simply cannot stop ourselves. You may intellectually know the type of ideal job, companion, or living arrangement that you want, but why is it that you keep getting pulled into the same painful patterns over and over again? These are often indications that you have programs that are looping.

Take a look at your life: what items or parts of your existence are looping? If you are serious about this work, I will share with you some key tools to help you reprogram your subconscious mind. First of all, you need to understand that you are not your reactions. This is a liberating and powerful realization. Although this is hard to discern in the midst of a reaction, this is in fact the truth. Your reactive system is just a series of programs, information, or data that is impaled into the subconscious mind with the ability to cause powerful emotional states that color your perception of reality. They are inherited and preconceived and are not authentic to your nature. The I, the Chooser, and conscious being is separated from the reactive system. Secondly, it is your birthright to rule and control the entire contents of your subconscious mind. Others have done it and so can you.

Thoughts Control Everything

Here is the way our ascended elders have done it. They realized long ago that all emotions follow thoughts. Our emotions are powerful palettes of colors that can easily distract us from this basic universal truth: thought creates everything. Our emotional reactions are, in the first place, the by-products of thought systems that slipped into the subconscious mind. If you want to assume control and achieve self-mastery, resist your emotional reactions. You are not a victim; you are the Chooser of what you feel.

By changing your thought, your emotional body and reactive system will follow. Thus your autonomous reactive system and its biochemical alteration of the body will shut down. This may be the only moment in life when we actually exercise free will.

Doing this is reminiscent of becoming lucid in a dream, realizing that the force that has taken you on a ride is completely incidental and that you are in charge of your perception of reality. As powerful as the reactive emotional system may seem, changing your thought quickly creates and alters your perception, emotion, and reaction and transforms it to a different and equally powerful experience of reality. As the creator of your experiences, your emotions are the color that you apply to the canvas of life, but it is your consciously created thoughts that decide what kind of scene, subject, backdrop, and color this composition takes.

Golden Keys to Reprogram the Negative Ego

Our job is to identify and separate that which is authentically you from the subconscious programs. To do this, you have to become reflective and watch yourself. Our South American shaman brothers teach that one has to "stalk self." It is your responsibility when seeking mastery to monitor and observe self like you would an outside entity. And for that to happen, you have to be detached from your experiences. Step outside of yourself while you are in the throes of an emotional reaction and see if you can identify the authentic from the fake, the illusion from reality. This takes training and time to master but is essential in the process of self-realization.

To move you in that direction, I recommend that you do "the daily Bardo" exercise. Bardo is a Buddhist concept that states that after your death, you go to a three-day examination period where you evaluate your successes, failures, and the degree to which you fulfilled your purpose. From this understanding, you begin to plan your next incarnation. Here is the thing: why wait for the end of your life to do this? You can do this on a daily basis. At the end of every day, write the highlights of the day in a journal. Once this is done, ask yourself this key question: If God/Goddess were walking in my footsteps today, would he/she have acted the way I did? If the answer is no, then you have adjustments to make. Remember to be kind to self. For in the process of doing this exercise most students spot only the mistakes and do not identify when they have acted in alignment. When you are in alignment with Spirit, give yourself a gold star. You are an outside observer impartially noting the good and the bad, the aligned and the misaligned. Once identified, write down the appropriate behavior or reaction and make a spiritual vow in front of all that you hold as holy that if that situation were to repeat itself, this is how you would respond. If you do this for just one month, your self-awareness will vastly expand and will not be the same.

To be honest, you will not at first be able to catch yourself before the behavior happens. In all likelihood you will realize this after or halfway through being engaged in the unwanted reaction. At that point, remember the way in which God and Goddess would have behaved, which you had written down earlier. With the focus of your will and intent, change your thought and behavior and react in that manner, or if at first this too hard to do, walk away from the situation and try to calm down. Over time, you may be able to realize and identify the program as your reactive system that has been triggered.

The purpose of this exercise is for you to become self-aware and remove the blind spots. Typically, the way in which the negative ego system and fear justify themselves is to blame the world and external events for your reaction, and therefore, the reason you feel pain and suffering is because of "them." You know, it's the idea that "if everyone in the world were to do exactly what I think, the world would be a great place." This is a clear example of a blind spot. Wake up. Don't get caught up in the canvas and hologram that you are in charge of creating.

If you are in the middle of an emotional reactive event, follow these simple steps of the One, Two, Three Step protocol and navigate yourself into pro-active control. First, realize that it is a test. Detach from your reaction and more importantly realize that it is an opportunity for you to overcome your negative ego. Second, count to ten. Literally, don't react for ten seconds: one, two, three, four … and so on. Hold your reaction for ten seconds. Here is why this works. In the middle of your brain is the hypothalamus, the chemical factory of your body, and it produces all the hormones, which are powerful body chemicals that trigger emotions. When a hormone is released, it moves rapidly through the blood stream and blends into the cellular structure, changing and altering it completely to the color, mode, and feeling associated with the specific emotion. If you don't react for ten seconds, the hypothalamus shuts down and the hormone flow stops. Finally, do the opposite of what your reactive system was telling you to do. Remember, it is your thought that creates reality. Now that you have stopped the emotional reactive system, it is time to program in some-thing different. By thinking, acting, and behaving like the opposite of your reaction, you are putting a new program into your subconscious mind.

If you are interested in accelerating the ascension process, it is in your best interests to also have a teacher, spiritual coach, ascension buddy, spiritual circle, or outside entity who is going to further help you identify the blind spots. This is a relationship that has to be maintained on a regular, preferably weekly basis. Just like having a gym or running buddy, this relationship with an outside entity who is working toward the same goal will accelerate your spiritual growth. It is not only a means to quickly identify the blind spots by having someone else mirror our behavior, but it is also a way to get encouragement on the day that we don't feel like doing any work. Additionally, the buddy will hold you accountable for promises, goals, and intentions made to self, asking you to explain why these things did not occur when you said that they would. Further, if the relationship is that of a buddy, you can return the favor. When two or more are working toward a common goal, an energy much greater than the sum of the parts is created, which propels the collective forward. The relationship that you will have with your ascension buddy or group is a powerful way to move rapidly through the ascension process.

Although it is true that you can do this work by yourself, it is slower and more complex. You will have to hold your own feet to the fire to be held accountable for your progress or lack thereof. It may help for you to cultivate a relationship with one of the Ascended Masters as a guide and outside force in a similar manner to the buddy system. Additionally, be brutally honest with self about the discovery of your own blind spots— something that is hard and time consuming, but not impossible to do.

The key question here is: how sincere are you in your intention to ascend? To what degree do you really want to discover your blind spots? Are you serious about the reorganization of your consciousness? The answers will come in proportion to the measure of your dedication to the process. It is unflattering grunt work that, once done, will move you into a realm of self-mastery.

If you are up for the challenge, follow me in this journey toward self-discovery.

Chapter 3

Personal Power

Lord, where we are wrong, make us willing to change;
where we are right, make us easy to live with.

– Peter Marshall

Of all the effects connected to the emergence of the ego, personal power is the key and fundamental quality of the expression of will. It is the ego and self-awareness that make you realize that you are different and separated from others and which give you the ability to make choices and decisions and chart your own course, individually and personally, away from the collective consciousness. It is one thing to realize that you are different, but you need your personal power to give you the courage to move against the grain and plot your own course. It is at the root of the expression and manifestation of your will. It is the center of your authenticity and autonomy. It is through the continual and progressive expression of your will, fueled by your personal power, that the bread of shame or negative ego program will eventually be removed. Therefore, your personal power and will are the most important rights that you have as an individual. Do not give them away. Do not give them to me, the Masters, the Angels, or even to God. The Masters, the Angels, and God do not want them. God wants you to remove the bread of shame program, and the only way this is going to happen is by you doing the work, not by giving the responsibility to someone else. God wants you to co-create with

Him. If you have given your will and personal power to a news commentator, leader, priest, teacher, or a Master, take it back. The age of the guru is over. Unlike the events of past ages, no avatar or world teacher is coming to save us. This age is the time in which men and women become Gods and Goddesses. The expression of your will and personal power is the key to the fulfillment of this prophecy. Own your personal power.

The entire Christendom is waiting for Jesus to save them. How sad for them and poor Master Jesus. Energetically, they all have anchored cords into the body of Jesus, which are holding him back from higher solar and galactic advancement. All the people around the world who are "waiting on Jesus to save them" are holding him back. It is much easier to wait on some external thing to redeem us than for us to do the work. The desire for the panacea is a powerful and alluring illusion that is rooted in laziness. I do not want to gang up on Christians for it is not a Christian thing, it is a human thing. No one wants to do the real work. What they should be doing instead is imitating His example. You are responsible for your own salvation. He is a guide, chariot, and trailblazer who laid down a redemption path. Walking the path is your responsibility. Granted, Master Jesus knew this and still volunteered to become the avatar of the Piscean age, but this is not my choice.

Guidance vs. Control

If I notice that any of my students are giving me their personal power, I will cease to be their teacher. They will be cut off. Keep your stuff to yourself. I am trying to create equality, not dependency, and no one, no energetic link, is going to hold me back from my continual spiritual ascension and evolution. This is not a popular position. Most spiritual and ascension teachers may say that they want you to own your personal power, but in actuality, they are creating devotees. In fact, they are often busy telling students what to do and how. True enough, as a teacher you have to help your students see their blind spots, but it is an entirely different thing to edit and control them.

There is a giant rift between guidance and control. I will tell you three times what I observe; beyond that, you are on your own. I will not mention the issue again unless you ask me. Furthermore, after telling someone about a personality defect three times, any additional repetition turns you into a nag. No one listens to you on the fourth and successive times. Besides, I have far better things to do than to waste my time telling you over and over about your subconscious and negative ego issues. Timing is everything. When you are ready to be helped, I will gladly show you how to create a reprogramming plan for the removal and deletion of the program, and that is it. I am not doing the work for you, nor do I have an attachment to how quickly you do it.

Giving Up Your Personal Power Unconsciously

Surrendering one's personal power is not always an act of laziness. It is at times unconscious, gradual, and incremental. I personally had a spiritual coach for many years, who helped steer me through some of my issues and blind spots. Over the four years of this relationship, I began to trust and rely on his opinion until the day that my ascension process began and he started saying to me that what I was experiencing was "maya, glamour, and illusion." These comments really threw me off, and it took me several weeks to process what was happening. I then realized that over those years, I had incrementally given him my personal power and right to veto me.

It took me several months to retrieve my personal power, for energetically he did not want to release the control and power that he had over me. Now I did not set out to do this. It simply occurred over the time that I had trusted him, because his guidance and coaching sessions were helpful and spot on. I gradually and incrementally gave him the right to veto me. It was a great lesson for me to learn that spiritual discernment must remain mine and be turned on at all times, even with the people whose opinion and counsel matter to me.

The Law of Noninterference

The ability to set our own course and to make free choices is a basic universal and cosmic right. Yet my choice must not influence or affect others without their permission or consent. I must embrace my free choice with all of its ramifications and consequences, but I cannot impose it on others. Of all the rules that govern our Universe this is the most fundamental. The law of noninterference states: I cannot comingle my energy grid with anyone or anything without permission and complete disclosure as to my intent. This is the rule that the fallen angels originally broke and are continually breaking. Life was originally seeded in this and other Universes as an experiment—a means by which the uncreated Source of all can fragment, manifest, and descend the dimensional scale; become self-realized; and ascend back into Source. The in- and out-breath of God—devolution and evolution.

Given the fact that all fragments have free will, the possibilities for choices and outcomes are endless. And for a while this purpose was being fulfilled—until groups of Angels and Elohim decided that they liked dimensional existence, fragmentation, and ego, and that the merging, reintegration, and ascension back to Source was not for them. They diverged from the original purpose by wanting to reverse or stop ascension back to Source.

To do this, they altered their DNA sequencing, but it did not stop there for they also began to influence and interfere with lower, fragmented dimensional expressions of Source by also changing their DNA sequencing. The way this was being done was through lies, deceit, and without disclosure or transparency. The law of noninterference was violated. The fact that they wanted to digress from the original purpose was acceptable for it was a free-will choice, which is a basic right; but influencing others without disclosure was a different matter.

Angelic Wars

This was the source of the angelic wars, for the Beings and Angels of the Light of God moved to block and oppose this aberration. The way the fallen angels did this was by shape-shifting and appearing as beings of light to lower forms of existence, promising them guidance and support. Who among us would not want that? It is a confidence game that they played and continue to play. They counsel the students wisely and give them great advice; expand their psychic powers; and bring them into the total confidence and trust that their best interests are being watched. The students, over time, give their personal power away; and then the fallen angels begin to lead them into perdition. Awareness of these facts can help you spot them rather quickly. Any advice coming from a so-called Master, Guide, Angel, or Spiritual Being that does not empower you to do things for yourself is not coming from the Light. If there is a lot of flattery about your level of achievement, assurances that they are going to take care of this or that, or that you don't need to do this work for you are already there, chances are that you are dealing with fallen energies. Remember the bread of shame and the negative ego. Spirit cannot and will not do the work for you.

I had a former student who found a channel who was connecting her to the Masters, and the messages were flattering her into believing that she was an important figure in Master Jesus's entourage; furthermore, that she was ascended and needed to do very little in this lifetime. She bought it and began to experience "false ascension," a fake bliss of believing that she was connected to Light, a bubble that worked like a prison to hold her from evolving and doing the negative ego work. Yet her mundane existence was chaotic and a complete mess. Let this be a word of warning to all past-life recalls of historical importance and the negative ego trap that they may hold. If I had a dime for every Mary Magdalene that I have met, I would be a rich man. This information may explain something about you and your purpose, but you still have a negative ego, and you still have to remove the bread of shame. If you were so high-and-mighty and needed to do no more work, what are you doing on earth?

Spiritual Discernment and Personal Power

One of the most difficult lessons for seekers on the path to understand is the ownership of their spiritual discernment and personal power. Just because Archangel Michael tells you to do this or that does not mean that you must obey. You are not sheep. In the words of the Oracle to Morphius in the third *Matrix* movie: "I expect you to do what I always expected you to do: to make up your own damn mind." Is the suggestion or advice in your highest and best interests? Every being that exists in dimensional reality has a filter or lens through which they are experiencing the Light of Source. That filter or lens may not align at this very instant with your own and true purpose.

Their perception may be higher than yours, but it does not mean that they don't have an agenda. That agenda may at times end up being harmful to your existence. Every time I say this, I hear students asking me, "How can an Archangel counsel me in a way that is harmful to me? It must not be the true Michael! It must be an imposter?" First off, Michael is not one being, he is a collective. All the Angels and Archangels are a choir and a legion of beings. In fact you can speak of the Order of Michael. Second, Michael's purpose is to defend and win the war against the fallen.

If you are a general going to war, you expect to have collateral damages. Some of your troops are going to fall. If you blindly obey orders from Michael or others, you may expose yourself and your family to immediate peril and danger. Is the command that you are getting making you the collateral damage? Put differently, if two bulls are charging each other on a prairie, do you think that they are concerned about the blades of grass across which they stampede? You are a blade of grass, and in the great scheme and purpose of these giants, you can become collateral damage. They are not thinking about your individual best interests, but how to strategically win. If you have played chess, you can understand how you may sacrifice a knight to checkmate your opponent.

Think of a cosmic chess game with the salvation of the Universe in the balance, and you may be close to the truth. Their advice is not necessarily nefarious, but at this very moment, it may be harmful to your immediate growth. Are you willing to be the knight? Is this what you want? You have to decide; it is your responsibility. Is this your battle? That is why you have free will. Do not follow anything or anyone unless it is in your interests.

Yet having voiced this warning, there is no better defense against attacks than Archangel Michael and his legion. When I call on him, he is always responsive to defend and banish darkness against infringements against my free choice and self-determination. All I am saying is that you must be aware that even higher spiritual beings have agendas. Although at times you may disagree with them and make different choices, if you are in need and you call upon them, they will always come to your aid. In our Universe, free choice is a right that all beings of the Light of God respect. There is no resentment even if you had said no to their guidance in the past. You were simply exercising your right.

Furthermore, everyone in the Universe has free will, and as such, the Angelic, Elohim, and Ascended of the Light of God have the ability to choose. What direction they will take is not a guarantee. Today, they fight for the expansion of the original purpose and the Light of God. It may not be so tomorrow. For reasons that you cannot imagine, they may choose to descend. Remember, ascension is not a one-way street. One can ascend and descend; after all, the fallen were Angels at one point.

Ascension and Descension

The movement and thrust toward the higher planes is not a straight line, but rather a wave with up and down fluctuations in the flow of the frequency. One student recently asked me if there is a point in the ascension process where one can no longer fall? The answer is no. At all points in dimensional existence, we have free will and can choose the path and direction that we travel. As I stated earlier, negative ego issues are not exclusive to the 3-D world. Free choice populates all dimensions. Even Lord Melchizedek, who is the soul that animates our Universe, has a specific lens and manner to reflect the Light of Source due to his negative ego perceptions. It is certainly less contaminated than the lenses of humanity, but it is a distortion nonetheless.

A word to the wise: it is your responsibility to constantly monitor the information that you are getting from the higher realms. Are they in alignment at this very moment with your free will and the authentic expression of your volition? If the answer is no, then don't listen to it. Don't follow it.

All sentient life in the Universe has the alienable right to change their minds, make free choices, and plot their own course. In your interaction with others, make sure that you have not given your personal power away out of habit. It is your responsibility to continually check for the alignment of your exchange with all beings with whom you transact and do commerce, 24 hours a day, seven days a week, even in your sleep.

Personal Power and Decisiveness

Personal power is not something you do on Sunday. It is the continual process of allowing or denying access to your consciousness by internal subconscious forces as well as external events and energy systems. If the proposed exchange no longer suits you, disengage. "No" is a complete sentence. It is not a whisper. It does not need explanation or a qualifier. And "yes" is a fait accompli. Your words and your actions must match. If your "no" and "yes" mean "maybe," then you are not in your personal power. The key is decisiveness and follow-through. Remember, personal power is actually the center of your will and authenticity. Furthermore, when you don't make a decision—by being lazy, by going along and not making waves—you make a choice.

We are decision-generating entities. There are hundreds of choices, if not thousands, that we need to make every day. Own it and take responsibility for your actions. No one is ever a victim. If you are in your personal power, no fallen, dark lords or negative extraterrestrials can engage with your grid. Indeed, they can only connect to you if there is an agreement. In all cases of connection, there is always an agreement. Now that agreement is often gathered by lies and deceits, but if you fall for the con, you have no one to blame but yourself. The way to verify that you are dealing with the fallen is to be in your heart space. The mind and heart coherence cannot be deceived. It is highly sophisticated and intelligent. Bottom line: energy does not lie. If you listen to it and follow it, you are never going to be wrong. These beings may lie, camouflage, and even shape-shift, but if you are in your heart space, they cannot deceive you.

How Then Do You Disengage the Old Agreements That You Have Already Made?

For every instance in which you capitulated your power to someone or something, your will split into fragments. It is in your interests to claim back your power by retrieving your fragmented pieces. If you have given your rights to family members, religious leaders, politicians, governments, or the media, take them back. You cannot be fully in your power until you have gathered all these fragments. What you are being asked to do at first is a solo act. No dependencies. You need to rescue self, re-assemble all aspects of your will and volition given away, and re-assume total responsibility for your future.

It is your total and complete four-body system that will ascend, not just one of the bodies. After ascension, you will eventually merge with your collective toward a shared consciousness and group awareness. If you had given your power away out of dependency and a sense of lack, do not waste your time trying to retrieve and re-negotiate every instance of capitulation. You are still giving away your power and ceding the upper hand to the forces who are outside of you. Granted, in the original exchange, they provided you with a sense of completeness and illusionary fulfillment. Typically, the relationship is a master-slave dynamic. You count on them to make decisions for you about your future. It comes from a program that says: I am weak and fragmented and I need you to decide for me. You can waste a lot of time negotiating, but this is not a debate. This is a control issue. Who is in charge, you or them? What you need to do is remove the program and sense of lack in your subconscious mind that allowed this to happen in the first place. Once this is done, all your will-fragments will be back. Full stop. Try "stalking self" by monitoring your consciousness to observe when you are doing this out of habit. Stop and count to ten. And then do the opposite.

Free Will vs. the Volition of Others

The expression of my free will should minimally impact and affect others. If I express my will based solely on my self-interests, the negative ego programming will win, and I will move to suppress the will and intent of others: survival of the fittest. This is a fear-fueled expression of will. What Spirit is asking us to do is to express our self-determination with love. Will without love to temper it is self-motivated, cruel, tyrannical, and fragmented. Instead of head-centered critical thinking and decision-making, we allow the heart-centered thinking to be expressed. It is in mind and heart coherence that one will distill peace, truth, and authenticity.

I am always asking my students to close their eyes and drop their heads into the center of their chests. When in that space, peace, calmness, and liberation rule, and one begins to perceive and understand energies, situations, and events from a 360-degree perspective. Head-thinking is limited and fragmented, and heart-thinking is inclusive and unifying. Both are necessary for balanced living, and blending both takes you to a holy place.

As an exercise and practice, try to hold your attention into your heart space for one week while going about your daily life. Most of us live in our heads, so this is a multi-tasking exercise for our awareness to be in our head and heart space at the same time. Once achieved, you will have moments when feeling of unconditional love will explode from your chest. Personally, when this happens to me, I cannot contain it. I step out of my office and hug everyone on the floor, telling them that I love them and that God and divinity adores them. Everyone who has tried this for a few weeks has reported similar experiences.

The Role of Guilt in Removing the Bread of Shame

In order to remove the bread of shame program, we evolved a sense of guilt about the bounty and blessings that we feel we are receiving for free. But the fallen beings do not have that issue. In the alteration of their DNA, they managed to eliminate any sense of guilt. They take for free without ever having any guilt. They are completely self-motivated with zero guilt. This DNA digression is also incarnated in the human population as the fallen have mixed their progeny with the daughters and sons of man.

Scott Peck in his book *The People of the Lies, the Psychology of Evil* says that about 10% of the human population is incapable of guilt. I have met these individuals, and they are not your serial killers or Nazi murderers; they are your average citizens, which make them even more difficult to identify. They are church-going, charity-giving friends, neighbors, and family members. But unlike the rest of humanity, they do not believe in a higher power, goal, or purpose. Some people believe in God, money, power, or sex. Everyone serves a higher or lower purpose. These beings believe solely in themselves. Whatever they do is justified. In fact, if humanity were to do exactly what they say, they believe the world would be a great place. No purpose is higher than theirs.

Redemption for All

With the understanding that the fallen DNA alteration was deliberately seeded among humanity by the fallen as a means to contaminate creation, these beings are incarnations of the aspects of the fallen beings. In a lot of cases, they are incarnated fragments of the fallen, who are seeking rehabilitation back into the Light. Some of them are seeking to revive and re-ignite the original DNA sequencing that is in alignment with the funda-mental law of this Universe: respect for the law of noninterference. They are trying to learn how to digest Light from Source instead of parasitically taking it from others.

A word of caution: do not attempt to re-habilitate any of these beings unless you are in complete spiritual alignment. Short of this, they will harm and damage you. You need special training to work with beings who spent eons drawing energy from others. If you were to work in a mental hospital, you would need to receive special training so that you could do your work without getting hurt by those you are helping.

I have had these beings as students and clients. Yet knowing all this, I often cringe and hesitate to teach or coach them. On a visceral level, I find their frequency repulsive. I also worry, given the openness and candid nature of how I teach, that they would corrupt the knowledge and information. Or even that they are spying on me. I had an instance where one came to me to be taught. When I expressed my concern to Spirit, I was told: "Pierre, love him unconditionally like you love everyone else. One of two things could happen: he could either become energetically incongruent and leave, or entrain into the Light." This was a real test for me. I did my best and loved him, and in time, I noticed some dramatic improvements. Yet at a certain point, he pulled away from me, becoming more and more incongruent as the vibrations that I was broadcasting were moving higher and higher in alignment with my evolving ascension process.

Having had that experience, I will now teach any of them anytime, for they are capable of revealing more light to the world than I. Let me use an analogy to explain. Let us say, if ascension is 1,000 volts, I am 100 volts, and they are 10 volts, their vessel has to expand further than mine to reach the ascension of 1,000 volts, and they would therefore reveal more Light to the world than I. If Hitler were to have done the negative ego work that was needed and had ascended, he would have revealed more Light and transformed a larger circle of influence than I could have. His ascension broadcast would have been wider than mine.

Typically, these individuals are seekers of free services. "I don't have any money now, but when I make my fortune, I will shower you with presents and gifts. Don't worry about your future; you will be by my side." I don't have a problem making special arrangements for individuals having financial challenges, but nothing is for free. Remember the removal of the bread of shame. There has to be an exchange of some kind. That exchange could even involve your helping me clean my house. I have made such arrangements in the past. I had a three-year experience with such a being who showed a voracious appetite for taking for free. I happened to realize that I had a karmic link to this person, which clouded my perception and judgment. I could not remember fully what it was that I did not do in the previous lifetime off-planet. Over the multiple experiences of him taking energy for free, I had three separate conversations with him. By the second conversation, I told him that he was cut off—no more free services. At the last and final conversation, I finally remembered what I had not said to him in a past life, and I told him: "John, I owe you absolutely nothing. Good luck in your journey." I felt a great release, and I knew that my karma was resolved and balanced, and the cord was cut. I have not spoken to him since then.

Fallen Spiritual Teachers

It is not just spiritual beings who are out to capitalize on your lack of discernment and decisiveness. Many spiritual teachers will do the same. Coupled with the fact that most people on the planet are looking for the magic bullet, you end up with a combination that is lethal for self-determination. On a planetary level, the age of the guru is over. This eon is about men and women becoming ascended Gods and Goddesses. Yet the old pattern lingers, as it is slowly phased out. I am convinced that most of these teachers, who have fallen but are not aware of it, did not start out dark. Their ascension process began sincerely by the same energy increase that I described earlier. But most did not do the negative ego re-programming that is essential for safe ascension. This increase brings with it the ability to manifest phenomena and attract a crowd. By now the negative ego issues are like a bad genie out of the bottle. The otherwise sincere, newly ascended teacher may struggle to either put the genie back into the bottle, or to keep the energy increase and adoration from the crowd and become a contaminated or unsuspecting agent for fallen energies.

This is the beginning of ascension—followed very quickly by descent. To the blind followers, their teacher is the savior, and whatever he/she says, it is the gospel. Many have followed these teachers to their deaths. Some will package Kool-Aid, telling their followers that it is the latest light technology from the higher realms, and they will drink it to their perdition. I have witnessed all of this. It is unsexy and far less delusional to take responsibility for your own growth and evolution. Who you choose to serve makes a big difference. You serve a guru and give them your power or you serve self and self alone.

Psychic Power vs. Spirituality

The thing that derails most students is witnessing the ability to manifest. Few understand that psychic power and demonstrations are not spirituality. I grew up in Haiti, and I have witnessed dark shamans with stunning ability to manifest. Yet they were harming people every day. Just because you can put on a great show does not make you spiritual or ascended. How do you tell who is ascended and who is not? Show me a vignette of the life and family environment of any would-be ascended, and I will show you

47

where the master is. If their family interactions are in spiritual alignment, they are ascended. You have eyes; perceive and witness the truth.

Reclaiming Your Personal Power

Since everything that we do and agree with for 21 days will drop down through the threshold of consciousness into the subconscious mind and become law, one can choose a set of beliefs and commands that empowers self into owning and reclaiming its power. Reclaiming your personal power is a process that can be initiated by a 21-day program that involves calling upon the help of specific spiritual beings for assistance and support and repeating out loud a series of positive and empowering affirmations. The process involves first the deletion of the sabotaging programs and then their replacement with appropriate ascended and supporting beliefs.

1. As you wake up in the morning while still in bed, you call upon The Mahatma, Lord Melchizedek, and Archangel Metatron and ask them to run their platinum light net through your four-body system and remove from it all negative, misqualified, and unbalanced energies. Wait a few seconds and allow this to take place. The Mahatma is composed of all the souls in the entire Universe that have achieved Christ ascension; Lord Melchizedek is the soul that animates our Universe; and Archangel Metatron is the Archangel of the Archangels. These three beings sit in front of the throne of God and can help you, but only if you ask them.

2. Remember the cosmic law of noninterference: no being can comingle their energy system with any others without consent. No spiritual being of the Light of God will come to your aid unless you ask. As you continue your morning routine, call upon Archangel Michael and ask that he create an impenetrable force field of Light and protection around you.

3. Next, ask that Master El Morya bathe you with the energy of the First Ray of will and power, balanced with love and wisdom. This is important, for will without love and wisdom to balance it will manifest as tyranny, control, and domination of others.

4. Then say out loud the following affirmations by Dr. Joshua David Stone:

   I am the power, the master, and the cause of my attitudes, feelings, emotions, and behavior.

   I am 100% powerful, loving, and balanced at all times.

I am powerful, whole, and complete within myself. I have prefer-ences but not attachments.

I am 100% powerful and decisive in everything I do.

I have perfect mastery and control over all my energies in service of a loving spiritual purpose.

I am the master and director of my life, and my subconscious mind is my friend and servant.

I am a center of pure self-consciousness and will, with the ability to direct my energies wherever I would have them go.

I am powerful, centered, and loving at all times.

I am powerful and centered at all times, and nothing in this external Universe will I allow to knock me off-balance or off-center.

I have 100% personal power, and I vow never to give it to my sub-conscious mind or other people ever again.

I have perfect self-control and self-mastery in everything I do.

The whole process should take less than seven minutes. Now proceed with your day, and if at any point you feel disempowered and overwhelmed, repeat steps one, two, and three.

In the evening, repeat the same steps and then add the following: ask Master Djwhal Khul to anchor into your body the core fear removal programming; to delete all core fears that are stopping your personal power; and to do this on a continual basis for the rest of the night. This is a spiritual technology of his creation, and it is the eraser that will delete all negative ego programs that are buried in your subconscious mind, which are robbing you of your power. It is funny how a process so simple can liberate your consciousness and connect you to your will, control, and power.

Repeat this process for 21 days, and I will guarantee that the alignment to your will center will dramatically improve. By the seventh day, the differ-ence will be a dramatic improvement in your clarity and sense of control.

Personal power is a process and not an event. Some may have to repeat this program multiple times to have the desired control and effect. I per-sonally have done this program several times and probably will do it at some point in the future. At any moment when I feel that I am not in my center and not the cause of my reality, I do this 21-day program to remind myself of what true personal power feels like.

In truth, personal power is a constant that must be maintained, for external circumstances will generate situations and opportunities that will attempt to erode your volition. Remember, the resisting force that was designed to make it difficult for us to gain back the Light is always at work. It is your responsibility to make sure that this does not happen. Vigilance is the key to accomplishing this. Personal power is not something that you do on Sunday; rather it is the ongoing process of approving and disapproving of all internal contents of the subconscious mind and all external events and energy systems that are trying to blend and lead your conscious mind. What may appear as an impossible task, becomes a simple matter of using the relentless ability of the subconscious mind to work 24 hours a day, 7 days a week, to manifest in favor of creating and supporting the blooming of your personal power. That is what this process is all about. If you do this 21-day program often enough, it will grow and bloom and keep you in charge of your will and volition, and nothing internal or external will stand a chance against it.

In order for you to help change the world, you first have to change yourself. This process will plant in the field of your subconscious mind a seed that will grow to become that foundation stone of your freedom from servitude. Do your utmost to allow this seed to grow, and it will become the filter through which you will experience everything. Like the phoenix that arises from its ashes, your personal power will blossom into an ascended, aligned, and bliss-filled consciousness. After all, ascension is self-awareness, and this will put you in charge, allowing you to direct and command your subconscious mind. The beginning of mastery is rooted here.

Chapter 4

The Inner Child and Unconditional Self-Love

Our first and last love is self-love.

– Christian Nestell Bovee

Self-awareness and the mind can generally be separated into three parts: the superconscious mind, the conscious mind, and the subconscious mind. The first two we spoke of in earlier chapters. Let us focus on the subconscious mind in some detail to see the mechanics by which it gets populated by programs. It is a vast network that far surpasses any man-made system. It connects and transmits data between various aspects of the mind and also to and from all sentient existence and energetic presences in the entire Universe in an attempt to manifest. It is a way by which unconscious sharing occurs, in order to keep all fragmented pieces of the Desire to Receive connected. Self-awareness and the conscious mind create separation, boundaries, and an individual identity, and the subconscious mind keeps and maintains a bridge and connection between all things. It also helps to attract people, things, and events to us on which we choose to focus our intention. It is the medium by which we co-create. The Swiss psychoanalyst Carl Gustav Jung has already written about the connection of our subconscious mind with the subconscious mind of everyone on the planet. I want to point out that this definition is very limiting. In truth, all life is connected by it. The animals, the plants, and minerals are plugged into it. In fact all energetic systems, like the oceans, rivers, air, and earth are part of it. Anything that has an etheric or energetic expression is connected to it. And since everything that exists in our Universe has an energetic signature and presence, everything in the Universe belongs to it. Carl Jung likens it to the vast and extensive section of an iceberg that floats below the surface of the ocean, dwarfing the part that is visible above the water. I will add that the ocean is also part of it as well. It is the largest and most extensive part of our psyche. It is everywhere.

Yet this network is not rational and does not have morality the way conscious awareness understands right from wrong. It simply manifests whatever intention is held and focused within it for an extensive period of time. Whether that thought or intention is positive or negative, if it is repeated enough times, the subconscious mind will be glad to continually loop it around and bring it to the attention of self-awareness over and over again. It does not care about the contents. It just serves a purpose. It will use its power to equally manifest the good or the bad intentions that happen to populate it.

Morality and the Subconscious Mind

As a servant and medium for creation, there is no better tool. It will attract and create for you the circumstances that permit 3-D manifestations to occur. But when self-awareness is not in its personal power and allows fearful thoughts to drop below the threshold of conscious awareness, the fear data and pattern will loop around ad infinitum, relentlessly bringing to self the toxic information that fell in. Now if self-awareness is disempowered enough to allow multiple fear patterns to drop below the mental level, you have a situation in which multiple programs are manifesting a reality that you may hate on a conscious level but have no control over now to change.

How the Subconscious Mind Manifests

Although there is a process by which these and all programs can be deleted and reprogrammed, let us see how they are created. Anything on which you focus your awareness for 21 days drops into the subconscious mind and becomes law. It is as though the thought, belief, or behavior coalesces into an independent splinter-psyche module with a specific set of instructions that travel this infinite network and seek out objects, people, and external events to demonstrate this law to you. If they happen to be ascended and self-empowering intentions, that is a great thing; but if they are fear-based, you have a problem. Of course, we want to keep the positive and ascended programs and delete and reprogram the negative ones into positive and ascended content.

Programs vs. Archetypes

These splinter-psyche modules are not created equal. Some are just patterns and programs learned from the environment in which we grew up, and others are archetypes—preexisting templates or formwork that populate our psyche prior to self-awareness—which get populated by programs. Just because we are human, we have certain pre-existing placeholders that exist in the subconscious mind. Like giant canals or grooves, they allow the flow of all the contents of the psyche. They are the veins and arteries that permit the flow of the matrix of life. Unlike the programs that have no prior existence, the archetypes can be described as riverbeds that pre-exist the flow of water. Now, how pure and clean the water is, the capacity of the flow, and the color of it are directly influenced by your first experience in this lifetime with an external environment that mirrors this pattern. For example, the mother/father archetype will be populated by the type of parent and caregiving that you had, which could have been positive, negative, or a bit of both. The placeholder is neither positive nor negative. It is Divine in its essence. It is your first life experience with the archetype that tints, polarizes, and gives it content. After 21 days of experiencing the externalization of an archetype in a specific way, you begin to believe that this is the way it is, and it drops down into the subconscious mind and becomes law or the filter for its expression. It is like a colored gel or lens on a light. Remove the contaminated and negative contents, and the archetype remains in its Divine expression, revealing the raw fabric of life.

The Inner Child

Of all the archetypes, the one that informs and influences the identity that you take in this life is the inner child. It is the first archetype that everyone on the planet populates. It stands to reason that if you can remove the contaminations from it, you would quickly regain your identity. Thus, it is the cornerstone archetype that can help retrieve your true self. Although all the archetypes play a critical and valid role in the proper functioning of the psyche, if I had to choose one to work on, it would be the inner child. Removing and clearing this program will reconnect you to the essence of who and what you really are.

The inner child is the key to your identity. Remove the toxic and negative programs from it, and you will liberate yourself. As infants, our parents and caregivers look like Gods to us. We grow up mirroring and attempting to please them. They, in turn, parent us by behavior modification—reward and punishment—to change our behavior to an inherited, preconceived notion that they believe will make us into better human beings. In the words of Don Miguel Ruiz: "We are domesticated similarly to how you would domesticate a pet." Most parents mean no harm; they just want us to grow up as functioning adults. But because they are not ascended beings, the patterns and behaviors that they are reinforcing in us, which causes them to drop into our subconscious minds, are contaminated with all kind of biases, toxic contents, and fears.

As if this were not enough, the school system adds its portion of negative programs and fears. Then the church engulfs us with more fears and re-strictions in an attempt to control our behavior. The village, the nation, the country, and the planet step in to add to the mix, and finally TV and mass media do a major number to dispense fear 24 hours a day. If we allow all these contents to drop into the subconscious mind, we end up with thousands of programs looping around, creating chaos and causing havoc in our life. But the key negative programs can always be found around the family.

Charles Whitfield, in his critical book *Healing the Child Within*, states that 80% of families are codependent and dysfunctional. Like all codependent dynamics, the family unit is enmeshed. These families are typically held together by a secret: something that polite society is not supposed to know and that every member of the family is busy trying to hide or compensate for. This secret could be a drug- or alcohol-addicted family member, mental illness, a handicap, or an abuse. Whatever it is, everyone, including children, move to hide it and compensate when and where the dysfunction occurs. If you happen to be part of the 80%, you were quickly robbed of your childhood as you evolved to accommodate for the lack of another family member. You lied and withheld the truth from others, and more importantly from yourself, in order to hide the family secret, and in the process you lost your identity.

Co-dependency and the Inner Child

In that kind of dynamic, no member of the family is whole. Everyone is a fragment wobbling along, needing the other members to be complete. No one's authentic nature is allowed to flourish. As a child in a codependent family, you become an adult quickly and develop survival mechanisms that allow you to cope with the dysfunction. If the family unit was abusive, the child may rationalize that "it is my fault; I need to be better" and thus becomes a fixer or a people-pleaser. He may have decided that "the world is not safe; I am going to fight the world" and move against the world by becoming angry and aggressive. He may have internalized that "I will never let anyone hurt me again" so he will be become self-sufficient and will need no one. He may even have concluded that the pain is too much, "I will not allow myself to feel anything," and become frigid and emotionally disconnected to self and to life.

Now as long as the child is in the abuse environment, the survival mechanism serves him, but as he grows to become an adult, the programs do not magically disappear. They are still running, controlling, and blocking him from further and future development. Unless an intervention is performed to address and reprogram these survival mechanisms, they will loop the antiquated patterns ad infinitum. As an adult, the child is stuck in the past as the survival mode causes him to recreate the patterns and prevents him from having a healthy and fulfilling emotional life.

Dysfunctional Family Dynamics

All dysfunctional family dynamics behave in a similar manner. They project the same deficiencies toward the child and cause him to compensate for the deficiencies by manifesting survival mechanisms. Here are some of the negative and unhealthy dynamics of dysfunctional families:

Inconsistent: Words and promises mean nothing in a dysfunctional environment. What the caregiver promises is not delivered and moreover "yes and no" actually mean "may be." If you are a caregiver, children will test you and your integrity and will quickly determine if the family environment is consistent or not.

Unpredictable: Routine and predictability is important to early childhood development. Is there a curfew time that is consistently being broken? Schedules that have been established should be kept to help maintain and hold a safe and predictable environment for the child. Is the family dynamic continually being uprooted by emotional drama?

Arbitrary: Are decisions and behaviors of the caregiver arbitrary? Children need to understand why, and they will often ask you that. Granted, not all decisions need to be explained, and some need to be explained to the level of the child's mind, but if you yield and refuse to explain what and why changes are being made to the family unit, you are creating an arbitrary environment, to the child's mind.

Chaotic: Are family pressures and external events creating an emotional rollercoaster environment for the child? Is the child not feeling safe and protected? Are dangerous and threatening situations and events causing trauma and damage to the child?

Abuse and Neglect: Neglect is directly related to abandonment and lack of caregiving. It causes all kinds of damages. The emotion connected to this experience is being unwanted and thus not being valued. Abuse on the other hand takes many forms: mental, emotional, physical, and sexual:

Mental abuse can appear as someone who manipulates a family member in order to control them.

Emotional abuse is common and ranges from unspoken malice, meanness, and verbal abuse; angry and vile expressions of emotion; and manifestations of rage. If you are on the receiving end of these displays, they will terrorize you.

Physical abuse boils down to a family member striking or beating other family members. This also creates terror for the child who is subjected to this.

Sexual abuse is seriously damaging and may take years to repair. It involves inappropriate sexual contact and behavior of an adult with a child. During a hypnotic regression, one of my clients discovered that the source of her addiction to sex was a sexual abuse incident by her grandfather. As she described the details and emotions that she was experiencing, I began to cry. I quickly realized that the emotions were very familiar to me and recalled an incident that I had apparently blocked of a scoutmaster trying to fondle me when I was 12 years old. I was grateful for this discovery and moved to address the damages that were done to my inner child. Sometimes when you give a healing, you get a healing.

Sexual abuse does not always involve penetration. It certainly was not so in my case. It may have involved an adult playing with your sexual parts or an adult exposing themself in front of you. It may be the fact that adults are walking into your private moments or that you don't have any privacy. All sexual abuse causes the child to be exposed to sexuality too early. This initiates major dysfunction, for at this stage in his development, the child is innocent and should be getting unconditional love and not be used as a sexual object. He thus internalizes that the only way he can get the love of the caregiver is to perform and be sexual. And this type of behavior can continue for years into adulthood or until it is addressed and reprogrammed.

While coaching a client with goal setting, he began to tell me about an early sexual encounter that he had with a married man when he was 10 years old, with a sense of disconnect and an almost matter-of-fact manner. I then told him that the man was a robber of his childhood, that this was a violation and an abuse, and further, that this is not what he should have experienced at that age. He then began to cry hysterically and further recalled 13 other adult men that had abused him. I am glad that I was present to help him through this realization and lead him in the path of recovery.

Guilt: Having guilt is not necessarily a bad thing. It is a means to control undesirable behaviors and wants that may cause harm to others. For example, having guilt about stealing from others is justified. But if we have guilt about wanting to be successful and abundant or being appropriately sexual, this type of guilt is rooted in a negative program. The caregiver should be careful not to instill or pass on his fears in the form of guilt to the child.

Shame: Of all the above-mentioned dysfunctions, shame may be the most damaging. It is the belief that there is something internally wrong with you: a stain, an irreparable internal damage, or catastrophic filth that nothing can fix. If the child buys into this type of program, it will take a lot of effort to deprogram it. Typically, an abusive situation will reinforce this program especially if the abuse is being done to one child and not the other children in the family unit.

Institutions like the church are famous for controlling humanity through shame. You are a sinner just because you were born. The sin is so great that no one living on earth has the ability to overcome it. Moreover, you had nothing to do in the making or creation of this sin, but just because you are born human, you are a sinner. Of course, the only way that original sin can be removed is by the sacraments of the church and through Jesus Christ. This means that someone or an institution external to you is the key to your redemption. What a crock! This is nothing more than a brilliant and successful marketing campaign to erode your personal power and to control your mind and consciousness. This is the greatest lie that has ever been perpetrated on the human race. You are not a sinner. You are innocent. To allow this program to take root means that you will always be running after the train, begging someone else to let you on board. Thus, you are not self-reliant and not in your power and are measuring your salvation by someone else's standard. You will always feel that you are not good enough. You will always feel undeserving and fall short of expectation.

The reason why this type of program is easily rooted in the consciousness of humanity is that the Desire to Receive is still running the bread of shame program, which is the underlying program that caused the original descent. Remove the shame program that is overlaid on the inner child archetype and your divine essence will shine through. Truth be told, the inner child in its archetypical, divine, and original expression is the cosmic child, the son of God, and the son of man. When you own and restore that identity, you realize that you need to do nothing to be deserving.

In fact, all the blessings of heaven and earth are yours just because you exist. Own that belief and you will move into a state of effortlessness, and you will begin to ascend. This is the allowing and letting go of the basic core fear program that rules this realm, which was designed to resist us and, by the same token, give us an opportunity to earn back the Light. If you successfully release the shame, the letting go will initiate the expansion of consciousness, increase your energy, and trigger the beginning of your ascension process.

Healthy Parenting and the Inner Child

To heal the child within involves us becoming the unconditionally loving parent and caregiver to our inner child that our parents were not. But to most, the mother/father archetype is already contaminated by the kind of mother and father figure that we experienced in early childhood. Thus you do not have access to the Divine, archetypical, and primordial expression of the parent archetype. Under these conditions, any self-parenting would come from an imperfect and tainted model.

To do the work properly, you need first to understand what healthy parenting looks like and restore the Divine archetype of the parent. This looks like an unconditionally loving parent that loves and supports the child, but is not permissive and provides the child structure and discipline. If you are unconditionally loving and say yes to all the desires of the child, you will raise a brat. On the other hand, if you are too disciplined and judgmental, you become the abusive and critical parent. You have to find the medium point between unconditional love and discipline. The following are some basic needs that healthy family dynamics and good parenting should provide the child:

Safety and Security: The family unit should be a safe place for the child to grow. Of all the mammals, humans are born completely dependent on the mother or caregiver for food, shelter, love, and survival. In nature, when certain animals are born, they learn within minutes how to walk. It takes a child several months to a year or two to develop the same motor skill. The parents are responsible for picking up the slack and providing security and safety to the vulnerable child.

Touching: A child should be lovingly touched. From the soft grabbing of his cheeks to the holding and rocking of the baby softly in your arms, the child needs to feel the caring and loving embrace of the caregiver's arms and hands around him. This is a necessary need for proper developmental growth.

Attention: The child needs attention. The caregiver has to respond to the crying and constant needs of the child. He/she has to figure out how to interpret the crying to discern what it is that the child needs. The child needs to know that you are within arm's reach to respond to its basic needs. Mirroring and Echoing: The child needs mirroring. From your enthusiastic response to the baby's cooing, to your loving facial gesture, and the baby-talk response attempt at communicating with the baby, the child needs mirroring, echoing, and encouragement.

Guidance: The child has to feel that you are present to guide and navigate him when he is confused, doubtful, or lost. It is your presence, response, and clarification to his confusion and doubts that will allow him to feel guided and cared for.

Listening: The child has to be listened to. Whether he is asking why or sharing his discoveries and explorations, the child needs you to listen to him. This means attention to the details and responses when it is necessary.

Support: The child has to feel that you are there for him—that no matter what happens, you are going to support and encourage him. You need to demonstrate your support toward him and what is of concern to him. It is as if to say, "You can always come to me for help."

Trust: The child has to trust the caregiver, and trust is not automatically given. It is something that you earn over a period of time. It is through the consistent demonstration of your care, love, and support that the child will begin to trust you.

Fun: There has to be playtime. The child needs to have fun. The caregiver has to schedule playtime that will allow the child to express his joy and have fun playing games and doing activities for no other purpose then entertainment, celebration, and laughter. Moreover, the effervescence of life will flow through the child, and boundlessly overflow, giving the child endless energy and resiliency. Playtime is a means to channel this flow.

Healthy Sexuality: The child will notice that there are two separate genders and will ask questions about the differences, similarities, and more importantly, why it is so. It is the caregiver's responsibility to explain healthy sexuality in a manner that is age appropriate. No parent has ever felt that they handled that conversation correctly. What the caregiver has to watch out for is that they do not transmit their shame and taboos about sexuality to the child.

Nurturing: The child has to be made to feel that the home environment is nurturing. He has to feel that he is being allowed to grow and evolve without judgment and that his strength and innate abilities are permitted to develop, grow, and mature.

Unconditional Love: The child has to feel unconditional love from the caregivers. This means that their love is not based on performance. He needs to do nothing to have it. It is an automatic and spontaneous flow without any restrictions or conditions. Granted, the caregivers may at times dislike the child's behavior and hold him accountable for the lack of judgment, but their love is automatic, unceasing, and boundless.

If you can hold all these principals to be true and stalk yourself, over time you will restore your mother and father archetypes back to their original templates. But it takes time and a lot of courage to do this work. To move into the business of re-parenting your inner child means that you are not only dealing with the wounded inner child, but also with mother and father archetypes that are imperfect. Yet this is the only way that you can proceed to help restore your psyche's health and the authenticity of your being. So your attention will be at several places at the same time: the inner child and the mother/father archetypes, and more importantly, the exchange between them. To jump-start and initiate this re-parenting process, the following guided meditation may be helpful.

Introductory Meditation to the Inner Child

Close your eyes and take a deep breathe. Relax your body, mind, and soul as you slowly inhale and exhale. Imagine that you are seated under an old tree in an idyllic meadow. It is a sunny day. There are beautiful white clouds floating past in the sky. You can smell the scent of the flowers and hear the birds singing. There are butterflies moving all around you. You feel at peace, safe, and supported.

From the distance a figure approaches. It is your father in this lifetime. As he stands in front of you with all his flaws and im-perfections, the Divine Father appears and towers over him. The

Divine Father moves into your father and overrides the flaws and the imperfections, and what remains is a perfect expression of the father archetype. Now allow this blueprint to blend with your being and correct any and all imperfect imprints of the father archetype. You are transformed by this experience.

You stare out into the meadow, and a second figure approaches you. It is your mother in this lifetime. As she stands in front of you with all her flaws and imperfections, the Divine Mother appears and towers over her. The Divine Mother moves into your mother and overrides the flaws and the imperfections, and what remains is a perfect expression of the mother archetype. Now allow this blueprint to blend with your being and correct any and all imperfect imprints of the mother archetype. You are transformed by this experience.

In the distance a third figure approaches. It is your best friend holding in his arms a child. He asks you to babysit for him for a while and walks away. As you hold the child in your arms, you take a closer look and realize that it is you as an infant. You look into your inner child's eyes, and you tell him that you love him unconditionally. You bring this fragile blessing closer to your heart, and you allow your heartbeat to blend with his. You let your love swell up inside you and envelop this beautiful expression of Divinity. You now make a promise that from this moment forward you will be the unconditionally loving, but disciplined, parent; that you will be there to support, guide, and protect him to maturity.

Remain in that space for a while, and let the energy of this self-loving oath surround you. This meadow is a safe place where you can come at any time to visit and dialogue with your inner child. It is your sanctuary for intimate and private communication with the most precious and important part of you. Ask the child if there is anything that he wants to communicate to you and wait and listen for a response. As you prepare to leave the meadow, remind the child that you will always be there and that you are only a heartbeat away. You put the child in a bassinette and say goodbye, and you take a deep breath and open your eyes.

Unconditional Self-Love Protocol

Remember, you are not just re-parenting your inner child, you are learning how to be a better parent to yourself. At times you may catch yourself being the abusive or the permissive parent to the child within. It is up to you to stalk self and monitor the progress, evolution, and growth of these two archetypes and make sure that contaminations are not influencing the relationship. In addition to periodic and continual return to the meadow, communication, and care of the inner child, it is very helpful to do a 21-day unconditional self-love program.

1. As you wake up in the morning, ask the Mahatma, Lord Melchizedek, and Archangel Metatron to run their platinum light net through your four-body system: the physical, emotional, mental, and spiritual bodies.

2. Start your morning routine, and while taking your shower, imagine that that the water is turning to the color blue, the color of the Second Ray of love and education. Ask Master Kuthumi to infuse your being with the appropriate amount of self-love.

3. Ask Master Djwal Khul to anchor into your body the core fear removal programming, to remove all core fears that are blocking your self-love, and to do this continuously for the rest of the day.

4. Now ask Archangel Michael to create a golden armor of light and protection around you.

5. Before you begin your day, repeat aloud the following affirmations from Dr. Joshua David Stone:

   I love and forgive myself totally for all my mistakes, for I now recognize that mistakes are positive, not negative.

   I now fully recognize that I have worth because God created me, and I do not have to do anything to have it.

   I now recognize that I am a diamond, not the mud on the diamond.

   My worth is unchangingly positive because it is a spiritual inheritance. It is not increased by my success nor decreased by my mistakes.

   I realize now that I have total worth and value as a person whether I learn my lessons in life or not.

   I now recognize that everything that has ever happened in my life has been positive, because it all contained lessons I needed to learn.

   I choose to live in the "now" and not hold the past against myself.

I hereby choose to approve of myself, so I do not have to go around seeking approval from others.

I deserve love because God created me, and my mistakes are not held against me.

I realize that everything that happens in life is a teaching, a lesson, a challenge, and an opportunity to grow.

I now realize that I am the "I" person, chooser, consciousness, and spiritual being and that this part of me deserves unconditional love at all times.

I am the light and not the lampshade over the light.

I deserve love because my true identity is not what I do in life. I am the "chooser" of what I do.

I now understand that I am here to learn lessons and grow in life, but if I make mistakes, I am still totally lovable and unchangingly worthy.

I hereby choose the attitude of being very firm with myself and unconditionally loving.

I am the master of my life, and I choose to be my own best friend instead of my own worst enemy.

I choose to love me as God loves me—unconditionally.

I now choose truly to understand that I want to be perfect, with the understanding that the mistakes are positive and part and parcel of the growing process.

I now realize on the level of my true identity being the "I", the chooser, the person, the spiritual being, the soul. I am a perfect equal with every other person in the world.

I now choose to awaken and recognize that it was only the faulty thinking of my ego that has caused me not to love myself.

I now choose to undo all the faulty thinking society has pro-grammed into me and replace it with self-love.

I choose to recognize that I deserve love, and so do other people.

I choose to recognize that I am guiltless and sinless, because all mistakes are just lessons and opportunities to grow. Mistakes, in reality, are golden nuggets of wisdom and are positive.

I now realize that God does not hold my misuse of free choice against me, so why should I?

I love me. I forgive me. I approve of me, and I commit myself from this moment onward to treating myself in a spiritual manner rather than in an egotistical manner. I now fully realize that the way in which I think is the reality in which I live. I have been living in my own self-created hell of faulty thinking. I now choose to and will live in my self-created heavenly state of consciousness. It is really that simple.

I unconditionally love me because I am a son/daughter of God, and my misuse of free choice or faulty thinking is not held against me.

Could what God created not be lovable and worthy?

I love me because I am innocent and not guilty.

The only thing in this infinite universe that says I do not deserve love is my "ego." I hereby reject my ego and its false attitude and get back in tune with my true spiritual attitude and self.

I now, once and for all, release the ego's game of "having to do" in order to deserve love and worth. I now fully recognize I have always been lovable and worthy and will always be so.

In the evening, before you go to sleep, repeat the above-mentioned protocol, minus the affirmation. Do this for 21 days and you will find that the internal shame program will progressively dissipate. I have personally done this program more than once, for the shame program is deeply rooted. Each time I have done it, I have felt better. Remember, this a process, not an event. In some ways, it is like peeling an onion. Without complete acceptance of self and unconditional love toward the inner child, there is no ascension. You deserve unconditional love from the Universe, and there is nothing that you have to do to get it. Aur, the Light of the Creator, is the most abundant thing in the Universe. It is the God particle and exists everywhere that can create and become anything. It is all around us. In fact, we are swimming in it. But due to our shame, most of us cannot accept the Light and its endless gifts and bounties. Remove the bread of shame and restore your original identity and watch your life flow into a state of effortlessness.

Conditional Love

The overwhelming majority of people on the planet express and expect conditional love. For instance: You have to do something in order for me to know that you love me, and when those actions and demonstrations stop, the loving ends. You have to give me affection, cook for me, take care of me, and give me money, sex, passion, or whatever the external condition may be for me to know that you love me. This is conditional love. When that condition ceases and the flow stops, it is clear that you do not love me anymore. By the same token, I have to reciprocate the actions and conditions for you to feel loved.

This is the dynamic of most family and romantic relationships. Once that demonstration stops, one party feels abandoned and unloved, and the relationship unravels. I have to share with you that if any of my past romantic partners were to walk into this room right now, I would light up like a Christmas tree. If love is unconditional, it is not a faucet that can be turned on and off. Granted, some of my past partners may be the most toxic people that I could attach myself to right now, but it does not stop the fact that I will always love them, wish and hope the best for them. Seeing them would bring joy, happiness, and yes, unconditional love to my heart.

Unconditional Love

Unconditional love is love received as a primordial right. You need not do anything to have it. It is the fact and realization that you want the best for the one you love without any expectations in return. I don't need anything from you, but I love you nonetheless. It is love without attachments or conditions. The fact that this incredible feeling flows through me is the greatest gift that I can receive from you. I don't need anything from you. You could be close, you could be far, but the level of my love will not cease.

Now what happens when you unconditionally love yourself? What self-transformation occurs when you mirror the Universal love and project it toward your inner child? No performance, show, or demonstration is needed: I love you, my inner child, because that is your birthright. I adore you because you are the most beautiful thing that I have ever witnessed. I bless you because you are everything to me: the alpha and the omega. Let the grace of the divine, unconditional self-love, abundance, and all the blessings of the heavens fall on you always.

Chapter 5

Removing Fears

*Tell your heart that the fear of suffering is worse
than the suffering itself. And no heart has ever suffered
when it goes in search of its dream.*

– Paulo Coelho.

There exist in the Universe two basic emotions: love and fear. All other emotions are a derivation of these two. Of love, we spoke in the previous chapter. Love inflates, expands, and unifies, whereas fear deflates, contracts, and fragments our energy grid. Fear is often misunderstood. In dimensional existence, it serves a purpose and plays a role in the functioning and manifestation of the ego and self-awareness. Yet too much of it causes further fragmentation and separation from Source.

Fear and the Creation of the Ego

Let us take a look at its origin. When the Desire to Receive said "no" to the Light and endless gifts from the Desire to Give, the Receiver experienced fragmentation and separation for the first time. The primordial Receiver was infinite and endless like the Giver. They were both everywhere. This first act of free will, as a reaction and attempt to remove the bread of shame that was building up inside the Receiver, disconnected him from Infinity and created finite dimensionality: height, width, and depth. Immediately, the Receiver was as small as a pencil head. This happened in an instant.

One minute, he was endless, and the next, he shrank and contracted to the size of a pencil head. The positive outcome of this was the perception of boundaries, edging, limits, and the emergence of the "id," the precursor to the ego and individuality, but it also created panic, fear, and the realization of separation from the Giver. For the first time, the Receiver experienced fear—fear that he had lost the connection to the infinite realm and that he was now in exile from a blissful state. The Receiver had changed state and dimension and was now fragmented and fallen from a higher into a lower dimension. The descent from infinity into individuality came at a price. It brought with it vulnerability and exposure to now unknown forces.

The shift from an infinite and endless state into a finite and limited existence brought with it separation and loss of abilities, faculties, and powers. This loss and lack created fear. Fear is the loss of control over the predictability and maintenance of the status quo. It is generated by the introduction of an unknown factor that appears to threaten survival. Individual self-awareness coexists with a degree of fear. How much fear you are holding will determine your level of evolution and spiritual reintegration with God.

Thoughts Create Emotions

I want to bring your attention to the sequence of events that led to the creation of this core emotion. It was the free-will act of the Receiver saying "no" to the gifts of the Giver. It was a thought and intention that initiated the fragmentation and separation from the infinite estate. Thought then created energy, and emotion followed. That intention and act of restriction was the cause. From this cause, a contraction into lower dimensional existence occurred. Then emerged an awareness that was not present before: "I am small and limited." At that point, fear and a sense of great loss for its former estate overwhelmed the consciousness of the Receiver. The thought and intention came first; then came the energy or change in dimension or state; and finally an emotion was registered.

I am not splitting hairs, but I want to make you aware of the sequential order in which all things manifest in the Universe. The vast majority of humanity live in their emotional bodies. Their desire and emotional bodies rule them. There is no mastery, restraint, or control over their emotional reactive system, which is triggered by events and the emotional states that they elicit completely on autopilot. If you are a slave to your emotions, you've got it all wrong. It is your thoughts and intentions that are supposed to control and rule you. If at any point you are experiencing a set of negative emotions, change your thoughts. This will cause a change of state, and your emotions will follow.

Our emotions are powerful filters that create holograms, colors, or lenses through which we perceive reality. It is not actuality, but in the throes of the emotional state, we perceive it to be so. The Receiver was in such great fear over the perceived separation and fragmentation from the infinite estates that it sent a desperate call to the Giver to return and restore things to the way they were. But the Giver knew that the only way to remove the bread of shame program was to create an arena or universe where the Receiver would further fragment into multiplicity and would learn to give and receive from the various aspects of itself. In this process of giving and receiving, it would make a real effort that would allow it to feel deserving of the Light. This was (and is) the only way for redemption to occur.

The Descent and Fragmentation of the Receiver

In order to fragment the Receiver into multiplicity, separate identities had to be created. Our Universe is multi-dimensional and at every step of the descent into dimensional existence, the Receiver further fragmented into multiples of itself and, consequently, more contraction, separation, and fear, which manufactured additional individual identities. When the Receiver perceived itself as having limits and boundaries, individuality was created. Thus a level of fear, a sense of separation and fragmentation, were needed for ego identification.

If the Receiver were still everywhere as a unified consciousness, there would be no multiplicity. But if I end here, and you and others begin there, separate identities are possible. This disconnection from the unity consciousness and the rising degrees of fear and fragmentation in the multiple aspects of the Receiver were needed to initiate this redemption process. Where there is self-awareness and ego, a level of fear must exist. Where there is infinite awareness and endless existence; unity, merger, and love exist. Love is the energy of fusion, and it binds and blends all things together. Fear is the power of fission, and it separates and fragments all things.

The Degree of Fear Removal Equates to Your Level of Ascension

As aspects of the Receiver, the amount of fear we experience and allow to register in our consciousness is directly proportional to the amount of bread of shame and fear we have removed. It is the continual process of removing fear from our awareness that will close the loop and allow us to return back to infinity consciousness. As stated earlier: ascension is a letting go and an allowing. Let go of fear, judgment, and separation, and we ascend. As we ascend there will come a point at which individuality will vanish all together and in its place will arise collective awareness. Now since the percentage or degree of fear, fragmentation, and judgment that we hold will determine our level of ascension, it stands to reason that some individuals are running more negative-ego programs than others.

The greater the number of fear programs that are running in our sub-conscious minds, the more reactive we are and the more disconnected we are to unity consciousness. And if we are more reactive than average, we are not to be pitied. There is a great gift and light hidden in someone who is totally reactive and living completely in the throes of the reactive system. If Hitler were to do the necessary work to reconcile his actions and redeem himself, he would reveal more light to the world than you and I could release. He would have to expand his reactive system and consciousness from being totally self-possessed and egomaniacal to realize that every living entity is an incarnated aspect of God and himself. This process would release more potential light and power into the world than the average individual could attain. No matter where you stand in terms of your sense of separation from Source, you are redeemable. Even Lucifer is redeemable. In the end, all aspects of the Receiver, including the fallen ones, will be redeemed. Redemption for all. Do not compare yourself to others, but just start the process of removing fears and worries from your consciousness, and allow unity to flood your soul.

Positive vs. Negative Aspects of the Ego

The emergence of the ego boundary caused fear and a sense of separa-tion to be experienced. It is one thing to realize that we are separated from others; it is an extreme corruption to register this realization as a license to move against the world and attempt to dominate and control everyone. There lies the difference between the positive and negative aspects of the ego. Knowing that we are separate doesn't mean we are going to attack and control everything around us. The positive aspects we keep, for they are the mortar that cements individual awareness. It is the negative aspects that we need to reprogram. In humanity, this is triggered by our survival instinct. Any perception that there is a threat or danger will cause the release of adrenaline from our hypothalamus, a very powerful hormone. This moves in nanoseconds into the blood stream and locks into and changes the configuration of every cell in our body. Now arises in us the "fight or flight" preprogrammed behavior. It is a visceral, powerful, intense, and quick transformation that has saved many lives. There is typi-cally a rush of energy in our body, enabling us to see better, run faster, have great strength, and survive. This is an ancient and reptilian program that we share with every species on the planet.

However, humanity has evolved this into a fine art. We not only fight or fly, but with the negative ego corruption, we lie, deceive, justify, plot, kill, and manipulate with skill and cunning, making us, to date, the dominant species on earth. Yet often the perceived threat is just that. It is perceived and not real. But this does not stop or curb someone who is in the throes of this hormonal release from the negative ego behavior that follows. Sensing a threat or fear in our environment brings a perception to our consciousness. Analyze it quickly. If you are in physical danger by all means protect yourself. Otherwise, this is an opportunity for you to transcend a preprogrammed fear and remove bread of shame.

Golden Keys to Removing Fears

The following are golden keys and tools to help remove fears and worries. Let us enumerate several protocols and mechanics to help remove fears and master our reactive system.

Key #1 – Control of the Reactive System

Ascension is self-awareness. You have to be the decision maker at all times. No preprogrammed or internal reactions are allowed to run and alter your behavior and consciousness without your approval and consent. You have to stalk self and realize that the fear that is registering in your gut is a test. The positive aspect of the ego, the I, the Chooser, has to determine if the perceived threat is real or not. If it is real, allow the instinctual reaction to keep you safe. If, however, the threat is perceived or just a lens, follow The One, Two, Three Step protocol as described earlier and here repeated:

1. First realize that it is a test and an opportunity to grow.

2. Hold your emotional reaction for 10 seconds. Do not do anything; simply detach from the situation. Become an observer watching what is taking place. Imagine that you are observing yourself from far away, from the core of the Universe. You need to become blank, disconnect from your feelings, and just observe them like an outsider. Remember that it takes 10 seconds of nonreaction for the hypothalamus to shut down and stop releasing adrenaline in your blood stream. This typically brings great insight and wisdom to the situation and people-dynamics that created the perceived threat.

3. Once the shutdown is effective, move to expand your reactive system by attempting to do the exact opposite of what your instincts were telling you to do. This is probably the hard part of this process. You might have to fake it before the I, the Chooser, can actually

command the energy and emotional bodies to follow. For example, if you are experiencing anger, command your energy body to feel love toward the situation. This is not forcing an opposite emotion; it is a mental process in which you focus your thought and intention on the opposite condition and your emotion simply follows. Remember, it is your thought that creates everything. Energy and emotion have no choice but to follow. Do this and it will demonstrate to you a superior level of mastery and control.

Similar to the will of the Receiver saying "no" to the Giver, which initiated a dimensional descent and eventual ascent, your thoughts and intentions control everything. Your will is the most powerful force in the Universe. Not even God can overrule it. Your free choice will bring into alignment your energy and emotional bodies. Choose what course you want to follow, hold that intention for a short period, and watch your emotional reaction and mood change. It is that simple. This is what mastery is all about. Be in your personal power at all times, and fear and worries will have no chance to alter your mood and consciousness. This is not an event, but a continual process of approving and disapproving of all internal and subconscious processes as well as external events and energy systems that attempt to trigger your reactive system. You are in charge; decide what effect and affect they will have. You determine the appropriateness and your emotional body will follow.

Key #2 – Archangel Michael's Dome of Protection

Every morning and night, ask Archangel Michael to create an impenetrable force field around you, a golden armor of Light and Protection that only the Light of God can enter, rejecting everything else. Reaffirm this bubble of Light continually to keep outside forces and events from penetrating your field and locking you into the collective fears and worries that the family, village, nation, or planet have agreed to experience. This will help you disconnect from the matrix and collective experiences that humanity is choosing. Unplug from the grid.

Key #3 – The Heart and Mind Coherence

Allow the heart and mind coherence to occur as much as possible, and begin to gather data and information about your internal processes and the outer world from your heart space. The mind is quantitative, linear, and exacting. Humanity lives in this consciousness, which explains the negative ego corruption. When you gather information about your internal state and the outside world from your heart space, you perceive quality, interconnection, and unification to everything around you. Be unconditionally

71

loving to self and others, and the separation and fragmentation will begin to dissipate. In its place will be inclusiveness, merger, and connections. Being in the heart space lets you see the interdependence that links everything, while the illusion, maya, and glamour of fear, chaos, separation, and fragmentation fall away.

Key #4 – Fear Removal from the Galactic Mathematicians

Ask the Galactic Mathematicians to help remove from you and your energy grid all fear programs, subprograms, and replicator programs on a continual basis until they are all removed. The Spiritual and Galactic Hierarchies are glad to assist us, but we must ask them for help. Remember that we have free will and they will never interfere with it. If you don't ask them, they will assume that you are making the choice to suffer. Remember the law of noninterference. They are not permitted to comingle their energy with any other form of life without consent and disclosure. I must tell you that these Higher Beings are literal. Whatever you ask them to do, they will do. No more and no less. Choose your words carefully. The Galactic Mathematicians are a wonderful collective of Galactic Masters who are responsible for the restoration of equilibrium and harmony for all things in the Universe. From subatomic particles to the proper distance between suns and planets, they bring all things into balance and alignment. All you have to do is call them; they will gladly remove all unbalanced forces and restore equilibrium into your various bodies by grace, in prefect ways. They are a kind, loving, precise, accurate, and exacting collective.

Collective Fears

It is not just the fear coming from subconscious sources with which you have to contend, but equally powerful is the fear from the collective to which you belong. You may be a positive and upbeat person, but if you walk into a room with 100 fearful people, you will begin to experience a shift in your energy grid. If your personal power and shield are not impeccable, you will soon begin to experience the collective fear. When any group gathers within which the individuals hold the same beliefs and intentions, a living force more powerful than the sum of its parts is created. The French mystics call this the "égrégore," or loosely translated, the group body. It is a living matrix created by individuals who share a common belief. The group body is nourished by continuous reaffirmations of these beliefs by members of the group. Now the belief may be false, authentic, or a combination of both. Therefore, the group body can have positive, negative, or bipolar qualities. For example, when you go to a game and everyone begins to chant the theme song of the team, a powerful energy begins to flow through the stadium, causing excitement and fever-pitch exhilaration. A family has a group body that is nourished by the gathering at a dinner table or family meeting.

Collective Lack and Fear

Now think about seven billion people living on earth in a perpetual state of fear and lack, creating a mighty and frightening collective hologram or group body. Every media outlet reaffirms this lack with the fear-mongering broadcasts required to keep the attention of viewers in a 24-hour news cycle. Advertisers are telling you that you cannot be happy unless you have the latest version of their car, phone, TV, computer, etc. It is new and improved, and if you have it, life will be better and beautiful. Your happiness is one purchase away. In a consumer-based economy, such is the game that one has to play to sell products and remain competitive.

This lack- and fear-based group body is alive, and like all living things, it is trying to survive. This group body hold is reinforced every time you experience fear while watching the news or feel you need the latest version of any product, even while the one you have now still functions perfectly well.

Use the tools mentioned above to disconnect from the grid. Remember that the I, the Chooser, must be in charge 24 hours a day, 7 days a week, even in your sleep. Try not watching the news for a while and see how you feel. Are you less or more anxious? I happen not to have a television, and I keep myself informed about current events via the Internet. I read what I want to read. If I feel that an article is biased or slanted toward the negative, I click off. Now one can argue that you can do the same with a television, but this is not what happens. One sits mesmerized in front of this box, watching negative report after report like a viewer on the side of the road watching an accident. Due to the general passivity of TV, we watch horrified, glued, paralyzed to the playing and re-playing of the same fear-generating video clip of some exaggerated reporting while our fight-or-flight hormones are being triggered and released, causing panic and fear.

Watching television is a passive activity while reading is an active one that requires the use of your mind and imagination. Your critical mind becomes engaged in the process. No wonder that modern man needs antidepressants. I don't mean to say that all news channels are reporting fear. Due to heavy criticism, some have begun to incorporate five minutes of feel-good news reporting in a one-hour news program. As a rule, the majority of the networks are just worried about the ratings and will do what is necessary to increase viewership.

Acts of Unreported Kindness and Love

I refuse to believe that the world is that dark. I see miracles happening around me every day. When you witness a young man helping a blind woman crossing that street or see a man giving his seat to a pregnant woman on the bus, goodness is alive. I view acts of kindness, compassion, and love throughout the day, and anyone saying differently is disingenuous. I suppose that this kind of positive news does not sell newspapers or attract viewers. Choose how you want the global grid or group body to interact with you. Do you want to be reactive to its stimulus or do you want to be unplugged and think for yourself?

Instead of the lower and base emotion of fear, what if the group body were a celebration of the highest for which humanity was aiming? What if it were a celebration of kindness, compassion, love, giving, interdependence, and the realization that separation is an illusion? In what kind of world would we then be living? The group body does not care about the content. It is we humans who fill in the blanks. If enough of us disconnect from the existing group body and hold a different set of beliefs, we would create a competitive hologram and, over time, we would overthrow the existing paradigm. This is a process and is really how a simple but fundamental idea can take root and change the world.

When Galileo proposed a heliocentric paradigm that contradicted the way spiritual and governing authorities viewed the world, there was a long period of struggle between the competing ideas. Galileo, as a scientist, just noted that the existing geocentric model, with the earth at the center of the solar system, was not supported by observation. Instead, the earth was a planet in rotation around the sun, he maintained. His observation-based paradigm and model threatened the spiritual and governmental authorities who justified the legitimacy of their rule by the earth's so-called central position in the universe. To their minds, they were the direct embodiments of the hierarchical angelic and spiritual legions that ruled over the entire universe. Therefore, the Pope, King, Queen, and so on, were acting as representatives for the Divine over the masses.

Dante's *Inferno* was a literary illustration of the popular collective belief and view of the world. This was a world where the earth was flat, with a precipice at the end; at the bottom of the precipice, all the wicked souls were frozen in ice, with Satan at the center. It may sound silly to mention this old paradigm today, for all of us grew up with the heliocentric model, but years of struggle ensued with spiritual authorities and apologists battling it out to the bitter end against empirical evidence. Galileo was even threatened with death, for the arms of the zealots were long and their punishments were just as quick. One paradigm had been inherited; the other was backed by science and observation. In the end, the heliocentric model of our solar system won.

Dismantling the 3-D Fear-Based Paradigm

We are in the process of dismantling the current planetary fear paradigm. New observations and experiences are disproving validity of the status quo. Global warming is creating rapid physical changes in the environment that are affecting our ability to survive. Who is to blame? Are the fear-based, egocentric past behaviors of man responsible for the frightening changes that we are witnessing around the globe? The mentality of fear and the perception of separation have caused us to accumulate and horde resources, giving us a false sense of safety. "Since I am separated, I will conquer and dominate everything around me." We have moved against each other in an attempt to become the top dog. We do this not only against each other, but we do it against the planet by extracting resources and polluting the environment without conscience.

These behaviors are unsustainable, and now the planet and the forces of nature are adjusting to restore balance. Extreme atmospheric and weather pattern changes are something with which our generation will have to struggle. If we stop the blame game and begin to look at what we must do to adapt to these changes, we may get to a solution set more quickly. We know that fear and separation fuel the top-dog mentality. What would happen if, instead, we perceive and feel the interconnectedness and interdependence of all things?

What if I live by the rule that every action I take, every feeling I allow in my consciousness, every thought I have affects someone or something else? I therefore share responsibility for the health and functioning of the whole. This awareness and desire would drive us to leave a positive footprint behind. It is already happening. For example, the Occupy Wall Street movement and the collapsing of the Euro Zone are leading the way and showing that a lack- and debt-based global economy is unsustainable. One percent of the planet cannot control 80% of its resources. Giving and receiving must happen in a balanced manner. After all, this was the purpose for the descent into this 3-D plane: to remove the bread of shame by learning how to give and receive from each other. If the majority of the planet is giving and a small elite is gaining and receiving, the bread of shame is not being removed. One segment of the planet giving and the other receiving is far from giving and receiving from each other. We all should be giving and receiving in a balanced manner. In fact, the elite are maintaining control by perpetuating a collective ethos of lack, scarcity, and fear. Giving and receiving in a balanced manner is the sustainable ideal for the future earth.

If history serves us right, this is only the beginning of a long struggle. Fear is a symptom and effect. At its core is the perception of a loss of control or a threat. Creating a new planetary group body or hologram of hope and equal exchange will be the means for us to remove and overcome the bread of shame program. The struggle required for us to install a paradigm of hope, love, and interconnection is the effort that will remove the shame and allow us to feel, individually and collectively, that we have earned the Light back.

Rescue self first. Begin in your own backyard by doing everything in your power to disconnect from the internal and subconscious fear programs and the external events and stimuli that cause you to experience the collective fear that the planetary group body is holding. If you disconnect from the grid and stop feeding the fear-based group body, it will become malnourished and die.

Claim your personal power and be the chooser of all internal and external processes. It is your birthright. Remember that to remove the bread of shame program that is causing your fear-fueled experience, you have to apply an effort that will allow you to feel that you have earned and deserve to have the Light back. Do this and peace, love, and ascension will be yours.

The techniques shared above—stalking self, doing the 1, 2 and 3 steps, being in your heart space, calling on Archangel Michael, calling the Galactic Mathematicians, and being in your personal power—will do just that. When you apply and live these techniques, your fear-based experiences will diminish and disappear because the effort exerted to maintain control over your consciousness will remove the original shame. Redemption is at hand. It is up to you to walk the path of salvation.

Chapter 6

Psychic Self-Defense

Put your sword back into its place.
For all who take the sword will perish by the sword.

– Master Jesus

We live in a world of opposites: light and dark, day and night, good and bad, positive and negative to name a few. The 3-D reality is bipolar. That polarity is typically separated by time and space. However, if the opposites are brought back together in the same space, they cancel and annihilate each other. The realization of our individuality and its precipitation from infinity brought with it limits and created the perception of separation from forces now outside of self that may have a different and even hostile agenda to self.

Time and space precipitated as the stage where the fragmented Receiver could now experience and interact with other autonomous sentient fragments. Fragmentation and free will allow each aspect of the fragmented Receiver to make different choices. These choices may be harmonious or amicable to self, or they may be hostile and even hazardous to your welfare. How do you preserve the integrity and best interests of self? The best and ultimate defense that you possess is to be in your personal power. No force in the entire Universe can penetrate your field if you are in your power. And this should be 24 hours a day, 7 days a week, and even in your sleep. When we believe and hold our consciousness in the hopeful, the miraculous, and the positive while being in our power, we create a force field around us that nothing can affect. Do not give your personal power to anyone. Not to me—I don't want it. Don't give it to the Angels, the Masters, and not even to God—they don't want it. God wants you to co-create with him. Giving Him your power would mean that you would merge with him and he would lose his reflection in the process. When we allow fear, judgments, and separation consciousness to take hold, that force field is broken, and since the Universe is not a vacuum and is filled with intelligences, parasitical entities, and predatory forces, something may attach itself to you or host in your field.

The Celestial Hosts and Twelve Root Races

In the process of descent from uncreated to manifested fragments, the aspects of the Receiver took on various forms and garments. There exist in dimensional reality various classes of beings who have played a critical role in the manifestation of all life. We can group them into three general classes: the Elohim, the Archangels, and the Angels. If God is the client, the Elohim are the architects and engineers, the Archangels are the general contractors, and the Angels are the subcontractors that collectively work on the manifestation of all life. There are classes of beings higher than these, but they do not exist in time and space.

Let us focus for a moment on the Elohim, the blueprint makers. They created the DNA templates that manifested all life. They not only created the template for the Humanoid race, but also for the Elohim, Archangel, Insectoid, Reptilian, Feline, Dracos, Aquatic, Amphibian, Dolphin, Bird People, and Dwarf races. All of the originally created races were ascended and sentient. This list only covers carbon-based life, but they also created templates for many more types of sentient life forms that were not carbon based.

The Law of Noninterference

Originally, the fragments and aspects of the Receiver operated and transacted with each other in dimensional space according to one rule: the law of noninterference. That law states that I cannot comingle my energy grid with any other forces without disclosure and permission. If I want to gift you or receive something from you, I have to disclose my intent, and you have to agree before the transaction takes place. And "no" is a valid and complete answer that needs no explanation or retaliation. This gives tremendous importance and respect to the freewill choice of every aspect of multiplicity—the ability to determine our own course and direction.

I can descend or ascend the dimensional scale as I choose at my own pace.

Evolution and devolution were progressing as the experiment in which the bread of shame program was being removed with the effort, or lack thereof, of the fragmented man within the confines of the law of noninterference. Two rules were driving the continual descent and ascent of all life: noninterference and the giving and receiving in a balanced manner. These are the MS DOS or fundamental programs that allow the Universe to operate.

The Fall from Grace

About 500 million years ago in our time line, a subset of the Elohim made a freewill choice that was contrary to these laws: they decided that they liked the descent and did not want the ascent. They liked the individuality and fragmentation, not the reverse wave of merger involving the effort and attempt to remove the bread of shame. Since everything in the Universe was wired with the return path encoded at a DNA level, the only way to put their plan into effect was to alter their DNA sequencing from that of all created and manifested life-forms. And since they were Elohim, engineers, and architects, they re-engineered themselves with 11 strands of DNA, eliminating and blocking the return path and code. Further, they manifested races created in their own image with the same altered DNA sequencing.

Over a period of time, their progeny married and crossbred with humanity. This meant that the original descending line of created beings with 12 strands of DNA and the race created by those fallen beings with 11 strands of DNA were procreating hybrid children. This was not an accident. The path of return for the unsuspecting victims was being deliberately eliminated by the fallen beings without disclosure or permission. This was rape and violation of the highest sort and an attempt to usurp the original purpose of manifestation.

All significant Light Beings who were outraged by this act gathered together and created alliances, cloisters, and orders to watch, defend, and eliminate this aberration and cancer that was threatening to take over and redirect the purpose of our created Universe. This is the true origin of the angelic wars that all sacred texts talk about, and for millions of years, this battle to restore the original purpose has raged. Many Light Beings and their agents have infiltrated, spied upon, and battled the nefarious intentions and the territorial and racial expansion of the fallen beings.

The Races of Fallen Beings

Now, I don't want to give the impression that these fallen beings are a cohesive group. They are not. They are composed of many races, groups, and subgroups who all share one thing in common: the desire to reverse ascension and spread that agenda throughout the Universe. The dynamic among the various groups is extremely volatile and contentious. They act more like the South American drug cartels fighting each other for territory and control. This fact actually serves us and buys us time, for if they were cohesive and unified, they would be a force that would be almost too powerful to deal with.

They are made up of many races, and a few of the leading groups of these notorious races are:

The Annu Elohim, the progenitors of the Annunaki, were a race of humanoid giants who were the gods of the Sumerians in Mesopotamia. They came from space and convinced the inhabitants of that area that they were angels or gods. They mixed their blood with that of the original inhabitants, creating them in their image. Basically, they altered their DNA and dumbed them down.

The Dracos are dragon-like beings who inhabit the Draco Galaxy. They are the most aggressive bullies in the Universe. The original dinosaurs that lived on earth were voracious vegetarians. It was the influence and DNA manipulation of the Dracos that created the Tyrannosaurus rex and other aggressive omnivores. They were trying to reproduce on earth and infiltrate our galaxy. The extinction of the dinosaurs has always been clouded in mystery. Let us just say that the intervention of the Dracos became such a threat that the Galactic Confederation of Planets, the collective galactic body that oversees the welfare of the Milky Way Galaxy, sent a weapon that annihilated them all in three days.

The Greys are a misunderstood race of beings who are trapped around our planet in a time-dilation bubble, unable to leave. They are originally from Zeta Reticuli and from a future time line in which they were extremely advanced technologically, but with little or no morality or ethics to match. This led to a great war in which they managed to destroy their home world and, in the process, ripped the fabric of the time-line continuum in their quadrant of space. The radiation fallout from this event made them infertile, and they then had to clone themselves to survive. But over a long time of making copies of a copy, degradation and weakness of the gene pool was inevitable. One proposed solution was to go back in time, before the catastrophic event, and stop the destruction before it happened.

Since the time line around their world was ripped and unstable because of the radiation, they selected earth, a similar planet, with the hope that once they were back in time, they would travel from earth to their world for the rescue. Their calculation was incorrect for when you go back in time, you create a time-dilation bubble or field that did not extend to Zeta Reticuli, and thus they have been trapped around the earth since 1947. To survive, they have been abducting humans and attempting to create a genetic hybrid: half human, half grey.

There are many other groups and subgroups of lesser repute but of equal malice, like the dark Orions and Pleiadians.

Implants and Devices

These beings can no longer assimilate energy directly from Source due to their DNA alteration. They must now parasitically exist by taking second-hand energy from others. For that purpose, they implant unsuspecting humans with devices that are designed to drain them of energy during sleep, or they implant transmitters for ease of location and later drainage.

Additionally, there is a second kind of implant that may host in humans. They are elemental implants. Thoughts are things and are alive. Suppose that in a room, long ago, a murder occurred. This act of violence created an imprint in the ether, and unless someone transmuted and moved the energy, it was and still is ever present in that space, even many future years forward in time. If you happen to walk into the same room at a moment when you are not in your personal power and your field is open and porous, this negative etheric elemental implant will attach to you like a leech.

This happens often and even multiple times a day. I was taking a yoga class not long ago. We began by chanting and then moved into the basic positions: at first, the salutation to the sun and the downward dog. As soon as I tried to do this, an excruciating pain began to radiate from my lower back. All I could do was to roll on my side and get up. What is the first thing that most people on the planet do when they feel pain? They claim it by saying: "I have a pain in my back." If you do that, you agree and claim it. Instead, I stood with my eyes closed and asked: "Is this coming from me or is it from someone else?" In other words, did I pull my back or is this from a foreign origin? The answer came quickly. I had picked it up from the mat. The previous user had left this imprint in the ether around the mat, and it was trying to host on me. I simply called Master Djwhal Kuhl and asked him to anchor into my back the Core Fear Removal Programming (see Chapter 9) and to remove this pain continuously until it was all gone. Within two minutes, the pain was vanished. It is your responsibility to stalk self all day long and check to see if the energy system that you are feeling around you is from you, or someone or something else. This is your job, and this is how you remain in your power.

Parasitical Astral Entities

These are not the only beings with whom we have to contend. The astral realm is polluted with all kinds of parasitical existences that are looking for a means to continue to be: astral demons, negative emotional imprints, negative ETs, dead and lost souls, or parasitical elemental entities, to name a few. This is not personal. They are doing what every other form of life is doing in the Universe: they are trying to live. If you don't want to be the host, protect yourself. Every time I hear students talking about going into the astral realm as if it were a badge of honor, I cringe. Granted, the higher level of this realm is benevolent, but the rest is the sewer system of the Universe, and for you to voluntarily go there and not get soiled is almost impossible. Yes, you may unintentionally travel there in dream time, but even that can be corrected before you go to sleep by setting the right intention to travel into higher realms.

The Importance of Lucid Dreaming

Most of us are not lucid or self-aware in our dreams. This is a problem for us and is an opportunity for forces that are looking to influence you. If you are not self-aware, you cannot have discernment. You cannot approve or disapprove content that you don't even know is being implanted. Many people don't even remember their dreams and dismiss them as insignificant.

When I watched the movie *Inception*, I thought I was looking at a glamorized version of my early childhood in Haiti. The movie is about a group of people using technology to go into others' dreams, implanting and retrieving information without their consent. Anyone who grew up in a shamanistic culture has lived this. I did. This technology is also known and used by the cabal as "remote viewing and remote influencing." It is an insidious and devious method of implanting ideas, memories, and programs in someone's consciousness without their awareness, which can begin to define and control them over time. This kind of infection can grow to become a full-blown false identity. So many people are walking around with false implanted memories and identities, and they don't know it. They are behaving and acting in a manner that is inauthentic, and there is nothing in their psychology to explain it.

Creating Boundaries

The basic defense against any invasion, short of counterstriking, is to have impenetrable boundaries. There are many methods that one can use to create a psychic wall, energy field, and a ring-pass-not. A lot of them involve calling upon higher spiritual beings to defend and protect you. Archangel Michael is probably the most called upon to create defensive walls, and since his purpose is to defend humanity, his order is happy to comply. Yet no matter who you call and what method you use, if you cannot create emotional boundaries, you cannot create psychic ones. If your "no" and "yes" are actually "maybe," there will be back doors in your psychic constructs that malevolent intelligences can penetrate. If, every time you say no or yes, one can wear you down into a maybe position and even change your mind, you do not have good emotional boundaries. No is a complete sentence, and it does not need a qualifier. Yes is a fait accompli. Your words and your actions must match. Do not blame the ritual or the higher beings for the failure of your defenses, blame yourself.

Charles Whitfield in his book *Boundaries and Relationships* explains how you can diagnose and evolve emotional boundaries. It is a must-read for all students on the path of ascension. In 80% of family dynamics on the planet, there exists a secret that polite society cannot know. This could be an abuse, a handicap, a drug or alcohol addiction, etc. Every member of the family moves to keep the secret by lying, overcompensating, and covering up to hide the perceived shame. This creates emotional enmeshment in which everyone in the family is intertwined, sharing one psyche. Not one member is whole, and all members become handicapped while trying to sense the needs and desires of others, then compensating for them. As long as you are not whole, your emotional boundaries are weak, and you cannot create impeccable psychic walls. It is therefore in your best interests to become emotionally whole as quickly as possible, for your psychic defenses are suffering as you read this.

Spiritual Battling vs. Neutrality

What I am about to discuss is taboo in the Light and Spiritual community. I know of no one who dares mention this without being labeled an agent of darkness. If this is the hat that I must wear, to tell the truth—so be it. The angelic war has been going on for 500 million years. The great pendulum swing of Light vs. Dark has moved back and forth over the eons too many times to count. Many battles have been fought, many campaigns have been won and lost, but the end of the war does not seem in sight. There appears to be no exit strategy. The great Light and Spiritual elders of our

Universe have gathered armies, choirs, and hordes of beings in their ranks. They have even enlisted the help of many incarnated lightworkers and starseeds to help them battle their campaigns. I have seen and heard so many of my brothers and sisters going into battle for the Light, swords in hand or power animals at their sides.

In my youth, I believed in the rightness of such a cause until I was schooled differently. When I was growing up in Haiti, the mother of a friend and neighbor was a "right-hand" Voodoo priestess. She served the Light and loved me like a son and would share her wisdom and insights with me. She told me that some years back, while she lived in the South of the Island, a group of women came to her, warning her that a dark "left-hand" Voodoo priest in the village was plotting her end. She laughed out loud and told the ladies that this was joke, that this man was one of her best friends. As soon as the ladies left, she went into her temple and cast a spell so that the dark priest would forget that she had ever existed. I was puzzled and asked her if she did not have the strength to fight him. Her answer was revelatory. She said it was not about strength, for whatever she could throw at him, he would gather and throw back, escalating until one person was dead. She added, "That way I live long and he lives long."

Every time you pick up the sword to battle against fallen beings, something or someone will block you—even if you are receiving messages from your guides, Ashtar Command, Michael, the Pleiadians, or any other celestial host. Ask yourself if this is in your best interests and if this is your fight? What will be the consequences of your actions? And if it is not your fight, don't do it. Remember that you have freewill choice. What if these Light Beings were using you as pawn in a gigantic chess game?

Some years ago, I knew a man who would get periodic commands to become bait for angelic forces in dream time, at which point the Angels would move in to destroy the darkness. My question to him was: when you go fishing, what happens to the bait? I did a clearing for him; he was infested from head to toe with implants. And I could not argue his lack of discernment about being bait, for I was just a man and he had angelic hordes at his side that would protect him, or so he thought. He was glamourized by the honor of having such personal relationships with celestial hosts. He was angry with me and unwilling to listen. Furthermore, the gain from battle—the powers, objects, and abilities retrieved—is perceived as things that you truly earned. Wake up people; every being that exists in dimensional existence has lenses or filters through which they reflect the Light of God. Granted, the Archangel Metatron filter is probably closer to the Light than mine, but I am not going to give him my personal power and believe blindly everything that he says.

Personal Discernment in Our Transactions with the Celestial Hosts

Everyone has an agenda. Is this agenda in alignment with my best interests? Every time I mention this, someone always asks how an angelic being could make a decision that would put anyone in harm's way. It must not be a true angel. Please don't be so linear; open your consciousness to the nuances of higher truth. Don't be so naïve and willing to capitulate your personal power to others. If a general goes into war overseeing an army of 100,000 troops, he knows that there are going to be collateral damages. Deaths will happen. Sacrifices and destruction will take place, but the goal is to win the war. Anyone who has played chess knows that you need to sacrifice knights for you to checkmate your opponent. Do you want to be collateral damage? Moreover, every sentient life force has free will and can decide at any point to ascend or descend. Your guides can also change their minds. They can decide to support the original purpose or digress at any point.

That same choice is available to the fallen beings as well. From their fallen position, they can choose to ascend. Keep this in mind when you are receiving your transmissions and commands from your guides. Free choice, personal power and will are not events, but processes that are continually becoming. There is no stationary or static position in an evolving Universe. Be discerning and make your own decisions accordingly.

Additionally, the beings that you are attacking for the Light are ancient and immortal. They have long memories and deep grudges. As soon as you attack or become bait, you are noticed. They will wait forever for a moment of weakness to attack you. And if you are so well protected that they cannot get to you, they will get what or who you love most. They will create chaos around you and destabilize you. If this work is your choice, your friends, loved ones, and family members will be at risk. Are you prepared to let your loved ones be attacked by principalities? We have a proverb in the Caribbean that says: "Animal with long tail don't jump fire." Your tail is what you love the most, and if you fight them and jump fire, you will get burned. Among the groups and individuals I know who are doing battle, all of their personal lives are in chaos.

Spiritual Battling on Earth

This warning about battling is not limited to disincarnate hosts, but is as valid if you were ever to be attacked by a black magician. In the work that we do, there is always someone who feels you have stepped on their toes, even if all that you are doing is spreading Light without any sword in hand. These attacks often reveal themselves in dreams. Let me say that none of these attacks can attach themselves to you unless you react in fear. I have had numerous dreams in which dark, nasty, evil-looking beings and situations of disempowerment were projected toward me to create a moment of fear. If you experience fear, the attack penetrates your shield. Remain an observer without objection, as if you were an outsider watching the situation, and nothing will break your boundaries. If you control and restrain your emotional body, the power that was sent will dissolve on its own. Under no circumstances are you to send a reciprocal attack or projection back to the point of origin.

None of the Ascended Masters will behave that way. If you begin to battle with a dark magician, the battle will never end until someone is dead; and even after death, they will know how to torment you in the hereafter. If you are actively under attack, you can ask Archangel Michael for protection. And you will immediately receive this protection even if you had said no to Archangel Michael and refused to be a pawn in his campaign. The angelic races are not as petty and retaliatory as we can be. They are created for a purpose and will do what is necessary to fulfill that end. We have the alienable right to determine when, where, and how we proceed on our paths, and if we exercise that right, they hold no grudges against us. I know of no power greater than Michael's to create protection shields. If you have worked on your emotional boundaries and ask Michael for help, a shield will be created that will repel all attacks and return everything to the point of origin without any effort on your part.

Reconciliation

Ascension is a solo act. It is an act of spiritual autonomy. Do not capitulate your personal power to anyone. In some ways, it matters not if you serve the Light or Dark, for as long as you are keeping duality in motion, the end is not near. The angelic war is 500 million years old and will continue for another 500 million unless we do something different. Of all the positions to take that will resolve this ancient conflict, the Ho'oponopono is the closest to an exit strategy. It is the path of reconciliation of the Kahunas, the keepers of secrets, of Hawaii. In the wise understanding of these native healers, all toxic relationships are being held at two points. Whoever is my tormentor now, I have tormented in a past life so old that I may not remember. In order to avoid the endless cycles of battle and retaliation of toxic energy back and forth, one side has to acknowledge that they have wronged the other. The blame is to be shared 50%. No one is a victim or spotless. Both parties are co-creating the unhealthy relationship. If you acknowledge responsibility, ask for a sincere forgiveness, replace any animosity with unconditional love, and let go, you are cleaning up the mess and getting to a resolution. Here is my version of the Ho'oponopono Liturgy:

Divine Creator, Father Mother, Son as One…

If I, my family, relatives, and ancestors

Have offended you, your family, relatives, and ancestors

In thoughts, words, deeds, actions, or inactions from the beginning

Of our creation to the present, I ask for your forgiveness…

Let this cleanse, purify, release, and end all negative memories, blocks,

Energies, and vibrations and transform these unwanted energies to pure light…

And so it is done!

If you can repeat this prayer over and over again every time you feel victimized or attacked; if this becomes your mantra every time you perceive toxic emotions and counter-attack thoughts coming from your own subconscious mind; if you mean what you say when you repeat this prayer; then a powerful release, peace, and resolution will be achieved. This is not an instant solution; rather it is a continual process of making amends for eons of struggle and battle. It will take time, persistence, and dedication to retrain your consciousness to a new way of perceiving, reacting, and being. I have benefitted greatly from this, and I encourage you to do the same.

Neutrality

Although we exist in a bipolar and dualistic Universe, there exists a third state in nature. The triad is alive and well. At the atomic level, elements have **protons**—which are positively charged particles; **electrons**—which are negatively charged particles; and finally there are also **neutrons**—which are neutral with zero charge. If we can select which part and role we play in maintaining duality, then it would stand to reason that we can also select neutrality. You have free will, and you can choose the state in which you exist. Having plunged into battle with sword in hand on behalf of the Light in the past, I choose neutrality in this life and future lives.

This was not something that fell from the sky one day; rather it was an evolutionary process. I was under psychic attack by a small group of individuals who were convinced that I was interfering with their mission. I received multiple psychic projections and attacks from them. A friend suggested that I throw everything back at them, returning the projections back to the sender. I told my friend that I could not do that. When you are a giant and know your strength, you act gingerly. I knew that if I threw anything at them, I might kill them. I simply chose to remain fearless. They went so far as intercepting my mail and breaking into my house when I was not home. When I returned, I was truly spooked by the intrusion and violation, and after talking to a friend who calmed me down, I retreated into a deep meditation, going into Source and asking God for help.

The connection was so powerful and pure that I entered a rare blissful state: a complete and total stillness. I sat for what appeared to be hours and then sensed the presence of a face materializing right next to my cheek. I was startled for it was not an apparition; it was a 3-D materialization. The being did not speak, but I seemed to understand him telepathically. He told me that he was from the Guardian Alliance of Light and that he was going to teach me a field of protection that nothing in time and space could enter. I told him to proceed and was taught how to create 12 counter-rotating torsion fields of light and neutrality, with zero-point energy around me and my house.

This was my introduction to the Guardian Alliance of Light and to the concept of neutrality. Neutrality is not allowing the Dark to win by not doing battle. It is not a disengagement from the injustice that exists around us. Every time I try to explain this concept, many perceive it as an escape and betrayal of the purpose of the Light. It is not so. It is a means to address injustices without being polarized. Instead of being black and white about what is going on around us, one can choose to find sustainable solutions that are holistic and resolve conflicts permanently. It is about having preferences and not attachments. It is the perception of a fear and a threat that initiates polarization, and if it is a fear, it is about fragmentation and separation. Every time we get viscerally upset, we acquire a charge and are polarized. If we perceive an injustice and attach no charge to it, but make a choice to seek a means to resolve the conflict for the greater good and ultimate sustainability of the purpose of creation, we stand a better chance of finding a permanent solution than if we run to the opposing corner.

The Danger of Blending Light with Dark

It is not a blending of Light with Dark either. There are many twilight masters and grey magicians who are attempting to blend the Dark with the Light. This path is a minefield, for there are aspects of the Dark and the Shadow that cannot be redeemed and brought back to Light. Once a force enters into a deep level of decay and decomposition, one cannot breathe life back into it.

I know of what I speak. I attempted in my youth to face my shadow, and the result was catastrophic. I am still living with the regrets of my actions, influenced by the shadow during that time frame. There are parts of the subconscious that must be allowed to decompose until they become compost for future creation. To attempt to bring them back will do nothing more than bring putrefaction and sewage into your face. You cannot re-gurgitate the contents of your bowels into your mouth. Any beings who are attempting to do this are a danger and menace to themselves, their families, and students, for by their actions, they will allow equal play to the Light and the Dark. They hope to balance Light with Dark and gain power by this blending.

From my personal experience, I can categorically say that the primordial and archaic part of the Shadow cannot be tamed. If the Light is about organizing and bringing life into manifestation, conversely, the primordial Darkness is about death, decay, and entropy. It has no morality, and there is nothing that you can do to give it morals. Now, I am not referring to the negative ego, which of course can be reprogramed, but to the archetypi-cal darkness. Let me just repeat here that these parts of the Dark are so frightening, you cannot bring them to the dinner table for a civilized con-versation. They will consume you and everything around you, spreading chaos, pain, and suffering—just because they can.

Neutrality is the ultimate form of conflict resolution. If opposite forces are brought together in time and space, they annihilate and cancel each other. Typically, there is a short circuit or explosion. Therefore, opposite forces are separated by space. They must exist away from each other. Upon entering zero point and neutrality, a charged particle is presented with a field of infinite possibilities and is allowed to balance the charge in an ac-celerated manner without a short circuit or explosion. Any charge or issue that is brought into neutrality is faced with its scalar invert and allowed to resolve the potentiality deferential in a safe and nonexplosive manner.

Torsion Field of the Guardian Alliance of Light®

The Torsion Field of the Guardian Alliance of Light® is a specific torsion field mechanism that the Guardians taught me to allow the creation of neutrality around any person, place, or thing, with permission of course. It creates a neutral frequency and band of noninterference around anything while allowing it to resolve any and all internal conflicts in an accelerated time frame.

It can be the end of pain and suffering, or it can create great ease of pain and suffering, depending on your readiness to accept and integrate resolution. I have seen people's problems disappear in 5 minutes and have seen amelioration of discomfort and need for additional treatments. That is how it works. It turns out that everything in the Universe that has a magnetic field has a torsion field or torus. The geometry is in the shape of a doughnut, with energy flowing up and down and all around the surfaces of the doughnut, with the person or object in the center. Since almost every object in the Universe creates such a field, this geometry exists everywhere. It is the building block of creation.

The Guardians that exist outside of time and space create 12 counter-rotating torsion fields of light and protection around you, with your permission. In effect, this allows you to move up the dimensional ladder with each torsion field, until you are outside of time and space and into Source and the blessed field of total neutrality. If you create it around someone else, the size of their problems and issues are not relevant to you. It is not your burden to fix or do anything. You just facilitate the creation of this field and take them into Source outside of time and space. There, you throw them and their problems into the field of Light and let go. You wait for a transformation and change to occur. You do not do anything but observe. When it is done, you bring them back into 3-D. This also was understood and foreseen by the Galactic Regent Council. If you are interested in learning the details of this technique, I teach this on a regular basis in my classes and in workshops.

Neutrality as Accelerated Conflict Resolution

Since we all have free will and the right to control our path of evolution, neutrality will only bring you to the level of conflict resolution that you are ready to accept. I have seen instantaneous change and transformation and have seen others struggling after several treatments using this mechanism, for they were still battling and polarized in some deep and internal way. For pain and suffering to end, you have to stop fighting through and through. How many of us have contentious and difficult relationships with family members, co-workers, bosses, neighbors, communities, municipalities, etc.? How many times have I done battle for the Light or Dark or both since the beginning of time until now? None of these are examples of a neutral psyche. If we are to embrace neutrality, we have to find a means to become neutral to these past events and have no charge to these relationships.

The Ho'oponopono is a phenomenal way to own responsibility for our actions. The short version of this prayer is: *"Please forgive me. I love you and I let go."*

Since everything that viscerally charges me is a mirror or a reflection of an internal conflict or fear, then whatever is causing me to fume is an externalization of an internal polarity. Besides, everything in the outside world is an aspect of the original Receiver. How can a cell fight against another cell that is part of the same body? When this happens in the physical body, it is called cancer, and it is often fatal. So as I say the Ho'oponopono, I am not just asking my apparent tormentor for forgiveness, but more importantly, I am also recognizing the shame, fear, and unsustainability of my polarized psyche and asking myself for forgiveness for holding this polarity against myself. Doing the Ho'oponopono with that consciousness will create deep and profound healing, and will allow you to accept neutrality and be in total spiritual rectitude and verticality.

Neutrality vs. Physical Threat

Now I am not telling you to remain neutral in the event of a physical threat or attack. By all means, move to keep yourself safe. But for all other matters, do not let fear motivate you and make you reactive. Be neutral and choose how you are to behave, as a premeditated act and not as an automated response. Like all spiritual and evolutionary states, neutrality is not an event, but a process to which we continually draw closer and closer.

So having taught this to my students, I thought I had a handle on the nuances of this energy until a woman schooled me. She became one of my students after attending one of my lectures. Two months later, she came to me for a counseling session and during the session revealed to me that she was serving a fallen angel. I did not react to the revelation, but as soon as she left, I asked my guides for help? "What should I do?" The Guardians were forthcoming with advice: "What did you think neutrality was? That only the Light was going to come to you? Many Dark Lords are aware of the unsustainability of this angelic war and are seeking a way out. She not only serves this fallen being, but she is an incarnation or aspect of this being." I then asked: "What do I do?" They said: "Love her like you love

91

everyone else. One of two things will happen. She will entrain and learn neutrality, or she will leave if the frequency becomes too high." So after every class, I made it a point to give her a great hug and pour love into her.

She studied with me for two years, and I did notice remarkable improvement. She stopped coming to the classes as I began to increase the volume of neutral frequency around me by removing my internal polarization to past events and situations. I know, however, that a seed was planted. How quickly it takes root is not up to me. This taught me that some of the fallen are also looking for an exit strategy out of this battle and conflict in the heavens. I have to say here that if they so desire, they can realign all altered DNA sequencing back to the original purpose and be redeemed. The original pattern and sequencing is dormant but can be revived with the right intention.

How do you go there? Simply by projecting your consciousness into Source outside of time and space and allowing the neutral and blessed field to solve all lack, pain, and suffering that you may have. It is not your purpose and need to solve or do anything. Just bring yourself and your issues into Source. Allow the field of endless possibilities and solutions to solve all conflicts and bring them into neutrality. Bliss out on the peace and stillness.

Chapter 7

Blind Spots

Every man takes the limits of his own field of vision
for the limits of the world.

Arthur Schopenhauer

As we proceed down the evolutionary path, it is sobering for us to understand that what we perceive with our five senses and what we allow to register in the field of our consciousness are vastly different. We perceive with our mind and not with our senses. All of our senses can be reduced to electrical responses that are interpreted in our mind as a sensation. For example, when light reflects off an object and the photons come to the lenses of our eyes, they are transformed into electrical impulses that our nerves carry to the back of our brain to the visual cortex, where they are reorganized and interpreted as an image. It is, however, not a perfect or accurate transmission of what exists in the outside world; rather it is a filtering of a vast array of information and data into patterns with which we are already familiar.

Experiments have been done in which one eye was given a slight distortion from the other eye, but the distortion was not perceived. The brain interprets the perceptions of both eyes and fills in the blanks to match what is expected. Anything that does not match the expected and agreed-upon patterns is rejected and does not register into the field of our awareness.

Visual light, which is a few bandwidths of the electromagnetic spectrum, allows us to perceive and experience the world. Right now, radio, TV, and a multitude of waves and frequencies are swirling and moving through and around us. We do not perceive them, but that does not mean they do not exist. We see in color, though other animal species see only in black and white, while the mantis shrimp at the bottom of the ocean perceives 10,000 colors. We are only perceiving and experiencing a narrow fragment of what is actually happening around us; to the rest we are blinded.

The Limits of Our Perceptions

Neurologists have determined that the human brain picks up 400 billion bits of information per second, yet only 2,000 bits are registered on the field of our awareness. They are related to our perception of space and the outside world, the limits and separation of the body from that of others, and the linearity of time. Why only 2,000 bits? It is because our brain and the neural net connection that interprets the world will only match nerve impulses to neural net synapses that already exist. Anything outside the realm of the expected is rejected and is not registered into the field of our awareness. We are busy editing and matching and holding reality to what we expect it to be. Any perception that does not match the pre-existing patterns is ignored. We have so many objections and fears that we become blind to any perceived data that does not match the expected or agreed-upon paradigm. We are busy maintaining the status quo.

There is a story about the Indian shaman standing on the seashore looking at the ocean and the disrupted waves for days but being unable to see Christopher Columbus's caravelas because he did not have a matching or familiar point of reference or pattern of them. After staring for a few days, he finally saw the caravelas, and when he did and told his tribe, they saw them too.

The Interconnectedness between the Observer and the Object

In addition to our limitations of perception, we must also consider that the observer is affecting the object being observed by projecting his expectation of it, thereby co-creating the reality that he sees. To better explain, let's use the now-famous double-slit experiment:

On an atomic level, when photons or particles of light with a discrete mass are passed through a single-slit and then double-slits created on a shield, the light is registered on the sensitive background in a specific pattern. If however a light wave is passed through the same single-slit and then double-slits created on a shield, a different pattern is observed.

On a sub-atomic level, when scientists bombarded the same single-slit shield with electrons, the smallest sub-atomic particle, the expected pattern was observed. But when they tried the double-slit, the registered pattern was that of a wave.

How could that be? An electron is an object or particle with a mass and not a wave. So they decided to put a measuring instrument on the back side of the shield to observe what was really going on. When they did, the pattern observed changed from a wave to a particle. The only logical conclusion was that the act of observing and measuring affects the outcome and changes the pattern from that of a wave to a particle. This is a mind-blowing and paradigm-shifting conclusion indicating that the observer is projecting an expectation, and the object is matching that projection.

This means that we are reality-creating beings. The responsibility of the reality we are experiencing falls in our lap. What we are experiencing, we are co-creating. Take a look at your life and think of all the joy, lack, pain, and suffering that exists. They are your creation because you expect them to be there. You are creating your own hologram or movie. What is even sadder is that this hologram is not even an original creation, since we are conditioned to match the patterns that we know; we are creating the expected and familiar.

The inherited rigidity of the world, which our brain and neural net are re-affirming, is also projecting and creating the trap that is limiting the expansion of our consciousness. After all, ascension is an expansion of perception and consciousness. If we want to evolve and grow, we have to explore the path less travelled. We have to consider that things may exist in manners that we have not considered before.

Blind Spots That Are Limiting Our Perception

We all have blind spots, areas of our life that we falsely perceive, which may be visible and clear to others but invisible and blind to us. Our internal wiring is designed to match patterns in order for us to survive. It is motivated by the original perception of fear that accompanied the realization of limits, edgings, and boundaries when the Receiver shrank down to the size of a pencil head. This illusion of separation and the fear that it creates in our core are constantly being supported by the filtering mechanism of our five senses and our matching neural net perception.

Releasing Fears and Judgments Associated with Our Perceptions

As aspects of the Receiver, we have been holding this fear in place for a long time. How do we let go of this core blind spot that is limiting our perception and blocking us from accepting the bounty that exists around us in the blessed field of the Giver? We have to figure out a way to remove the bread of shame. The problem is not the fact that we observe the world through our five senses, it is that we have objections, judgments, opinions, and fears about what we observe. If we can perceive without objections, a world of endless possibilities would open up to us. One way to do this is to take stock of ourselves and make the necessary changes and adjustments of consciousness that are needed to release the fear that accompanies our perception.

This is a long road of struggles and slow, incremental progress. However, there is a quicker way to accomplish the same thing. If we repeat the short version of the Ho'oponopono like an endless mantra—"Please forgive me. I love you and I let go"—over and over while directing it at all fears that accompany any sensation we perceive throughout the day and night, and even in our dreams, we will eliminate the fears and objections that are often associated with our perceptions. Do this as you walk down the street, buy groceries, or talk to your co-workers, boss, and family members. Repeat this mantra as you feel, sense, and smell, and more importantly when you think about anything, for that is when the opinions, judgments, and fears will creep in.

The end result is that you will stop fearing and trying to control the world around you and start believing and accepting the miraculous place where you exist. Doing this will bring tremendous healing, releasing loads of baggage, pain, and suffering associated with a fragmented consciousness. It takes 21 days to train the subconscious mind to create a new habit, and after that, muscle memory takes over and causes the manifesting engine that is the subconscious mind to loop this new program forever. The blessed field is worth this small effort on your part.

For those of us who have done and continue to do this, it brings great freedom and lightness. I am not responsible to do or remove anything. Because there is no fear, the burden to do and fix anything is released. Instead, I allow the endless possibilities of a benevolent and gifting Universe to manifest. I receive with graciousness and gratitude. It is a consciousness-expanding way to move about the world, for all kinds of synchronicity happen when you are in a state of gratitude.

Without fear, your neural net will allow the expansion of things and bits of data outside the inherited and accepted realm. Over time, the blind spots will begin to lift to reveal the landscape that was under your nose. At first this is disorienting. For one thing, bliss begins to wash over you at the strangest of places and times. Second, your perceptions are expanded, and you know, feel, smell, hear, and sense things that are outside the normal way of sensing. This is because the higher senses are being brought online. Behind the normal range of our five senses exists a higher and more expanded capability to perceive and know the world.

Our Higher Senses

Let me just say here that language will limit how you and I express this expanded perception. We often hear psychics say "I see," when in actuality what they really mean is "I feel," "I sense," "I know," or "I hear." I have often explained this in my classes for those who feel and do not see and who may think that something is wrong with them or that they lack necessary skills. Not so. We typically have a predominant sense and, if we are lucky, maybe two.

Now what happens is that as you do this work, new neuron connections are created to match the new perceptions that you are allowing in. This may manifest with the expansion of existing predominant senses or may result in new senses becoming activated. Finally, as you continue on this path, a synesthesia of your senses may happen, which is when two or more of your senses are fused together. The most common type is for words or hearing to trigger color perception, or for reading a word to trigger color as well. But it is not unusual to have words or hearing trigger an image or some vignette like a window that opens in the mind, or for words to create a smell. As you remove fear and allow consciousness to observe without objections, more neural net connections will be established, and your perception of the world will expand into larger and larger territories. The first blind spot is thus your organ of perception.

The Domestication Process of Children

As children, our caregivers are like gods to us. We want to emulate and please them. Good parenting involves our caregivers "domesticating" us like you would a dog at obedience school. Positive or negative reinforcement goes a long way toward forcing the weak will center of a child into agreement with what is expected of him or her. It is not done with malice, but with the desire to help us become agreeable, well-mannered, functioning citizens. Statements like "good boy" or "good girl" substitute for treats and go a long way to bend a young mind into "acceptable" behavior. This process continues at school, church, through the media, society, and the environment, with all of them trying to bring us into docile acceptance of the status quo. These continual bombardments reinforce the neural net connections of what is acceptable, and weaken and dissolve the connections and beliefs that are ignored.

By the time we are teenagers, our awareness has been domesticated to mirror, accept, and reflect the knowledge and agreements of our ancestors. The collective agreement and neural net of the family, lineage, and social groups with which we identify ourselves are by now incorporated into our psyche. As we grow up, our view of the world gets more and more limited, rigid, restricted, and inflexible the more we identify with social groups. But remember that rigidity and inflexibility come from the perception of a threat or fear. Slowly and incrementally, we have capitulated our authenticity, neutrality, and freedom to become good team players at the cost of our individual and personal growth, exploration, and evolution.

Ascension is, however, a solo act. This is not to say that you will not have companions along the way and guides in your journey, but that the ultimate merge with God that you seek is a personal and individual reflection back to Source; it is when you realize that the "Father/Mother and you are one," that the out-breath of God will reverse into the in-breath. It is a path of self-discovery and self-mastery in which one takes responsibility and lets go of inherited beliefs and allows in the possibility that what lies beyond the fear is not a threat, but a blessing in disguise.

Our God Concepts as Blind Spots

Of all the blind spots that have caused wars, death, destruction, separation, and divisions among men, none is more polarizing than our "god concept." More individuals have been killed in the name of God than for any other reason. How many millions have been killed in the Crusades, witch hunts, and ethnic or spiritual cleansings?

Our god concepts and religious beliefs are inherited and are often based on dogmas or Holy Scriptures that may predate us by thousands of years. The followers are asked to have faith, to believe in the words, and not question any aspects of the Scriptures. Yet the teachings are not from our personal experience; they are given to us as laws that we must obey for the promise of a salvation or after-life. Anything that falls outside of the belief is heresy and must be viewed as a threat, dealt with by an attempt at conversion or by the destruction of the heretics and their beliefs. Although spiritual idealizing and devotion has at times done great good and converted lost souls onto a path of righteousness, it is also limiting in that the followers by their nature will only obey and at times interpret in fundamentalist ways what was given to them as guidance in the Holy Scriptures.

Anything outside of the Scriptures is viewed as a threat. Yet life is ever continuous and expansive, and the experiences, decisions, and responsibilities that we are now facing were not anticipated by the writers of the Holy Books. To ignore the changes and transformations that are happening around us is to put our heads in the sand like an ostrich. Ascension is a personal and self-engaging path of continual growth and evolution. If the god concept of your grandfathers is what you are holding today, then you have blind spots and objections and have not allowed new experiences in, like personal ascension. I am not suggesting that you reject what you know but that you build upon it; make this an endless journey of exploration and ever-expanding awareness about your highest spiritual concepts. Ten years from now, your god concept and your understanding of your relationship to your Creator should evolve and be broader. If the god concept that I am explaining in this book remains unchanged for you ten years from now, you have not evolved.

A wife once brought her born-again husband to me for a healing of pain and suffering. Since I need permission and must disclose the nature of what I am going to do, I explained to him that I was going to channel all the Ascended Masters for the healing. Further, that in my studies of all religions, I saw more similarities than differences: whether you call them Christ, Moses, Mohammed, Buddha, or Krishna, they were all the same state of God realization. He answered: "If it does not come from Jesus, I don't want it." How sad and limiting for him. I did not do the healing, and as of today, he is still suffering.

Socio-economic Blind Spot

The social and economic level in which you grew up will also blind you to the struggle, difficulties, privileges, experiences, and perceptions of someone at the opposite end of the socioeconomic ladder. The neural net connections that are fused with the memories of your experiences given your social and economic status will blind you to possible difficulties or ease that someone at the opposite end of the spectrum may have. These blind spots will narrow your views to the expectation that everyone should understand and interpret the world the way you do. If you were at the lower end of the economic ladder where you had to struggle to achieve, you may end up being an overachiever, or the struggles may have developed into an entitlement mentality in which you feel that the world owes you for the lack of privileges that you did not have. If you were at the upper end of the economic ladder, your privileged status will blind you to the fact that someone else at the opposite end has to work twice as hard to get the same recognition, to accomplish the same things. Furthermore, you may also feel entitled, that the world is your plaything, and that whatever you want should be given to you. If you grew up having everything you wanted, becoming an adult will not change the expectation that the world is a kind and giving place where you can have what you want. At the opposite end of the spectrum, you can perceive the world as unfair, skewed toward a privileged class that gets everything with ease while you work very hard to accomplish and achieve anything.

When I was growing up in the Caribbean, my family was considered to be middle class; the perception of higher status was not related to money and economics, but rather to education. What school you went to and how well you were educated was the barometer that determined your status. In my family, I heard things like: "You can lose money and fortune, but what is in your mind can never be lost." During my entire childhood, I watched my single mother sacrifice everything to put the four of us through private school. This had the effect on me of judging those who went to public school as being somehow inferior and myself and my siblings as being superior to them. Going to a private school does not guarantee that you are learning or getting a better education, nor does going to a public school mean that you are not learning or are getting a bad education. I had to learn this.

One thing that stands out with class, social, and economic blind spots is entitlement. This is the perception that you and your group have special privileges and are superior for being included in said class. The unstated part of this perception is that those not included are inferior or lesser somehow. This judgment is about separation, and it comes from fear that what lies outside of the group is a threat to the integrity and functioning of the perceived superior class. In truth, if you and your class were indeed better, the outside would not be any threat.

Moreover, the Universe is not black or white. There are too many shades and colors in between that are just as valid as the experience that you had. Maturity opens you up to the possibility that your perception is one lens out of multiple possibilities that exist. If you are lucky, you will realize this and allow your consciousness to expand and incorporate other lenses in an attempt to widen your awareness.

Racial Blind Spots

Your skin color and racial background will cause you to have specific experiences that will lock in a particular neural net configuration, giving you blind spots. If you grew up Native American, Black, Asian, or White, your experiences will be different from one another. Again, each race is perceived as having certain stereotypical benefits, privileges, and limits. Many years ago, an African American member of the temple to which I belonged was educating me on the injustices that White men committed on the African American community. I listened to him politely. He was getting more and more excited and agitated, saying that the Black race was being held back because they were superior. I knew that part of what he was saying was true. Yes, African Americans have been wronged and held back by the White race, but to believe that any race is superior is a blind spot. Racism exists in this world because of fear of an ethnic group's appearance and apparent differences from another. Anything that creates separation and fragmentation is an illusion. I simply asked him this question: "Tell me, what color is the soul?" He could not respond. If all human beings have souls and the soul has no color, how can one race be superior to any other?

This is probably the second most polarizing type of blind spot to have caused wars, injustices, death, deportation, and destruction in our world. The Black trade that legalized 400 years of slavery has killed, uprooted, and destroyed the lives of millions of Africans. More recently, the ethnic cleansing and genocide of Bosnia and Yugoslavia showed that humanity has not progressed far from the dark episodes of the Black trade and the Holocaust. How can we as a civilized society let these horrible events occur? They did not take place overnight or in a vacuum. Neighboring nations watched for months, if not years, the systematic slaughter, deportation, and destruction of an entire ethnic group before international pressure caused an end to the injustice. The fear, vitriol, and hatred that we are projecting on any group or race is an attack against our own body. No one exists outside of me, since everyone is a fragmented piece of the original Receiver. How can I attack, kill, or hurt a cell that exists in my body? This is lunacy.

Gender Blind Spots

Your gender can blind you to the needs, feelings, and behaviors of the opposite gender. If you have ever felt that you could not understand why your partner or spouse behaves the way he or she does, that is the reason. Growing up as a male or female carries with it the biological function and role that each gender plays. Moreover, the physiological differences of your gender will limit your perception, understanding, and connection to the opposite gender. We are wired differently; our sensory assimilation, approach, and understanding of the world are processed differently. For example, a man can be angry and get into a fight but let go of the memory of who started it and said what to whom afterwards. On the other hand, a woman who gets into a fight and argument remembers all the details: who said what and what was said. Men tend to identify with their jobs while women identify with their emotional relationships, although in today's patriarchal society most women react and identify to their jobs just like men. Women give birth and are often better nurturers than men. They also live longer than men. Some of these differences are wired while others are learned.

Some of the physiological differences can be overcome if one undergoes gender reassignment surgery. To date, women are still the only gender to carry a child and give birth. Because gender identification is not synonymous with genitalia, but is rather related to mind, some males and females may see, understand, and perceive themselves as the opposite gender. The transgender population has the right to be who and what they perceive themselves to be. If you are biologically male or female but feel inauthentic as that gender, you need to be true to that with which you identify.

Gender relations and the battle of the sexes have been going on for centuries. Women have been abused, oppressed, and suppressed by men because of fear of their differences and of the power that women and feminine energy possessed. The killing of "witches" by the Inquisition in medieval Europe was not just about religion, but about the wise ancient herbal tradition that European females possessed. Millions of women were burned at the stake because of oral and ancient healing traditions that they were perpetuating.

According to early Christian doctrines, women did not have a soul. Only Mother Mary, the mother of Jesus, possessed such a unique gift of a soul and as such she became the Queen of Heaven. The dominant cultures on the planet have moved from matriarchal into the patriarchal, and for centuries, male energy has dominated humanity. Look at the precipice on which we are standing: greed, self-interest, and the desire to control and dominate others are the goals that most seek. I am not just suggesting that female energy should now take over. I am certain that if the pendulum were to swing the other way it would create some now-unforeseen ill. I am saying that the yin and yang must be balanced. No being can ascend without balancing the male and female that resides within them. It is an alchemical marriage, whether you are a male of the Anima—the inner feminine—or a female of the Animus—the inner masculine. Once this is done individually, then the entire culture will follow.

Countries of Origin as Blind Spots

The geographical location or country of your birth will bring with it blind spots related to how your nation views itself. If you grew up in America, Africa, Europe, Asia, China, the Middle East, or India, your perception of yourself and how you fit into the world will differ from others. When I was growing up in the Caribbean, my perception of the United States was mythical. To me it was a land of plenty where one could get "stuff." When I arrived in the USA, I quickly realized that it was a land where you go into debt because you want to buy "stuff" to keep up with the Joneses, and now you have to work two jobs to pay for it. Back in the Caribbean, I did not have any debts, nor did I have a lot of "stuff," but plenty of time to enjoy life and connect with family and friends. In the USA, this is reduced to holidays because you are busy working to pay for "stuff." A White male in the USA and a White male in Europe view themselves differently. An African American male in the USA and a male from Africa are different for the same reasons. They expect different things from themselves, their family, government, and the world. They address and solve similar problems differently. The culture in which you grew up domesticated you into a collective belief, and these beliefs differ in other collectives found at geographical points all around the world.

One of the most useful and practical ways to remove your blind spot about other cultures is to travel and see the world. Take a two-week or, better yet, a one-month vacation. Become an exchange student. Serve in the Peace Corps. When you are immersed in a different culture with people speaking a different language, living life with different values and priorities than your own, it changes and influences your perspective. I find that after every time I travel for a month, I make changes in my life when I return home. Having a passport and using it goes a long way to cross-fertilize ideas, values, and priorities, more than reading and all the television shows in the world. It is like comparing apples to oranges.

Your Professions as Blind Spots

If you are an attorney, architect, doctor, or sales associate, your view of the world will be influenced by the professional group with which you identify yourself. The knowledge base of a doctor, architect, or shoemaker is different, one from the other, and gives each group specific blind spots that limit their understanding of what the other profession does. You may have a general understanding that a doctor is a healer, but you don't know what it is like to walk in his shoes. Thus, trying to have an in-depth understanding of how a physician arrives at a diagnosis is comparable to you trying to be an astronaut. It is a fantasy; no more, no less. There is a wealth of information and years of training and experience that shape the professional into what he is and separates him from the layman.

Emotional and Psychological Blind Spots

Emotional and psychological blind spots are the most difficult and tricky to identify and overcome. They may be visible to others but completely hidden from us. When we are in the throes of an emotion, it is a herculean task for us to realize that the emotion is but a color, flavor, or lens, and that in truth, we can change the emotion by changing our thought. It can be done, but it takes training, time, and experience. To that end, it is helpful to have a spiritual coach who will hold you accountable and help you see your blind spots. Short of that, it is helpful to have "ascension buddies." These are one or more friends with whom we agree to pair up, to focus on the goal of helping each other ascend. Just like gym or running buddies, they will help you during the days and moments when you can't help yourself. In return, you will do the same for them. The limit of this system is that if the ascension buddies are sharing the same glamour and blind spots as you, you will reflect them back to each other ad infinitum. In fact, you will enable and amplify them in each other. Even with this limitation, having someone outside of yourself to help you and point out your blind spots can accelerate your ascension process and save you years of poking around in the dark.

Additionally, you have to be teachable. You have to be willing to entertain the fact that your perspective may be limited. If you think you know everything and you have all the right answers, then there is nothing that anyone could add. However, let me just say that what you think you know is not authentically representing your experience, but comprises the inherited and collective beliefs of the groups, égrégore or collective, and group bodies with which you identify.

Human knowledge, whether accumulated by inspiration or empirical means, is limited and in time will be surpassed by a greater and more profound truth. Agreeing and defending a fragmented and limited perspective lacks wisdom. These agreements are keeping you in compliance with the accepted truth that is blocking your evolution.

Ascension exists outside of your comfort zone. To reach it, you have to be willing to traverse a landscape laced with unknowns, fears, and doubts. You have to move away from the status quo. It is overcoming the fear and threat of what may exist outside of self and the accepted norm that will eliminate your blind spots. Once you pass this territory, you enter a world of new possibilities, a blessed field of expansion and evolution. It is not that the status quo is wrong, but that it is a limited perception or lens. Creating space for the new possibilities opens you up to a wider and broader perspective.

While human perspective is limited, the insights of the planetary Ascended Masters are far greater than ours. Their scope of vision is wider, and that of the Galactic Masters is even broader. At a Universal level, Lord Melchizedek has multi-Universal lenses, but that is nothing compared to the God lenses that include everything. Since ascension is merger with God, the process of removing blind spots does not end until we are back into the bosom of Divinity. Keep that in mind and be ever teachable.

Chapter 8

Manifesting

*Everyone sees the unseen in proportion
to the clarity of his heart, and that depends upon
how much he has polished it. Whoever has polished it more,
sees more—more unseen forms become manifest to him.*

– Rumi

To foresee the future, to remember the past, or to pick up what exists beyond the veil of ordinary perception is the forte of the lightworker community. We are great at holding space for a vision of a better tomorrow, but how we bring this vision into physical manifestation eludes us. This is a major weakness in our community. How do we manifest our intentions? What is the mechanism of manifesting, and how can we excel at it?

The Three Levels of the Mind

Let us go back to basics. We are made up of three minds: the superconscious, the conscious, and the subconscious minds. The superconscious mind is our Higher Self. This is where the soul and inspiration from the Monad comes to us. When we see a vision or hear the voices of a Master or Angel, the superconscious mind is the medium for this communication. Every time we get a download from Spirit, this mind is being activated by higher energies dropping in wisdom, understanding, and knowledge for us to either accept or reject. We always have the free choice to agree or disagree and select our own course and direction. We have to use our discernment to filter what is not in our interests from what we want to do.

The vehicle that makes these choices is the conscious mind. It is the I, or Chooser, that makes the choice and selects the direction in which to go; that identity exists in the conscious mind. This is where self-awareness exists. It is through this medium that we are conscious of the 3-D world around us, and this awareness interprets and gives color to our experiences. It is also what allows us to understand that we are separated from others and that we have boundaries that end at the limits of our bodies. Because it is the vehicle through which we experience our separation from others, it can easily be contaminated by the perception of fear or threat from the outside world. This awareness is designed to be the conductor who decides what kind of reality we experience. Whether we select fear or love, separation or merger, it is up to us.

Whether they are coming from the outside world, the superconscious or the subconscious minds, all inputs and data must be interpreted and accepted by the conscious mind. This process occurs 24 hours a day, 7 days a week, even in our sleep. Instead of taking responsibility and deciding which information to approve or disapprove, most people on the planet simply choose to do nothing because of laziness. But the Universe is not a vacuum. When you choose not to make a choice, you make a choice. After lifetimes of not making choices, the conscious mind becomes completely reactive to the whim of external events and subconscious programs that hijack self-awareness and transform it into a tailspin of emotional and often inappropriate reactions. No control or mastery there.

The subconscious mind is an engine for manifestation. As a result of repetition and habitual behavior, whatever the conscious mind resolves to be true and real will drop below the threshold of consciousness into the subconscious mind and become law. This law, program, or belief becomes a goal that the subconscious mind will seek to prove, validate, and manifest by creating echoed events, circumstances, and synchronicities in the outside world. This program will never stop working unless one deprograms the information originally entered. It will operate 24 hours a day, 7 days a week, even when you sleep. If the program or belief is positive and constructive, that is great; but since the subconscious mind does not have morality and does not understand right from wrong, the potential for negative ego contamination and fear to drop into this fertile soil and grow is very real and probable.

Moreover, our subconscious mind is connected to the subconscious mind of every other living thing on the planet and all sentient existence in the Universe. The need of one subconscious mind will send messages into a vast and almost endless network, asking for the reflecting circumstances that will prove the held belief to be true. Understand that this belief is not actuality but is a thought or idea that was dropped into the subconscious mind by repetition. The subconscious is only creating and reflecting back the held belief—good or bad. If you were to have different beliefs, the subconscious mind would mirror back a different reality. Every experience that we have—good, bad, or indifferent—is of our own making. Whether you are experiencing joy, pain, or suffering, a program is responsible for having magnetized it into your reality, personal hologram, or movie.

The Process of Manifesting

In an ideal setting, the I, or Chooser, gets inspiration from the superconscious mind and makes a choice, selecting to accept or reject the inspiration. Once the decision is made, it commands the subconscious mind to manifest it. The subconscious mind connects to the vast network of the collective unconscious and creates the synchronicities and circumstances that physically manifest the command. However, most people on the planet are not in their personal power, and if you are not in your personal power, you are incapable of doing this. Remember, personal power gives you continual control and approval of all internal processes or external events. Because of this, most people are slaves, reactive to the desire body and the emotion du jour.

In other words, the servomechanism— the subconscious mind populated with all kinds of programs originally designed to obey the conscious mind— is now assaulting consciousness with programs running amok, manifesting chaos in our lives in the process. No wonder we cannot manifest our desired goals. Every time we have a clear intention and we focus our conscious mind on attempting to create this intent, multiple subconscious programs rise up to battle, contradict, and attack the intention.

Neurologists say that we intend and un-intend three to five times per minute. For example, we may intend to get a new job. As soon as this thought is released, a program from the subconscious mind arises, saying: "you never finish anything that you start," or "you don't deserve a new job," or both. These subconscious programs and forces, in trying to manifest their own internal laws, will interfere with your desire to find a new job. The result: you are not in control and you cannot manifest your intention. Yet the chaos, pain, and suffering are running at their own speed and causing all kinds of damage.

Uncluttering the Subconscious Mind

We know that the subconscious mind manifests whatever has been repeated over time. True, since our childhood, our environment has populated the subconscious mind with a clutter of negative programs, but if we could use this ability to deprogram the clutter and instead program positive, life affirming, and ascended programs, everything would turn around.

Until you have substantially reprogrammed your subconscious mind, you cannot manifest at will. It is therefore in your interests to start reprogramming your subconscious mind, divesting the clutter of negative programs that pollute it. We keep the positive program; it is only the un-ascended and negative ego programs that need to be brought into the Light.

Let us review some of the previously mentioned techniques: the Stalking of Self, the Daily Bardo, and the One, Two, Three Steps.

The Stalking of Self: Similar to a hunter stalking prey, you spend your time paying attention and observing how you react and behave. You become detached and watch how you respond and act at all times. Every time you catch yourself in the throes of an emotional reaction or subconscious program, you choose to act and behave in an ascended manner. Every time your emotions or moods are dark and self-absorbed, you are in fear; so you make a choice to acknowledge the positive and the interconnectedness that bind everything and uncloak that fear as illusion.

The Daily Bardo: The Buddhists believe that after our death, we spend three days examining our lives for successes, failures, and the accomplishments of our purpose for the planning of our next life. Instead of waiting for the end of our life to do this, do it on a daily basis. At the end of the day, write in a journal the highlights of the day. Once finished, ask yourself this critical question: If God/Goddess was walking in my footsteps today, would He/She have done what I did? If the answer is no, you have adjustments to make. Write down the desired and adjusted behavior and make a "spiritual vow" to behave in this manner if that situation were to be repeated. When the situation presents itself again, you may be midway into the behavior before you catch yourself. Just stop and walk away. Now behave in the manner promised.

The One, Two, Three Steps: When you are in the throes of an emotional response and are reactive, follow the One, Two, Three Steps. First, realize that what you are feeling is a test. This brings you detachment and self-awareness. If what I am feeling is a test, how do I pass this test? Second, count to ten: one, two, three, four, up to ten. Do not react for ten seconds.

Hold your reaction and go into a blank space for ten seconds. It takes ten seconds of doing nothing before a shutdown occurs in the hypothalamus, which is in the center of your brain and produces the hormones that rush into our blood stream to create an emotion. I once had a student who told me that it took him a count of up to 120 for the shutdown to happen. He nonetheless was so proud to have been able to do this when typically it would have taken days to calm down. And third, once the emotion is shut down, go to step three, and proactively act in the opposite way your reactive system was prompting you to do. This is probably the most difficult part of the process. You may at first have to fake it and act like you are feeling the opposite before the emotions and subconscious mind comply and follow your command. Remember, there are other voices and programs that are battling for control and that are trying to lead the conscious mind into a different direction.

The Power of Intention

Please remember the wise saying: "Thoughts are things." Our thoughts and intentions are the initiators and creators of everything. They command and all other bodies including the emotional body will follow. These are not just words on paper—it is Universal law. For most individuals on the planet, it is the other way around. What they feel appears so real and convincing that they cannot imagine having control over their emotions.

I had a coaching client who was always talking about how she felt. In the course of our sessions, she would say "I feel" at least 10 to 15 times. One day mid-session, I asked her to tell me her story without saying "I feel" for the rest of the session. She was mute for the remainder of the time. It is not that our feelings are unimportant; it is that they are one of the many ways that we react to information about the world. Indeed, the emotional body is a powerful holograph and immersive spice, lens, or color, but it is only an interpretation and one of many, probably endless, ways to view the same situation.

The Control of Our Thoughts vs. Emotional Intelligence

If the current lens or color displeases you, change your thought and the emotional body will follow. It is that simple. But for someone who is clairsentient or highly emotionally intelligent, it is like asking them to breathe under water. They have spent most of their life interpreting all their experiences through feeling. They can pinpoint the direction, the provenance, and the type of emotion they are experiencing with great skill and dexterity. They can differentiate what their feelings are and what they may be empathing through others. Yet they have no control and mastery over the timing and intensity of their emotions. They have no boundaries and simply exist in the sea of feeling completely disempowered.

I have watched them using the One, Two, Three steps and get to step two, but after counting to ten, instead of *thinking* the opposite, they try to *feel* the opposite emotion and bring the counter-emotion into the mix, hoping that it would balance the equation. It is painful to watch, time consuming for them, and never successful. Besides, one will not deprogram a neural net setting with the opposite emotion. It is the opposite *thought* and *intention* that will initiate the process, after which energy and emotion will follow. The neural net connection is created in the mental body, and emotion cannot reprogram it.

The Causal Body Initiates Change

To do this, the center of consciousness has to shift physically into a different location. The average person on the planet exists in his head. When in that space, separation and linear thinking rule. If I am separated from the world, the world may be hostile to my wellbeing, and I must act to remove and control any perceived threats that exist around me.

But the center of awareness can shift and allow different kinds of cognitive ability to come into play:

> *I am going to ask you to close your eyes and take three deep breaths. Once you are done, let your head drop into the center of your chest. This is your heart space. Now, notice what you notice. Realize that you can perceive energies in all 360 degrees around you. Now open your eyes. This quick exercise brought you into the heart and mind coherence and away from being solely in your head and linear space. In your heart space, you gather information from all around you. Separation is abolished, and you make decisions based on an understanding of the whole. Now please extend your hands straight above your head. Look up at your fingertips about three feet above you. You are looking at the bottom of the causal or spiritual body, which is where your consciousness should be to initiate the opposite and manifest anything new. The causal body has been described as a field of endless possibilities and potentialities. Now close your eyes again and take three deep breaths. Let your head begin to float above your body to a point three feet above your head. You should feel expanded and taller, as if you had become a giant. Notice what you notice. Realize that you have great clarity, single-mindedness, and focus. Now take a deep breath and open your eyes.*

These experiences are completely different from each other. When you get into step three of the One, Two, Three Step protocol, you should be in the causal body. After counting to ten and allowing the hypothalamus to shut down, let your consciousness rise from the sea of your emotional body and float above your head into the causal body.

Now think and intend the opposite for a few minutes. You have planted a seed into a field of endless possibilities. Now release and let go and let the Universe boomerang the effect back to your other bodies. Pay attention to the subtle changes that are taking place. Energies are rearranging themselves in and around you. You may already begin to feel the opposite emotion swelling up. Take a deep breath and open your eyes. Pay attention to how you are now sensing and perceiving the world. Is your perception different from before?

The causal body has many important qualities. It is a fertile field where accelerated growth and precipitation into the 3-D world is initiated. But for that to happen you have to understand that the intentions and ideas brought into that field are decrees that the entire Universe will obey and create. Be careful what you think and what you bring into that field, for they will manifest.

At times you may be unclear about what thought should be brought into that field. So you enter it, seeking clarification and posing a query to the field of endless possibilities as to the most appropriate response to your situation. Now wait for an answer. A short time thereafter, a solution may wash over you, like a bucket of water with information addressing your query. Sometimes it appears like an open fan with multiple solution sets radiating from one point; then one of them gets selected and comes into focus. Decree it and hold it in place for a short time. Then say thank you and have gratitude for the help and support that has been provided.

The Processing of Causal Intentions

The seed intention now planted in the causal body is promptly connected to a vast network that includes everything that is alive. The égrégore or group body will collectively process the solution set. Whatever information, data, wisdom, and support that are needed for manifestation to occur will be provided. At times, it may be all that is needed for an immediate transformation to occur, especially if you are dealing with an emotional state. In some rare instances, this process will appear to create manna from the sky where manifestation is almost instantaneous. However, in most cases additional follow-up has to take place for manifestation to occur.

If instead of a change in your emotional state, you bring into the causal body a complex issue like how to go about getting a new job, the causal body will begin to precipitate ideas or images into your mental body that you will have to carry out for the desired effect to take place. Let me just say here that the clarity of the causal body allows you to take abstract concepts, ideas, and emotional states and break them down into all their components parts, with detailed plans and accurate timings for the desired manifestation to occur. It is a how-to that will lead you to all the steps and sub-steps that bring manifestation.

For example, first you do A, B, C and simultaneously do D and E, and merge everything at F to arrive at the desired result. The proper rhythm, timing, sequence, and details of what to do will be visible to you. This energy brings ideas and creative concepts into manifestation. The nebulous and idealized ideas get focused into physical reality.

During your connection to the causal body, you get activated to the appropriate actions that will lead to the eventual manifestation of the thought and intention brought into this field of endless possibilities. It is a crucible that allows the abstract to precipitate into physical reality. Thoughts and intentions descend the dimensional ladder creating invisible and subtle codes, sequences that call in the lesser builders and elemental energies to bring ideas into physical manifestation. At every point of the step-by-step descent, the confluences of elemental energies followed by actions will be shown to you, to precipitate 3-D physical manifestation into reality. If you match the elemental descent with appropriate action, the Universe will obey, and manifestation will be grounded in the 3-D world.

Reorganization of the Subconscious Mind and the Power to Manifest

If you are to become master and co-creator with God, the subconscious mind must cooperate with you. For that to happen, the I, the Chooser, and self-awareness must be in charge, and the subconscious mind must play a supporting role in this equation. When you begin to look at the number of negative programs that reside in the subconscious mind, the work of reprograming them using the above tools seems overwhelming. I am saying this to make you aware that every seeker is initially paralyzed by the vastness of the task. It is often a mine field that makes many walk away in fear. There is an entire menagerie of all kinds of negative programs that are jousting for attention and control of conscious awareness. Do not be discouraged by the size of the task, but simply begin by reprogramming the issue that is in front of you at the moment. Proceed with what surfaces next, and keep removing negative ego programs one step at a time. Remember that any behavior that is repeated in front of the subconscious mind for a period of time becomes a law that will then loop ad infinitum. If you keep reprogramming negative ego programs using the same mechanism, you are setting up a new law that the subconscious mind will relentlessly operate, 24 hours a day, 7 days a week, and even when you sleep.

Before you know it, a little discipline and consistency will give you the upper hand in the reprogramming process, and all you have to do is become the lion tamer and be in charge. The I, the Chooser, will soon begin to control the subconscious mind, and when about half of your subconscious mind is reorganized, your thoughts and intentions put into the causal body will manifest before you within hours, if not minutes. A unified consciousness stops the mental chatter and self-doubts and allows the appropriate relationship to be restored between the superconscious, conscious, and subconscious minds. Inspiration and guidance coming from the superconscious drops into the conscious mind, which approves or disapproves, and then commands the subconscious mind to manifest.

Certainty

A few years ago, one of my students asked me to do hands-on healing for her roommate who was suffering from a popped-rib incident. Knowing the mechanics, she had tried to help but was only able to soothe the pain and discomfort. I could see the rib on top of the spinal cord, and I placed my hand on top of the location. I held space for neutrality to be created all around her and for her pain and suffering to end. I did not massage, push, or pull. I just gently kept my hand on top of the location, holding neutrality. After 15 minutes, the spot became warm and soft, and the rib dropped back into place. She immediately fell into a deep sleep. I went out of the room, and my student asked me what was the difference between what she had done and what I did. I told her the difference was "certainty." I not only knew the mechanics and followed them, but I had certainty that spiritual law would always operate. There was not one moment of doubt and hesitation in my consciousness. I knew that as sure as the law of gravity would always work, holding neutrality around her would end her suffering. The Zohar talks about this principle as the vehicle that allowed the passage through the Red Sea.

The Bible story says that Pharaoh's army was in hot pursuit of the Israelites after the exodus from Egypt. The Israelites were trapped, with the Red Sea in front of them and Pharaoh's army behind them. So Moses asked God for help, and God told him to extend his staff, whereupon the sea parted, taking the children of Israel to safety and drowning Pharaoh's army that followed them.

However, the Zohar tells a different story. When Moses asked God for help, God's response was: "Why are you calling me?" Essentially, God was telling Moses and the children of Israel that He already had given them the means to create their own miracle. So during the night, Moses led the 3 million Israelites into a trance state using the 72 divine names of God previously given to them. This brought all of them into a state of certainty and at sunrise at the shore of the Red Sea, a young Israelite moved away from the crowd and into the sea while everyone looked on in silence. He was in total certainty when the water was at the level of his waist. He moved further in, slowly and in certainty that no harm was going to come to him. The sea was then at the level of his shoulders, and the crowd looked on in silence and certainty. He kept moving forward, and the water was then at his mouth, but he was still in complete certainty that no harm was going to come; and as the water went into his nostrils, the sea parted. It was not Moses who parted the Red Sea, but it was the certainty of the young Israelite man.

Yehuda Berg in his ground-breaking and lucid book *The Power of Kabbalah* says about certainty: "Overcome your own reactive nature and the heavens will respond and help you overcome the laws of nature, for the two are intimately connected." When you believe in the hopeful and miraculous with every fiber of your being and consciousness, you hold a power that is as solid and real as gravity. Remember the double-slit experiment. The observer is creating reality and can change and affect everything that we are told is immutable.

Where you choose to put your consciousness will determine the outcome that you get. If you go into the causal body and place an intention with doubt, the result will be mixed. Whereas someone who goes in and decrees an intention with complete certainty will have immediate and miraculous manifestation. You are creating your reality and hologram. All the rules that relate to it are of your own making. If you clip your own wings by having doubts and believing things to be impossible, you have no one to blame but yourself. Believe in the miraculous and the impossible. Travel down the path of the road less travelled, and the miraculous and effortless will populate your life.

The creation and manifestation of the miraculous and impossible is our birthright. The only thing that is holding you from playing in the field of endless possibilities is your shame and fear. Remove the fear and shame and bliss will follow you. Remember that the rules of 3-D reality are not unbreakable rules. They simply are a means that the égrégore is using to keep you bound and domesticated to the group-body agreement. Hold your personal power and be the anomaly in the grid. Liberate your consciousness by creating a reality and hologram that suits your needs. You have the means to create your own miracle. Take responsibility for your happiness and existence. Manifest the reality according to your desires, and delete the hologram of pain and suffering that is the result of a lack of mastery and improper thinking.

Chapter 9

Overcoming Bad Habits
and Addictions

An over-indulgence of anything,
even something as pure as water, can intoxicate.

– Criss Jami

For the seeker on the path of ascension, overcoming bad habits and addictions is a big challenge. A bad habit is a negative habitual behavior that has dropped below the threshold of consciousness into the subconscious mind. Repeat any behavior or create any emotional association with any person or situation enough times, and the muscle memory of the subconscious mind then takes over; and this mind will repeat it ad nauseam. Since the subconscious mind does not think and has no sense of right or wrong, it treats a bad habit the same as a good one. It will endlessly seek opportunities to attract and mirror the behavior in the physical world, causing the physical, emotional, and desire bodies to react to it in the programmed manner. On the path of enlightenment and self-development, we want to keep the good habits, such as a burning desire to merge with God, meditating every day, or having compassion for the pain of others. It is the bad habits, such as over-indulgence of cigarettes, alcohol, drugs, food, sex, painkillers, shopping, gambling, sugar, other people, or seeking energy from others, to name a few, that we need to reprogram into God, Goddess, Christ, Buddha, Krishna, and ascended relationships. The goal is for the seeker to have preferences but not attachments, for attachments trigger the desire or astral body where all habits and addictions live. Having preferences means that you are going after your goal, but if it is not successful, you are not devastated by the outcome. You are still essentially happy, in your center, and at peace even if the goal is not achieved.

Now some of our habits are learned in early childhood development whereas some come from past lives. During our childhood we learn good and bad habits from our parents, family, school, television, peers, nation and mass consciousness. We are born into this lifetime with certain predispositions and habits that are inherited due to past-life experiences. Some of us may be born with an aptitude for math and science, the arts and music, or an innate understanding of crystals; others may have a tendency to drink, eat, and medicate self.

The Chemical Dependencies of Addictions

An addiction is a bad habit that has moved from the mental and emotional into the physical and material plane. Unlike a habit, an addiction has a chemical dependency component to it. The nicotine, alcohol, food, or drug is what the addict is trying to get. Let us clarify here that it is not the outward behavior to which one is addicted. The addiction to the medication or behavior is a substitute for a deeper pain that the addict is trying to cover up. Until the core pain is addressed, the addiction and dependency will persist.

Now if you are addicted to a behavior such as sex, shopping, people, or reading the energy from others, there is still a chemical component to it. If you will remember, the hypothalamus in the center of the brain is producing peptides, which are hormones that rush into the blood stream, attaching themselves to the cells and changing the cellular structure to create an emotional reaction. It is now the chemical and cellular changes, internally produced in your body but triggered by external events, which become the chemical component or medication for the addiction. This is much harder to treat and reprogram, for one can regulate with effort the contact with external chemicals such as nicotine, alcohol, or drugs, but when the drug pusher and supplier is your own faulty perception of reality triggering the brain's release of peptides, the challenge is moved up a notch. This is not to say that addiction to external substances does not have a hypothalamus and peptide component to it. If you will remember, the chemical addiction is a camouflage to hide a deeper pain. Once the external chemicals are removed from daily contact, you then need to deal with the real issue: the faulty perception that causes internally produced peptides to flow into the blood stream and change the body chemistry, creating an addictive reaction.

Addiction is a Camouflage or Escape for a Deeper Pain

Addiction is a means to escape a core negative feeling or a perception of pain and suffering and an attempt to replace it with a new feeling. Alcoholics drink to escape the pain and anguish they feel by trying to create a different feeling. Food may be used as a means to stuff feelings or to create a sense of love or greater protection. Drugs are sometimes used to create a high that helps the user bear reality. Gambling provides the high of a potential winning and the alluring escape from poverty consciousness.

In the light community, I have witnessed addictions that were specific to energy workers: individuals who would walk into a room, begin to read everyone's energy, and feel compelled to tell everyone what they saw. This was a violation of the boundaries of innocent bystanders who gave no permission. This reading was being done without their consent. Energy addicts do this compulsively and are always seeing dark forces and energies.

A man with such a problem came to me for a healing to help remove the dark energies that were haunting him. I told him to remain quiet for five minutes and began my healing protocol. No sooner had I begun than he started to moan and began to describe what he was perceiving and seeing. I told him in a stern voice, "Shut up! What part of being quiet for five minutes did you not understand?" The core issue for him was that he felt unlovable unless he showed people what he could do. "Please love me for I am special. Look at what I can do."

I have also met energy workers who walk into a room and begin to empath energy from everyone. Again, this is a violation of the sovereignty of others. It is psychic spying. These individuals have a great sense of the separation between themselves and others. They perceive others as a threat and are busy "feeling their energy" for information so that they can be in control. Unfortunately, anytime you comingle your energy grid with anyone or anything without their consent, you absorb their positive and the negative energies. Whether you do this by reading or empathing others, the results are the same.

The energy addict's field is constantly contaminated by the sewage and dark stuff that they are picking up from others. More importantly, this behavior of blending energy without consent is the true sin of the fallen beings. Like will attract like. The fallen beings will be attracted to the addict's energy grid, for they are perceiving a matching frequency. They will infect and pollute the addict's energy and even use them as a puppet. Even when you explain this to the energy addict, they cannot stop themselves. The chemical dependency resulting from the release of peptides is too powerful. They feel horrible being infected by the energy of others and will have to spend hours trying to remove and clear the negativity.

The Cellular Chemistry of Addiction

We have already spoken about the peptides rushing into the blood and changing the cellular and body chemistry, causing an emotional reaction. The mechanism by which the peptides lock into the cellular receptors to change the blood chemistry is no different than when a drug addict is injected with an opiate. Except now you are addicted to your own internal juice. In order for any behavior to become a habit or addiction, it has to be repeated a number of times. That repetition causes neurons in the brain to lock into a specific configuration, holding in the reaction associated with the behavior. As the subconscious mind attracts and creates synchronicities to manifest the reality of this behavior, the hypothalamus releases the peptides that change the blood chemistry and cause an emotional reaction, which then reinforces the neural net bonding. Because of the chemical dependency, more instances of this behavior will be mirrored in the real world, and the neuron will continue to grow stronger and stronger. This creates a vicious circle of a chemical dependency feeding a neural net bond, getting stronger and stronger with every instance and further solidifying the reality that we experience. Yet, if we can manage to not react or even do the opposite, the neural net will get weaker with every instance and will eventually disconnect and form a new bond based on an emotional reaction of our choosing.

Pain and Addiction

This may seem hopeless, but let us focus on what is at the root of every addiction. Behind the chemical dependency is a perception of pain and suffering with which the psyche is not ready to deal. This pain is so great that one has to hide it behind something else. It may be that in your core you feel unloved, vulnerable, misunderstood, victimized, and violated. But in truth, all these negative ego, fear-based, and fragmented perceptions are not reality. They are all the results of years, centuries, and eons of wrong thinking and not being in your personal power.

It is your thought that controls everything. If you hold the right thoughts, your reality will follow. If you think the thoughts of Christ, Buddha, Krishna, Moses, and Mohamed, your habits and addictions will cease to be negative, and the positive nature of this new perception will manifest a different reality. Remember that ascension is mastery of the spiritual, mental, emotional, and physical bodies. Bad habits and addictions affect the mental, emotional, and physical bodies: the mental body by the perception of separation and fragmentation; the emotional body by causing illegitimate pain and suffering; and the physical body by creating a chemical dependency. This is a great opportunity for you to overcome the negative ego programming and create self-mastery in those three bodies.

If you look at the spiritual psychology of the addict, you will notice that the mastery of the four bodies and their integration is lacking. The energy addicts may have psychic gifts by being great channels, mediums, empaths, and healers, but if the negative ego issues and the false perceptions of separation are not addressed in all four bodies, these gifts will be corrupted. It is in modeling yourself after your higher power and God concept that you will begin to rise from the depth of victimhood into the height of mastery.

If you have identified yourself in what you have read so far, don't despair. I will be enumerating a series of tools, exercises, and spiritual connections that will, with application, take you out of the field of chemical dependency and into the role of being in charge and in control of your destiny.

Core Fear Removal Programming

Let us begin with the Core Fear Removal Programming. Do this meditation for about 15 minutes every morning and night for 21 days. Close your eyes and take a deep breath. Now call forth God, the God force, Christ, and the Holy Spirit to anchor into your body, energy grid, and subconscious mind the Core Fear Removal Programming. Ask Spirit, the Masters, and the Angels to remove all core issue that are creating bad habits and addictions. Spirit, the Masters, and the Angels will remove from your energy grid and body the bad habits and addictions. They will be pulled out of your energy grid like you remove bad weeds from a garden. You will feel the removal and begin to feel lighter. In the evening add the following specification: ask Spirit to anchor into your body, energy grid, and subconscious mind the Core Fear Removal Programming for it to be done **continuously for the entire night**. This is a very powerful detail. Don't skip this. Between the fifth and seventh days, you will wake up in the morning feeling the best that you have felt in a while. You will perceive a marked difference in wellbeing.

Personal Power

Be in your personal power. The Personal Power Program is a 21-day process of psychological exercises, the shifting of awareness, and the connections to Archangels and Ascended Masters, who will bring you into the center of your will. The full details are in Chapter Three, but let us summarize here. As you wake up in the morning, ask the Mahatma, Lord Melchizedek, and Archangel Metatron to run their platinum light net through your four-body system—physical, emotional, mental, and spiritual—and to remove from them all misqualified, negative, and unbalanced energies. Now ask that Master El Morya of the First Ray drop into your energy body the right amount of the First-Ray energy of will and power. Let Archangel Michael create a golden bubble of light around you, a field that is impenetrable, rejecting everything except for the Light of God. Repeat the personal power affirmation aloud. Throughout the day, if you sense that your shield is compromised or that you are not the chooser of your reality, repeat the above-mentioned steps.

In the evening, repeat the first three steps and add to them the Core Fear Removal Programming night protocol, asking that they remove all programs and beliefs that are siphoning your personal power and that they do so on a continual basis for the entire evening while you sleep. Do this for 21 days and watch yourself move from being pushed around to being in charge.

Now let me just say that personal power is in truth the continual process of approving and disapproving of the internal contents from the subconscious mind and the external events that occur around you 24 hours a day, 7 days a week, even when you sleep. This is not a process that ends on the 22nd day, but rather something that you need to maintain and be vigilant about. But like all processes, if you do it enough times, the subconscious muscle memory will take over, and you will be doing this even in your dreams. A new neural bonding will be created, and as you reinforce it, it will create the synchronicity to manifest it all the time.

Spiritual Vow

Make a Spiritual Vow. "A life without a vow is like a ship without an anchor" (Mahatma Gandhi). One of the most powerful tools to help you overcome a bad habit or addiction is to make a Spiritual Vow to God, the Masters, the Angels, or your higher power. Vow that if the temptation were to present itself in front of you in a moment of weakness, you would summon your will to resist by doing the opposite. It helps if the vow is written: "I swear that I will surrender my desire body in the face of temptation to your Holy help." Now write down the appropriate behavior. I have personally found this tool extremely helpful. When the temptation is in front of me, I first sense the awareness that it is a test; second, I remember my vow; and third, I find that my desire to be true to my God is greater than the needs of my desire body. Although I sense that I am strengthened by the power of Spirit around me, I now can choose how I will act: to continue to indulge my desire body or to correct my course and overcome my addiction.

The weight and power of my connection to God and any promises that I make to him/her are far greater than any bodily, emotional, or energetic need. This requires that you first believe in a higher power and that you have a relationship to it. In the *Twelve Steps and Twelve Traditions*, the foundation of Alcoholics Anonymous, this is reflected as step number three: "Make a decision to turn our will and our lives over to the care of God as we understand Him." Of all the steps, I believe this one has the most transformative power. You have to realize that you have no control or power over your addiction and that only God or your higher power can help overcome the compulsion of the addiction. It is a surrendering, and it is the enlistment of the help and power of beings far superior to you that can intercede on your behalf and help you on the right path.

The problem is that the average man does not believe in a higher power and is too proud to surrender or ask for help. No wonder modern society is in such crisis. No spiritual being can help you without you asking them for help. Remember the law of noninterference. If the surrender is real and comes from a sincere place, help from your higher power will be provided. This also means that on some deep level you recognize and know that your addictive behavior has taken you far away from a place where there is no pain and suffering. Your God, however you perceive it, can help you get to that Promised Land.

The energy of your connection to a higher state is what drives this. If you only believe in the body and flesh and are not educated in spiritual psychology, then you will have no real ability to overcome any negative ego programming. The most famous historical example of this is the change and transformation of the life of St. Paul. He was a Roman and a persecutor of the early Christians, but on the road to Damascus, the Light of God surrounded and blinded him. The result was a spiritual conversion; from being a persecutor, he became a defender of the Christians and one of the most influential founding members of Christianity. This 180-degree turn can only happen when religious idealism is involved and the light, perception, and grace of a higher being is shared with you to help correct your vision and path. The same grace can happen with your addictions, but you have to ask for it.

Mirroring God

Do not let any thought or feeling that is not of God enter your mind. Deny entry to all thoughts, feelings, behaviors, and emotions that are not of God. Reject all negative ego, fear-based, and separative thoughts, feelings, behaviors, and emotions. Only allow into your consciousness what is of God, Christ, Buddha, Krishna, Moses, and Mohammed. Actively seek the Kingdom by mirroring it. Alter your negative ego patterns by realizing that you have the will, control, and power to change simply by choosing different thoughts. Immerse your consciousness, thoughts, and activities with what you think God/Goddess would do. Make all of your choices be of and for God.

For this to happen, you have to be vigilant for the Kingdom. Monitor your consciousness and thoughts, and only allow in ideas, feelings, and experiences that are elevating, expansive, and liberating. Let all fears and fear-based experiences be removed from your life by continually watching over your status in the present and making the choice to correct and delete what is not aligned with your highest purpose. The South American shamans call this process the stalking of self. This means that you have to observe and watch how self is interacting with internal subconscious programs and external events from an outsider's point of view. You must be detached from the experience and gain the advantage of an almost-impartial observer. To be immersed in any situation is like trying to understand a great work of art by standing one inch from it. You need to stand back and take the long view to understand the composition and appreciate the visual impact of the piece. Take the long view, monitor yourself, and make the needed God/Goddess and Ascended corrections.

The Power of Prayer

Pray to your higher power and God/Goddess on a daily basis. Why worry when you can pray? Every morning and every night call upon God, Christ, the Holy Spirit, your Mighty I Am Presence, and Your Higher Self with all your heart, mind, soul, and might, and ask their help in not allowing bad habits and addictions to overtake you. Remember that a prayer is like talking to God and meditation is listening to God. You need to ask for assistance and help. In fact you can do this all day long when you feel that fear is invading you or that the compulsion of your addictions is coming back.

There are two major components to reprogramming any negative ego issue: the deletion of the old and the installation of the new. About the deletion, we spoke at length; but in order for you to install a new habit, you need to repeat affirmations that are at the core of the correct belief for 21 days. You could also behave in a different manner than usual for 21 days, and it should have the same effect. You can choose the affirmations from Chapters Three and Four about personal power and unconditional self-love, or you can create your own. The affirmations in these earlier chapters are broad, so something more specific that targets your addiction will probably be more effective.

Think about how God/Goddess would behave and how you are currently acting. Write down the customized affirmation and code of conduct that the subconscious mind will, from now on, obey and make manifest to correct the addictive behavior. It is like writing the line and code of a computer program. Take your time to write from the point of view of God/Goddess, however you conceive them to be, and repeat for 21 days.

I have to make a confession. Over the years, I have done many 21-day programs. I believe the 21-day period is a way of installing the software, but often the program does not run until after several 21-day cycles. For example, I have done the 21-day Personal Power Program many times. I can even foresee a future moment when I feel that I will need a booster and will repeat the program. It is like reinstalling software, or since your awareness changes each time, it probably is more like an upgrade to the software.

Call upon the Holy Spirit or Holy Ghost

Ask the Holy Spirit or Holy Ghost to undo the root cause of your addiction. This is a very powerful tool, for the Holy Spirit is not a white dove that descends from the heavens, bringing peace. The core power of the Holy Spirit is to remove and undo what is not of God. If any of you have been in a Baptist Revival Church or a Charismatic Catholic healing ritual and have watched the crowd as the energy of the Holy Spirit moves through, you understand. People are screaming and rolling on the floor. Ask the Holy Spirit to remove dark programs, entities, and false beliefs. There is nothing peaceful about this. The energy of the Holy Spirit is similar to the energy of Shiva, the destroyer, in Hinduism. It is the undoing and destroying that is needed so that new programs and beliefs can be installed. If you are building a house, you have to excavate, dig, and remove dirt so that you can create the proper foundation.

For a period of 21 days, every morning and every night, ask the Holy Spirit to remove the root cause of your addiction. Remain quiet for about five to seven minutes after asking, to allow the Holy Spirit to move through you and do its job. You will feel things move and being lifted from you. Now if you do that first, followed by the 21-day affirmation program, it will go a long way to correcting your addiction.

Call Dr. Lorphan and the Twelve Galactic Healers

Ask Dr. Lorphan and the Twelve Galactic Healers to repair your etheric or desire body and your cellular structure from the damages done by the chemical dependency created by the addiction. For 21 days ask for this to be done morning and night. At night, ask that this be done on a continual basis while you sleep. Dr. Lorphan and the Twelve Galactic Healers exist at the core of our Galaxy. They are Galactic physicians and with your permission will assist you in repairing your etheric body. This is where your desire and need for the addiction exist. Ask this team to remove the need for this behavior, and it will be done.

To explain: When a peptide is released from the hypothalamus and enters into a cell, it penetrates through receptor points. As this peptide is more frequently released, the cells will exponentially reproduce, mutate, and create more receptor points to allow the docking of this specific, popular peptide, to the detriment of other receptors that the cells need to maintain vitality and cellular health.   This is how the etheric or desire body precipitates into the physical body: by creating cellular mutation that will process the more frequent hormonal releases from the hypothalamus. What you are asking Dr. Lorphan and the Twelve Galactic Healers is to repair the cellular structure of all the trillions and trillions of cells that exist in your body so that, at the next cycle of cellular reproduction, the cells will mutate back to having only a single receptor of that specific peptide. This is truly a powerful healing and an act of grace and mercy from the Galactic Core. They work together with a rod that emits a laser-like radiance, which moves through your bodies and repairs and restores the appropriate receptor points.

Clearing and Negative Implant Removal

In addition to this help, you may have to ask a qualified healer to do a clearing and negative implant removal for you. In my experience, the physical, etheric, emotional, and mental bodies of most addicts contain implants and devices.

What are implants? Let me explain: If you are always positive and believe in the miraculous, you have a defense field around you that nothing in time and space can enter. But if you are not in your personal power and you believe in fears and separation, you have doubts and judgments that collapse your field. And since the Universe is not a vacuum, parasitical existences penetrate and host in your field. Do not judge them, for they are doing what any living thing in the Universe is doing. They are trying to live. A virus does not know that it is harming your body; it is simply multiplying to survive. All addicts have implants in their bodies that have to be removed to give the individual a fighting chance of recovery. A clearing is a process by which a qualified practitioner scans your grid and asks the assistance of the entire spiritual hierarchies in removing the identified devices. Doing this will remove any external influences that have vested interests in maintaining your disempowerment. There is a great release following this process, and it will accelerate your recovery.

Dealing with Temptation

If you are ever tempted, immediately pray and ask God, Christ, the Holy Spirit, your Mighty I Am Presence, and your Higher Self to remove the temptation from your consciousness. Then visualize yourself holding Archangel Michael's Blue Flame Sword, the symbol of his will and power, and cut the cord of temptation. Say to yourself: "I have perfect self-control and mastery over my energies. I am the master and director of my life. Be still and know that I Am God." Take a deep breath and release as you assume control.

Calling upon the Names of God

No bad habit or addiction can withstand the names of God. If ever you are struggling with a temptation, immediately start chanting the names of God or a Mantra of God. Here are some Judeo-Christian examples: Elohim, Yod Hay Vah Hay, Adonai, Ehyeh Asher Ehyeh, El Shaddai, Shekinah, Eli, and Shaddai El Chai. Of course depending on your tradition and belief, you can call upon any highest One that you know, and ask to receive divine grace, intervention, will, power, and assistance. If saying the name of Jesus works, by all means do so. Whatever your god concept is named, call upon it and let it remove the temptation from you.

Call upon Spirit, the Masters, and the Angels

Call upon Spirit, the Masters, and the Angels to repair all your physical, emotional, and mental bodies and implement a chakra cleaning, balancing, and repair. Give them a few minutes to do this. Just wait quietly and let the work proceed. Now ask that all seven chakras begin to work like one unified chakra. Do this every night for a period of 21 days.

The Love Shower

Once a day, ask that Spirit, the Angels, Lord Maitreya, and Master Kuthumi bathe your bodies with a "Light Shower of Love." Allow this to happen every day for one minute. Ask that you may have a serene temper and compassion for self and others. Let peace and unconditional love enter into your heart. Let go and let God take over and be at the helm of your ship. Be at rest and know that you are safe.

Chapter 10

Balancing the Masculine and the Feminine

As far as I'm concerned, being any gender is a drag.

– Patti Smith

The patriarchal system has been the dominant paradigm for several thousand years. Today, masculine energy permeates all aspects of modern living. But in early human history, this was not the case. In the past, the feminine and the energy of the Goddess ruled the world. Some say that the return of the energy of the Goddess is imminent. Whether the controlling paradigm is the masculine or the feminine, neither will bring peace to self nor harmonious living to the planet. They both have positive and negative aspects with which to contend. Since both have ascended and un-ascended aspects, neither can create a peaceful internal state or a righteous society. It is in the balancing of the masculine and the feminine that true harmony and ascended living will come.

Fragmentation into Genders

Let us start at the beginning. In the process of the fragmentation and descent from infinite into finite, the original Receiver separated first into two opposites. This duality precipitated gender roles and identities: male and female. The male and masculine gender is strong, focused, linear, mental, goal oriented, and able to be quick and decisive. He is force in action. Biologically, he is prodigal in creating the seed that fertilizes a female egg. He ejects abundantly and with largess the endless flow that brings new life. Since he is force in action, the negative aspect of this gender will cause him to continue to move in a direction even if he is told that it is the wrong way. Because he is thought-centered, he is highly susceptible to the negative ego and the desire to dominate, conquer, compete, and expand territory. Men are wired to see the world and process information quickly and cerebrally. They compartmentalize well and can shelve and separate issues, topics, and emotions. Even when they acknowledge emotions, they are quick to move to the next topic, thoughts, or ideas. It is easy for them to let go.

The female and feminine gender is receptive, inclusive, conciliatory, feeling, nurturing, and able to create an environment for new growth to happen. She has the ability to create the form in which life can manifest. Biologically, she is the vessel in which new life gestates and where only one or two eggs a month are viable. Compared to the masculine overflow, she is highly restrictive to the masculine seeds. This selection allows her to carefully choose which seed, from millions of candidates, will fertilize the egg. She considers what is being presented to her with great discernment and selects what feels most viable.

The negative aspect of this gender is that since she is driven to create form, she will move about the world examining and selecting potential candidates for this fertilization process. This can apply either biologically or to projects and endeavors. Unless a clear choice is made not to create form, she will be driven to select a suitable match. She is curious and inquisitive. Additionally, women are wired to process information about the world through feeling. Because they are highly emotionally intelligent, everything becomes personal and is perceived as being done to them, for they are at the center of their emotional bodies. They are therefore highly susceptible to the subconscious mind as well as the emotional glamour, illusion, and programming that exist in the emotional body, all of which may hijack the center of self-awareness. It is difficult for them to let go.

Gender Identities and the Fall of Man

When the male and female genders come together and copulate, the cycle of life is maintained by the creation of offspring. From the Biblical story of Adam and Eve and the fall of man, one can learn a lot about gender roles and identities. The story goes as follows: Adam was told by God to eat and partake of the fruit of all the trees in the Garden of Eden, but not from the tree of knowledge. Adam proceeded as told and did not touch the fruit of that tree. Here, he is the linear, focused, and directed male gender personified.

Then entered the serpent that tempted Eve. It was the murmur of the subconscious mind pointing to the rising level of the bread of shame that both Adam and Eve were experiencing. Adam was not connected to his emotions and could not see it. He would be the last to feel the shame. Eve on the other hand, being highly emotionally intelligent, felt the shame. They were receiving everything for free and effortlessly, but without the ability to give back or earn the blessings received.

As in the life of many couples, it was the female that identified and analyzed the emotion and brought it to the attention of the male. Eve told Adam what the serpent told her. Basically, she unmasked the shame that both she and Adam were feeling. This realization was a major revelation for Adam, for as the initiator, he had to take action to try to solve this situation. They both ate of the fruit of the tree of knowledge and realized that they were naked. They allowed themselves to feel the shame and face the pain. Being naked is allegorical for exposing oneself to something.

As a result they were expelled from the Garden of Eden. The expulsion from Eden is the decision that Adam and Eve made to say no to the free gifts being giving to them by the Giver. That act is interpreted differently by different people. Some say it was a fall, a forced descent from an elevated state. Others say that it was a self-assertive step, an act of emancipation. Whichever school you believe in is not important; what is clear is that a decision was made to attempt to remove the bread of shame. Adam and Eve began to descend the dimensional scale, fragmenting into multiplicity, shedding gifts, abilities, and powers into 3-D density where all fragmented aspects of the original couple could learn to give and receive from each other, thus removing the bread of shame program.

But gender is not as clear-cut as it may appear. The story of Adam and Eve in the Garden of Eden represents an archetypical situation. Adam is the archetypical male, and Eve is the archetypical female. Today, no one is 100% male or female. In fact, we are all a mixture of both genders. All males have an inner feminine or anima, and all females have an inner masculine or animus. In his exhaustive writings, Carl Gustav Jung coined those terms and discussed the necessity of integrating our inner genders for the healthy functioning of our psyche. No one can ascend without balancing the masculine and the feminine energies within them. The Yin and the Yang must be balanced to bring us to the Tao, the perfect equilibrium of the two. The polarity and duality within must end if we are to re-enter the Garden of Eden. When we are sexist and reject the opposite gender, we are not just hurting beings outside of ourselves; we are in fact diminishing, tarnishing, and degrading our relationship to our inner opposite. We are in fact flagellating and hurting ourselves, destroying any hope of blending, healing, and merging our splintered and fragmented psyches back together.

Masculine and Feminine in the Kabbalah

The ancients knew better. This is evident by how they represented the inner workings of the masculine and feminine. In the Kabbalah, the "Tree of Life" is a glyph that holds within it the path of the descent and ascent of man. It is a series of symbols to which are assigned esoteric meanings and values. The masculine energy is represented by the sefirot or symbol named "Chesed," which is Mercy and Compassion. The feminine energy is the opposite sefirot or symbol named "Geburah," which is Strength and Fear. One would think that there is a mislabeling. How can mercy be associated with the male energy and strength with the female? Men are stronger and go about battling and conquering, which appears to equate to strength, and women are receptive and nurturing and would seem to be a better fit for the energy of mercy.

In actuality, the descriptions are spot on. Chesed is the overflow, gift, and exuberance that moved forth to initiate the creation of life. In the path of descent, there existed a blank field, an entire Universe that had to be populated. The male energy is the profuse flow of the creative impulse trying to initiate life and fill the empty Universe. Nothing can seem to stop it, and its endless gifting to the world is an act of giving and mercy. It is the benevolent king represented by King Solomon, the wise and merciful. Think of the endless and boundless energy of a youth, and you will be close to understanding the power, creativity, and miraculous nature of this gifting and merciful vortex. Within the masculine embodiment of strong physique and dominance is hiding the inner feminine quality and gift of mercy. However, these gifts cannot continue to flow unchecked. Think for a moment of what state you would be in if you were partaking in an endless all- you-can-eat buffet. You would become sick and eventually die. An energy system has to balance this out by saying, "No, I have had enough."

This is where Geburah comes in. She is the power of restriction and resistance that one must invoke to stop this endless flow and become discerning and selective. If you were to allow creation to continue without stop, we would end up in a sorry place. She is the vessel that will receive the creative flow and gifts of Chesed but will select only one or two gifts and reject all else. This is the restrictive force that has the strength to say, "No, I am full," and stop the exuberance. It is the power to select among the endless gifts and possibilities from Chesed the one that will work and deny all others.

Geburah has the power to purge and destroy that which is not suitable for life. It is this energy that causes women to naturally abort any fertilized egg that is not vital and suitable for healthy development. Before you create a house on virgin land, you have to first excavate and remove soil in order to create a solid foundation. She is the energy system that allows this to happen. It is represented by the Indian Goddess Kali, the destroyer. She is not death, but the ability to create after careful sorting and selection. She uproots and destroys that which no longer serves us. The creative force has to be balanced with an equally destructive energy so that equilibrium can be maintained. Within the weaker feminine body resides an inner strength that can send fear into the overflow of the creative force and destroy that which is not vital. This is the inner masculine power and strength that exists in every woman. Also, let us not forget that women are the stronger gender. They outlive men by several decades.

However, this does not mean that men have to be merciful and gifting at all times or that women must be restrictive and have strength in perpetuity. In fact, if this happens, there is no balance. A life focused on mercy alone would have catastrophic consequences just as a life focused on strength alone would create death and destruction. An evolving consciousness has to navigate the waters between these two vortices—male and female. When and where you need to apply mercy as opposed to strength is part of your soul maturity and only time and experience can grant you that wisdom.

The equilibrium and balance of these two forces create a third state, which is the sefirot or symbol "Tipheret," meaning Beauty. It is the center of the Tree of Life and is the point around which all other vortices on the Tree of Life rotate. This is the idealized state of the Tao to which we should aspire, a perfect blending of the masculine and feminine energies.

Female Energy in History

Yet this idealized state is not something that civilized society has embraced. In fact, instead of allowing both genders to exist as complements of each other, being simply the opposite side of the same coin, they have been competing for dominance. Gender war, battling, and suppression have been going on for centuries.

133

When the divine feminine energy was the controlling paradigm, the matriarchal system ruled autocratically around powerful, strong female leaders. Unfortunately, the patriarchal system has suppressed the matriarchal one for so long that few historical examples remain. However within the context of the male-dominated paradigm in which we exist, we can clearly point out examples of powerful, mythical female-warrior rulers who demonstrate the energy that female control can muster.

The Greek historian Herodotus feared the nation of the Amazon warrior women. They were an all-female society that allowed men in once a year for reproduction purposes. The male offspring resulting from the encounter were sent back to their fathers, while the females were raised by their mothers and taught agricultural pursuits, hunting, and the art of war. In a different version of the tale, during the Amazon war campaigns, they would capture male prisoners as sex slaves. The male offspring resulting from the unions would either be killed or abandoned as babies in the forest, while the females were raised by their biological mothers. They were ruled by a powerful queen named Hippolyta, who participated in the Trojan wars, having a magical girdle given to her by her Father Ares, the Greek God of War.

They built numerous cities, including Smyrna, Ephesus, Sinope, and Paphos, and later on moved to Themiscyra on the River Thermodon (the Terme River in present-day northern Turkey). They also spoke their own language. Greek history and myths are filled with battles, invasions, and stories about the active presence of the Amazon warrior women. They were a force that all Greek city/states feared and with which they had to reckon. Their mastery of battle strategy and hand-to-hand combat was unparalleled in the Greek world. As mythical as it may sound, this is giving us a glimpse into what unchecked collective feminine energy may have looked like.

During the Middle Ages, one female figure stands out as the most powerful and skillful head-of-state in her time: Eleanor of Aquitaine. She was the wealthiest and most influential woman of her time. She owned half of France as the duchess of Aquitaine and countess of Poitiers. She was the patroness of such literary figures as Wace, Benoît de Sainte-Maure, and Bernart de Ventadorn. She was an intellectual, a poet, painter, musician, warrior, and the most eligible woman of Europe, who married King Louis VII of France. During that time, she gave him two daughters and fought in the second Crusade in full armor. She had the marriage annulled and eight weeks later married Henry II of Normandy, who later rose to the throne as the King of England. She gave him eight children: five boys and three girls.

Her relationship with Henry II was contentious. King Henry II imprisoned her because she was trying to raise an army to overthrow him and place her son Henry as King. After the death of Henry II, her son Richard the Lionheart, became king and quickly released her from prison, and while he engaged his life on the battlefields of the third Crusade, she ruled England. She lived a long time and survived all but two of her children.

Eleanor of Aquitaine is a historical wonder, for in the midst of a patriarchal medieval society, stood the greater-than-life footprint of a woman of great power and sophisticated political cunning, who manipulated the highest corridors of government to her advantage. Her gender was never a handicap, and she used her wit and beauty to facilitate the expansion of her agenda.

If there is one historical female figure that personified the archetypical energy of Geburah, or strength, it is Joan of Arc. Born Jeanne d'Arc in Lorraine in 1412, she was a peasant girl who, as a teenager, began to have visions of God asking her to support the uncrowned King Charles VII. It was the time of the Hundred Years' War, and most of France was occupied and sieged by the armies of England. She was a charismatic, fiery, and passionate young girl, who managed to convince the uncrowned King Charles VII that God had sent her to support him and put an end to the English occupation.

She was sent to Orléans where she innovated battle strategies and overcame the military complacency of veteran commanders. She led the French troops to battle, and after nine days, the siege of Orléans was over. She continued to lead the French troops to several other swift and almost miraculous victories that ignited the spirit of the people of France. As a result, Charles VII was crowned King of France at Reims.

Although a guided military protégée, she was not a seasoned politician, and her rise to popularity and fame threatened many. She was being guided by a Divine voice that she obeyed with total abandonment. She could not be controlled or corrupted. She was betrayed and captured by the Burgundians, and transferred to the English troops in exchange for money. She was put on trial by a pro-English Bishop of Beauvais, Pierre Cauchon, and was burned at the stake for heresy when she was 19 years old. Twenty-five years after her death, an inquisitorial court authorized by Pope Callixtus III examined the trial, pronounced her innocent, and declared her a martyr.

Referred to by the French as The Maid of Orléans, "La Pucelle d'Orléans," she was the virgin female warrior that embodied the negative aspect of the archetypical energy of restriction, strength, and death. She led the French troops to many victories, but they came at a high price. This was the Middle Ages and warfare was particularly barbaric. People on both sides were brutalized, dismembered, gorged, disfigured, and decapitated. It was not just death; it was violent and brutal death. She was a teenager, and she was leaving a trail of blood behind her. Yes, she was guided, but by the negative polarity of the égrégore of her God concept. Indeed she has been canonized as one of the patron saints of France, but keep in mind the cost that this polarity shift caused. History has painted her as a martyr, but be aware of the thousands who died in battle for this swing of the pendulum. Could King Charles VII have been crowned king of France without her involvement? Could a different choice have been made? The answer to both questions is yes. There are always an infinite number of solution sets that one can access if one is open to the possibilities.

Recent history will prove that when women come to great political power and prominence, they do not necessarily display the pattern of behavior of the weak, nurturing, and motherly type. Women can more easily tap into the negative aspect of the female energy, fear, than men can and display unbelievable rigidity, will, and power.

One such example is Margaret Thatcher, the longest-governing Prime Minister of the United Kingdom in the 20th century and the only woman to ever have held that post. Known for her conservative and uncompromising politics and leadership style, she was almost unbendable. Her views were forthright, and she would bulldoze everything in her path to implement them. Aptly nicknamed by a Soviet journalist as the "Iron Lady," she deregulated the financial sector and the labor market, privatized state-owned companies, and reduced the influence of trade unions.

A second example is the fourth Prime Mister of Israel, Golda Meir. Before Margaret Thatcher was known as the "Iron lady," Golda Meir was described as the "Iron Lady" of Israeli politics. Although she was often portrayed as the strong-willed, straight-talking Jewish grandmother, former Prime Minister David Ben-Gurion called her "the best man in the government." She was uncompromising, direct, a labor Zionist, and a socialist who moved to Palestine with her husband and was one of the 24 signatories on the Israeli Declaration of Independence.

While you may not agree with the politics, views, and actions of these historical female examples above, the point was to illustrate the ease with which women can activate the negative polarity aspect of their gender. If strength is not tempered by mercy, you will end up with a cruel and brutal expression of the female archetype. Again, the balance of the outer feminine with the inner masculine is the key to internal and external peace and social justice.

Gender War

It will not come as a surprise to say that the dominant patriarchal system has not been kind to women. You would think that since both man and woman fragmented from one being, playing complementary roles would be the default setting. But that is not the case when you have a resisting force designed to resist the removal of the bread of shame program. This energy system, code-named satan (pronounced sa-'tan), fuels a man and woman's sense of separation and isolation, until fear of the other gender becomes an issue. "It is outside of me and acts, behaves, and serves functions that I can never fulfill, therefore it must be feared, and I must control it."

Physically stronger, men would hunt, battle, defend, and protect the family and tribe while women gathered herbs and plants, nurtured the family, and took care of the offspring. Men were stronger, skilled at battle, and could overtake an enemy with a combination of cunning and power. Their physical strength was something that women feared. What if it were directed at them? On the other hand, women have been feared by men for their ability to be the vessel for new life, their knowledge of edible plants, herbs and roots, their cunning, and resiliency.

Over the eons, the battle of the genders raged. At times women were dominant, and at others, men were in charge. The brawn of males gave them a physical advantage in the control for dominance in the gender war, and for the past several thousand years, the patriarchal system has ruled. In the male-controlled égrégore and paradigm, women played a secondary role. It was not until the 19th century that the church acknowledged that women had a soul. Up to that point, according to the church doctrine, only the Virgin Mary enjoyed such a privilege.

In the USA, women had to take to the street to gain the right to vote. Even today their reproductive rights are being controlled by men. In over three-quarters of the planet, women are viewed as property. In fundamentalist Muslim countries, women cannot go out in the street, drive, or travel without being accompanied by a man from their family. They are severely punished with public lashings for such simple actions as wearing western clothing or not covering their faces. And if they are convicted of adultery, the punishment is hanging or public stoning. We watch in horror when we hear of this news and say this only happens in Muslim countries.

But if we take a closer look at home, women are not doing a whole lot better. In the job market, they are not paid equal wages as men performing the same job. They are date-raped, physically and emotionally abused, threatened, and neglected by their male partners. We have a long way to go to achieve gender equality. Yes, we have women in high-powered positions in business and politics in the West, but for the vast majority, the attitude of the male-controlled media and news is that females are for the pleasure, entertainment, and adornment of men. The current reality shows and *Housewives* franchises, again dominated by a male-controlled executive body, perpetuate the negative stereotype of women being bitchy, loud, vindictive, and emotional lunatics. Like sheep, millions watch the *Housewives* train-wreck series of TV shows with forced, scripted, and improbable situations to the financial joy of the executives. Untold damages are being done to the psyches of young females on the planet, either by design or by greed. This is the model to which they are being told to aspire.

Finding a Healthy Balance of Female Energy

It is sad to say that in the patriarchal society in which we live, most business women think, act, and behave like men. They are copying a model of aggressiveness and business climbing that is masculine and foreign to the core of their gender. They are disconnected from their heart and have embraced the male model of bullying, intimidation, and conquest to get ahead. They have been so brain washed by the patriarchal system that they think the only way for them to be a success is to be like men.

This lack of authenticity is a major failure that at some point will cause them to have an identity crisis. You cannot ignore who you are for very long without your true nature coming back to sabotage your false identity and claim its place. What develops at this point is a great sense of regret, disorientation, loss of time, and living with shame over the pain inflicted on others in the process of business climbing. In their emotional relationships, their femininity is also lacking. They have difficulties relating to other women, and men find them cold and calculating.

I am not saying that women should not be in business, but they should climb the corporate ladder on their own terms. They should never forget that they are women and should use that as an asset. They are intuitive, inclusive, and can gather information in a way that men cannot. It is not always about numbers, linearity, and efficiency. Greed, conquest, corporate expansion, and the shareholders' bottom line without soul are unsustainable. That kind of environment has created the mess that the global market is in today. Where is the heart, the giving back, and the sharing? Allow the feminine principle of inclusiveness; pass on some of the blessings to the less fortunate and the consumers; and watch your business and brand gather a global and loyal following.

The Yin and the Yang

We are immortal souls and karma is a means for us to work out and balance the toxic energy dynamic that has been initiated in our other lifetimes. If you are inauthentic to yourself and your gender, or battle the other gender, you will probably find yourself incarnated as the opposite gender, to experience the disempowering state of which you took advantage in a previous life in order to balance the equation.

In fact, we all have been both male and female. In the initial descent, the Receiver created separation of the genders; the ascent is an opportunity to experience reversal and merger. For that to happen, you have to first be comfortable with your own gender. Additionally, you have to cultivate the buried qualities and characteristics of your inner and opposite gender. You have to allow the inner virtues, characteristics, and treasures of your gender-opposite to blossom and flourish in your life.

Although biologically we are wired differently, we can and should transcend our wiring and connect to a Universal principle where both genders exist. No one can ascend without a perfect balance of the masculine and feminine energies. Our relationship with the opposite gender provides an opportunity for us to empathize, assimilate, and recall inner qualities about the opposite sex that we may have forgotten. Observe attentively and remember that they are not outside or foreign to you. If they are riveting, protecting, nurturing, sexual, and loving to you, they are a reminder of what exists within and what you are trying to embrace. In fact, nothing exists outside of you. Your inner and opposite gender is an aspect of yourself, externalized and brought into your life by the Universe to remind you that you have to learn to integrate, absorb, and assimilate. Remember, the zip file and memory of this past estate of sexual merger and balance already exists within. You have to find it and extract the file.

The opposite genders are in your life to teach you where to look so you can begin the extraction process. Love, honor, appreciate, and respect them for they are your greatest teachers. If you are gay or lesbian, stay away from any misogynous or misandrist tendencies; celebrate, admire, and honor the opposite gender; and embrace all the gifts that it is adding to your spiritual liberation.

This is probably the most difficult test for the seeker to learn, for so many cultural and inherited stereotypes and taboos are telling you not to do it. It takes a secure, courageous, and confident man or woman to explore buried feelings of another gender within. Yet it is in the blending and merger of these feelings with your physically expressed gender that cellular equilibrium will be achieved, and with that, conscious immortality will be yours. The polarities and opposites must become completely neutral. Our redemption is linked to the embrace of our spiritual androgyny. Gender division is the most polarized expression of opposites with which we contend on a daily basis. When you exist in a state without gender separation in your psyche, you are in the Tao. You have reassembled yourself and the totality of who you are.

I know that most people on the planet are obsessively searching the outside world for their soul mates or twin flames to complete them, but the truth is, external matches are only "training wheels." The real and eternal partner lies within.

Chapter 11

Giving and Receiving

It's not how much we give
but how much love we put into giving.

– Mother Teresa

Before there was time, there existed only an infinite Desire to Give, and that Desire to Give was everywhere. It was a form of existence that was unlike anything we know. It existed but was not self-aware, since nothing was outside of it. For you to know that you exist, you need an outside, a mirror, or reflection. To address this, it created an infinite Desire to Receive, an opposite, inverse, or reflection. And for a time, the Desire to Give and the Desire to Receive reflected each other in a perfect spiritual marriage. Slowly but incrementally, the Desire to Receive began to feel bread of shame over the infinite and endless gifts that it was receiving from the Desire to Give, without any effort. Getting everything for free without any effort or ability to give back was too much to bear. That shame became so paralyzing that the Desire to Receive told the Desire to Give: "No, I don't want anything from you anymore."

Instantaneously, the Desire to Receive moved from being infinite and endless into being finite and as small as the head of a pencil. But the Receiver soon realized that without the Giver it was afraid and empty. Separation from Infinity created limits, boundaries, and a bourgeoning ego; therefore fear evolved that everything external to the Receiver could have negative intentions. So it called the Giver back, saying: "I made a mistake. Come back. I need you." The Giver realized that it could fulfill every desire the Receiver had except for the removal of the bread of shame, for the Giver was not equipped to receive. So it devised a plan to make this removal happen. As soon as the Giver touched the Receiver, it shattered it with a primordial spiritual detonation. The Receiver was now broken into multiplicity for the purpose of removing the bread of shame, which would be accomplished by the giving and receiving to all of its broken aspects. Each fragment manifested an ego or persona, and each individual had to remove the bread of shame by learning to give and receive from each other.

I want to emphasize here that unlike the primordial plan in which the Giver could not receive, we have to give and receive to each other. Both things must happen for the shame to be removed. If one person gives and another receives, the original shame program will be triggered. The fragmented Receiver has to find a way to earn the gift or give something back so that the shame will be removed.

Noninterference

Be aware that we are aspects of the original Receiver, overburdened with the bread of shame program, which we are all running. It is the basic operating software of this Universe. Additionally, in the process of giving and receiving to each other, we have to obey the law of noninterference. You cannot comingle your energy grid with anyone else's without permission and complete disclosure. In other words, if I want to give to you, I have to ask for your permission; and I have to disclose what I intend to give, and you have to agree. Reciprocally, if I want to receive from you, I have to ask for your gift, and I have to tell you why I think this is a good thing. All beings that operate under the Light of God follow these rules.

On a spiritual level, we give and receive energy from each other. This can take the form of energetic healing, prayers, or positive and supportive intentions. Since we all have free will and the right to choose our course and direction, I cannot give you healing or send you a prayer intention unless I have your permission. So many lightworkers violate this rule multiple times a day. This is the sin that was committed by the fallen angels. Your healing and prayer intentions without permission are violating someone else's sovereignty. If you don't have permission, do not interfere with the will, volition, and intention of a sentient life form. Even if they appear to be dying, they are sentient and have the right to make that choice too. For reasons that you may not understand, that being may choose to suffer today. Every choice is respected. Those who know me can tell you that even if someone asks me to heal and pray for them, the first thing that I will do before I proceed is to ask them: "Do I have your permission?" If the individual is a minor, is in a coma, or is mentally incompetent, I will ask their Higher Self for permission and wait for an answer. Until I sense a "yes" or an energetic release or letting go, I will not proceed.

None of the Ascended Masters will interfere with our will. They have a lot of abilities and powers that could assist us. But we have to remove the bread of shame—it is our job and it has to be a real effort. If we feel that right now we need to experience pain and suffering, they will support us in that choice and do nothing. A true Ascended Master will never volunteer or push their help upon you. They will wait for you to ask. When you ask for help from any spiritual being of the Light of God, they will do exactly what you ask them to do. The Ascended Beings so honor this law that they will follow your request to the exact letter. No more, no less. Choose your words wisely.

Thoughts, Perceptions, and Projections

On a mental level, we give and receive by holding thoughts and intentions about each other. We project thoughts and judgments on others all day long. The average person on the planet has three to five intentions per minute; often they are projected toward others, and most of them are not ascended in content. Even if the thought was positive, did the recipient give you permission? Mind your thoughts. This is an aspect of mental mastery that needs clarification. Thoughts are things and create everything. A thought projected is not just an idea that came across your mind, but a decree that you are now forcing on another sentient life form without consent. What do I mean by projected thought? Let me explain: During my interaction with others, if I discern that they are behaving from a negative ego standpoint of disempowerment, it is my perception, understanding, and realization. But if I now want them to change by sending them thoughts of self-empowerment, I am violating their right. From an ascended perspective, the best thing that I can do is to embody and demonstrate what self-empowerment is and hope that they will learn from my example. If they don't ask me, I don't project or see them empowered, without their consent. It is a hard lesson for the seeker to understand that with his increased ability, he cannot go around trying to "help" others without approval.

Our consciousness is constantly accessing what is around us. We are coming to conclusions about situations, people, places, and things in our environment. It is the value that we place on the result of these conclusions that are projections. This is good, bad, evil, light, dark, positive, negative, ascended, and unascended. When we do this, we become polarized, and this projects and holds an energetic filter or lens on the external experience and relationship. The goal is to observe and assess without objection. In other words, can you observe the dark or light without having a visceral charge about it? Everyone on the planet is addicted to making judgments and creating these endless projections on each other.

This is one of the reasons why the web of karma is so difficult to untangle. Every time a projection is made without consent, a cord is created between you and the target, and that toxic tension must eventually be brought back to equilibrium. That restoration and balance can happen in this or future life times. It is done privately, in silence, and with the speed of thought. It is a good thing that our energy body is not large enough to allow our thoughts to manifest instantaneously, for if that were so, we would catastrophically hurt and damage each other.

Let us add to this one-on-one scenario the group or collective dynamic. Where thousands or millions of people are holding one thought, it creates a group body, and that now becomes the rule that will govern and operate the functioning and interaction of this collective. If it happens to be fear, rage, or disempowerment, the group body will manifest this model just as well as if it were love, respect, and peace. As a means to unplug yourself from this addictive behavior and personal or group karma that it creates, repeat the short version of the Ho'oponopono like an endless mantra, and direct it toward all thoughts, conclusions, and judgments that are exiting your consciousness about others: "Please forgive me. I love you and I let go." Very quickly this will bring you into neutrality and negate the toxic cord that is being created with every judgment that you make. Do this and watch yourself become free of entanglement and drama. Neutrality creates liberation.

Giving and Receiving on an Emotional Level

On an emotional and psychological level, we give and receive to each other by listening, encouraging, supporting, and loving others. Every time you do a kind deed directed toward another, you give them a helping hand. Every time you say a kind and supportive word to a stranger, friend, coworker, and family member, you extend support. Every time you go out of your comfort zone to help someone else, you not only give to another, but you expand your vessel and increase your capacity to hold more light. At times you will give support and at others the Universe will bring you support. Make sure that your support and help is wanted. Remember the law of noninterference. If you offer help to a friend who appears to be in trouble and they respond that they don't want to talk about it at the moment, respect their wish and walk away. On the other hand, when you allow fear into your consciousness and move to attack, diminish, control, and dominate others, your vessel shrinks, and you reduce your capacity to broadcast Light.

Being Neutral to Projected Fears

Even if we limit the moments when we allow fears in, we all know people who have a propensity to dish it out or give us a hard time. Keep in mind that an attack thought is a loss of control and an attempt at getting it back. By all means do not allow yourself to be victimized by someone that is acting out of fear. Create proper boundaries so that you will protect yourself. Be understanding of the fact that they are coming from a state of lack and fragmentation. It is therefore an illusion. If and when you have to resist or oppose them, do not come from a place of vengeance, rancor, or fear. That would polarize you to match their frequency, and on some level, this is what they want. Simply act to resolve the conflict from the perspective of the removal of the bread of shame. This is the ultimate goal. Remain neutral and simply act to make sure that their actions are not robbing you or anyone else of the opportunity to remove your shame. Remember, when you overcome fear and realize that there is no separation, shame is removed and fragmentation ends.

Money and Prosperity Consciousness

In our modern society, one of the fundamental ways that we give and receive to and from each other is with money. All businesses sell goods or services, and the cost of the transaction is determined by supply and demand. If today this item or that service is in high demand and short supply, we assign a high monetary value to it. Yet the value and consciousness that we attach to money itself is often contaminated and distorted. I remember years ago that a Wall Street friend of mine told me his father once said to him: "He who dies with the most money in the bank wins." For him, earning a six-figure income and putting the money in the bank was the key to fulfillment. The purpose of his life was to accumulate more money; he worshipped money like a god. If this is your belief system, then greed and corruption are not far behind, and the negative ego, limited lenses of instant gratification, and me-first behavior will cause you to be spiritually out of balance and bankrupt. This is an example of someone who only knows how to receive but is unable to give.

145

There is nothing wrong with wanting to receive and be rich; in fact, God wants us to be prosperous, for with our abundance we can help manifest God's plan on earth by sharing with others. Abundance and prosperity come from God, not from the amount of money you hold in a bank. If your focus is money, you are worshipping a false god. On the other hand, there are those of us, along with plenty of lightworkers, who fall into that category and are able to give but find it hard to receive.

I met this beautiful soul a while back who would give you the shirt off her back. She was one of the most generous people that I have ever met. I later found out that she had a nervous breakdown, and as it turns out, she was giving not because she was full, but because she felt worthless and empty. Due to lack of self-love and negative ego contamination, she interpreted receiving as ungodly and dirty. More to the point, she did not believe that she deserved to receive from anyone for she did not have any positive self-worth. But if you don't receive the bliss, inspiration, and downloads coming from God, you will find very quickly that you run on empty and your world-service work becomes ineffective.

These two examples are illustrations of the extremes. What we are called to do is a bit subtler, for we must give and receive at the same time. We have to allow the blessings to come from God and others, and give and share with the world what we receive. Furthermore, when we give to someone, we must allow them the opportunity to remove their own bread of shame by reciprocating back to the degree that they can. I once sent a few hundred dollars to a maid my family used to have. I had heard that she had fallen on hard times. For me, it was only a few hundred dollars. But for her, living in the Caribbean, it was an overwhelming blessing. She wrote back to me very gratefully but said that she had to give me something in return. I thought about it and asked her if she could give me an embroidered handkerchief. When she sent it to me, her shame was removed. I could have easily said that I did not need anything, but that would have caused her to run the bread of shame program and would have sabotaged the blessings she was enjoying.

In truth, currency is energy, and the exchange of energy between giver and receiver must be done in a balanced manner. The money and paper that you have in the bank or your wallet is not the actual source of wealth. It is simply a symbol and value that we collectively attach to what is in demand. Wealth, abundance, and prosperity are states of mind and come from proper balancing of the desire to receive and give in everything that we do. It is not about the money and currency, and it is all about the energy exchange and not creating blockages in giving and receiving. When receiving, we have to earn the blessing; and in giving, we give because it is spiritual law that we share with others, and we allow the receiver to earn his or her blessing.

Removing the Bread of Shame

If you look at nature, nothing is free. There is effort attached to the survival of every species. Spiritual effort is the key to connecting to true wealth and prosperity, and it can take many shapes: a mailed handkerchief, a new job, self-love and acceptance, prosperity affirmations, giving to charity, an act of service to the world, re-programming the negative ego mind, etc., or it could be a combination of all the above. We have to earn back the Light of God and remove the bread of shame or the negative ego program. The moment it is done, the blessings are yours to enjoy. It is not that bliss is not all around us; we simply have to earn it. And it will be revealed to us, for it is our shame that is holding the bliss back, and that shame can take many forms.

I recently held a workshop and met a couple who were experiencing financial difficulties but had a serious interest in attending the workshop. They asked if I could make some special arrangement for them. I lowered the admittance to whatever amount they could afford. They were one of the most enthusiastic participants of the workshop. It was as if they had been walking in the desert for years and had just found water. Later that evening, one of my students who had left with them told me a fact that I did not know. They had given the last penny they had for the workshop and did not have any food in their house for dinner. But God is great! That student arranged for them to eat that evening.

The spiritual effort that they put in getting to the workshop was more than equal to the dollar value of admittance. There was no bread of shame. They earned the entrance fee, for it is not the amount of money spent, but the effort and energy they put into getting there. Additionally, I welcomed them and saw them as equal participants in the workshop. As spiritual leaders, we have financial obligations and concerns that can cause us to be reticent to make these kinds of arrangements. Or worse, we agree to them because we think it is what we should do but have doubts about our giving, thus contaminating it with questions, fears, and worries about how we are going to solve our own financial crisis. This kind of consciousness blocks the blessings from God that such an act should bring, and the act of giving becomes soiled with the negative ego program. My gift to this couple was free of such concerns; I really wanted them there.

I have witnessed the inverse of what I just described: lightworkers and spiritual teachers who would not ever alter the cost of their services under the claim that the potential students had prosperity issues that they had to solve in order to attend their classes and workshops. This is a brilliant negative ego justification for individuals who are amassing a fortune and yet are blocked, for they do not know how to give. They are no different than the Wall Street guy I mentioned earlier.

On the other hand, I have seen potential students who were chronic beggars of discounts and free services. They would flatter the teacher by telling him or her how brilliant he or she was, that at the moment they were experiencing lack, and could they attend the event for free. They further promised that when good fortune came their way, they would shower the teacher with money and gifts. These types of students are incredible seducers, but their words are empty.

This is also a negative ego contamination for they don't want to provide for themselves. They feel they are entitled, that the world owes them, and that they should get what they want without any effort. Ten percent of the planet's population is wired this way.

As spiritual teachers, we have to stop enabling these students by refusing to give them free services. Nothing is free in the Universe. If you have the capacity to hold only 2 volts and you try to capture 10 volts, you will short circuit. Until they start to remove their bread of shame program, they will live on a roller coaster of apparent gain and rapid losses. They may initially get some items for free, but they will dramatically and quickly loose what they receive, for you cannot keep what you did not earn.

Being Present in the Act of Giving

A few years ago, I was taught a valuable lesson about giving from a beggar at Sai Baba's Ashram in India. I came out of my hotel only to be followed by a mother and child, her hand outstretched asking for what I thought was money. I put my hand in my pocket to get a few rupees to give her. But something unexpected happen; she refused them and said: "No money… Baba says: no money…Food for baby." And she began to drag me by one arm to a street vendor. When we got to the street vendor, for the first time in the exchange, I looked at her and her child and I asked her: "What would you like?" She replied: "Milk." So I bought milk and gave it to her. For me it was an epiphany, for I realized the number of times in the past that I dismissed beggars by giving them money. I would give to them quickly so that they and their problems would go away. This time I was engaged in the act of giving. My consciousness was in the present, and I gave with full and complete intent.

The Short Circuit of the Global Financial Institutions

On a global scale, the financial institutions are "short circuiting." The greedy corporations who pursued the accumulation of money without ethical standard in order to gain personal and shareholder profits are failing and going under. The free market of supply and demand is a model easily contaminated by negative ego programming as it can fall into the trap of demanding more and more gain at any cost.

The burst of the real estate bubble was not without reason. It was not that the banking institutions making these bad loans did not know that the home buyers could not possibly repay the loans with their low incomes; they were just going to sell these bad loans to other banks and pass the problem to someone else. And for a while, their predatory lending practices toward the borrowers created great corporate profits. CEOs and shareholders were happy over the gains. But these were the ill-gotten gains of corrupted banks who seduced the borrowers and other institutions and ultimately the entire financial market.

This should not come as a surprise for the very foundation of the global banking system is based on creating free energy by receiving without earning or removal of the bread of shame. If you borrow $100,000 from a bank, the bank is required to put down in real currency only $10,000. The balance of $90,000 is electronically created. It does not exist, but the bank has the legal right to create it out of thin air. Your note from the bank says that you owe them $100,000, and for the next 30 years, you will pay back the principal and interest on money or energy that did not exist. The bank is gaining and receiving, without earning, after putting down only 10% of the value of the loan.

If you and I were to try to do this, we would be arrested. If you were an alien looking at the planetary financial system from afar, you would conclude that everyone on earth must be brainwashed to allow this to happen. It is done because we are being told by our politicians and government that it is good for the country and for business, and like sheep, we believe them. There is no disclosure or transparency for the banks about the true nature of the gift or loan that we are getting from them. They are bypassing the law of noninterference. It is a spiritual abomination, for this system is circumventing the removal of the bread of shame, the very reason that dimensional existence was created: so that we can earn back the Light.

It is however a bonanza for the fallen beings who are trying to reverse the ascension process and hold us from merging back with the Light of God.

As long as the banks are allowed to do this, no giving and receiving can be done in a balanced manner. The bank's free gain is antithetical to spiritual law, and because of this, the bank and you are caught in a toxic relationship and karmic imbalance in which you are the victim. This must then be rectified in some future lifetime. In other words, ascension is delayed and put back for a future time, for only the removal of the bread of shame can permit merger back to Source, and that requires effort from all sides of the equation.

But no man or institution can get away from this spiritual law: "You cannot keep what you did not earn." What we are witnessing around the planet is the short-circuiting of the financial world because of its attempt to create wealth for a few from energy received for free. Remember, it is not about the money. Spiritual effort must be equal to the gain achieved. Think of it as an equation: both sides must be equal to each other. When the receiver takes more and more without giving, the equation is out of balance. When the giver supplies more and more without receiving, the equation is also out of balance.

Furthermore, any forces or energy system that is out of balance will ultimately be brought into a state of equilibrium. The global financial meltdown is spiritual law trying to equilibrate what is out of balance. At that level, the forces in motion have no morality and do not care about collateral damages. Learning by karma is always painful. What governments around the world are attempting to do to address the situation is not a solution. Having an entire nation pay for the energetic inequity will not balance or correct the karmic debt. Remember again, it is not about money; it is about energy.

Giving and Receiving in a Balanced Manner

True balance can only come from sharing of the planetary resources with all. This is the consciousness that God wants to install in the grid of the planet. There are enough resources and wealth on the planet for every man, woman, and child to be fed and sheltered. The spiritual destiny of humanity is to share with each other—a continual exchange of effort and energy in giving and receiving. Last October, Lady Gaia spoke of this in these words: "No personal ownership. God and Gaia own everything. You are just the current stewards and your purpose is to share." I am also reminded of something Dr. Joshua David Stone once told me: "You can only keep what you are willing to give away." As lightworkers, soldiers, and volunteers in God's army, it is our role to help facilitate and anchor this template. So when you hear in the media about the global economic meltdown, do not fear, for to fear is to buy into the negative program and world karma. Instead, welcome this as an opportunity for you to help co-create a new paradigm of sharing. The only thing that doesn't change in the Universe is the law of change. See this so-called financial meltdown as an opportunity to help shift first your consciousness and then that of the planet as a whole.

Be cognizant of where your consciousness is when you give or receive. Are you running a negative ego program that is blocking you from earning what you receive? Are you giving to others with full and complete aware-ness that sharing is spiritual law manifest on earth? Are you fearing lack in your act of giving or are you consciously aware that it is in giving that we receive? If not, adjust your consciousness accordingly, for it is your thoughts that will help create and anchor this vision from Spirit and the Masters. Try keeping a journal of the state of your consciousness for 21 days while giving and receiving in all aspects of your life. What program were you running when you were at the supermarket checkout counter, the gas station, paying the rent, receiving your pay check, losing a contract, giving a hug to a friend or family member, donating a few hours at the hospice, etc.?

All interactions and exchanges that we have with internal subconscious forces or external forces and beings are acts of giving and receiving. Are these exchanges occurring without contamination and in an uncondition-ally loving manner? If the answer is no, then adjust your consciousness to that of the unconditionally loving God/Goddess that you truly are. Create a reprogramming plan and correct the negative ego contaminations, replacing them with Ascended thoughts, feelings, desires, and emotions. Make a spiritual vow that if the situation presents itself in the future, you will handle it in a Christed manner. After 21 days of journaling, your conscious mind will begin to do this automatically. Your prosperity, peace, health, and happiness is at hand if you can only discipline your subcon-scious mind not to react in fear, panic, and habitual, shared responses that the news and media are feeding you. And when enough of us can do this, the collective abundance and prosperity grid of the planet will shift as well.

My brothers and sisters, you have two choices in front of you. You can choose to do nothing, let the tide of global karma take over, and seek balance by draining the world's overinflated financial resources. This path is like an avalanche rolling down the side of a mountain. Nothing will be able to stop it until it reaches the bottom and buries everything in its way. Or you can yield to the change, be proactive by making the spiritual effort necessary to alter your individual consciousness, and reprogram the negative ego fear-based thoughts and belief systems that you shared with the planet, which caused this crisis in the first place. This is the only way to equilibrate and balance the inequity of the gain, for as you choose to make this effort and your neighbor and neighbor's neighbor do the same, a critical mass will be achieved, which will turn around the tide of karma. After all, the spiritual effort must equal the gain. Since karma is "correction" and not punishment, when the balance is achieved, the crisis will be over. Choose to assimilate this lesson by grace, for hidden in this crisis is the opportunity to learn how to unconditionally share your energies and resources with others. Manifesting this will greatly accelerate your ascension process and help anchor God's plan on earth.

The Future Earth

Imagine: a planet where all natural resources are equitably shared and extracted in a sustainable fashion; a green eco-friendly environment in which all decisions are made with the needs of the collective and the planet in mind; a place where no woman, man, or child is homeless, hungry, or uneducated; a planet where all geographic locations are on the same stage and level of social and economic development; a place where giving and receiving are exchanged in a balanced and spiritual manner in which the gain is always equal to the effort. This is the paradigm that God, Spirit, and the Masters are installing in the grid of the planet, and this is the essence and core of the energy of the "Age of Aquarius," the age of brotherly love.

That idyllic dreamscape description is, in truth, an illustration of the spiritual law of "equal exchange" taken to its logical conclusion, and anything in the Universe that does not obey it will short circuit and cause equilibrium to be imposed by crisis and karma. This fundamental principle is learned in high-school chemistry: If you want to change liquid water into gas, you must heat up the water. The amount of water that changes state from liquid into gas is proportional to the amount of heat supplied. If you want more or less gas, the amount of heat must be adjusted accordingly. Both sides of the equation will always equal each other: equal exchange. We all seem to understand that this law applies to the transformation and transmutation of physical and natural objects, but we are completely clueless to its corollary importance, effect, and impact on our emotional, psychological, psychic, and spiritual behavior and interaction relating to how we give and receive to and from each other. If we are not exchanging equally with anything or anyone on all these levels, we are creating karma and will short circuit at some future point in order to equilibrate and correct the equation. Add to this the learned negative programs and behaviors of a family unit, a small village, an ethnic group, a nation, and a planet, and you begin to understand the level of toxicity and negative ego programming running the planet's grid, which needs correction either by grace or by karma.

The healthy future of financial exchange may lie in creating a crowd-funding-based banking system that lends against collected and real value gathered from contributions of members and not by creating value and money out of the thin air. As I write this, many places on the planet are going through severe financial recession and are experimenting with the battering system. In Greece, entire regions are functioning and exchanging with this system. Necessity is the mother of invention, and a solution set to the planetary financial crisis is out there. We just have to find it. In fact it is already here; we merely need to allow the laws that govern giving and receiving to operate while the bread of shame is removed.

In October 2007, Gaia showed me a vision of a small village being run on these principles. She also told me something curious: "No personal ownership—everything belongs to God and Gaia. Pierre, this is a template. Anchor it anywhere on the planet, and it will spread to the earth's grid like wildfire." As the world leaders are moving to install rescue package after rescue package to help revive and shore up the free market system, remember the law of equal exchange: "the gain must be equal to the effort." If the financial remedies do not obey this principle, they are doomed to fail. Now the free market system is based on buying low and selling high to make a profit. A profit-driven economic system is based on gain without effort, which means that someone, some group, or some nation, is holding the short end of the stick while the top dog, corporation, or nation is reaping all the gain. It is in the corporation's or capitalist's interests to invest as little as possible and take short cuts to maximize profit. This is why 90% of the world's wealth is controlled by 1% of the earth population while entire countries and continents are ravaged by wars and famine. This is a system ruled by the negative ego programming of me-first. Furthermore, nothing in the Universe is free, and free is usually expensive.

Creating an ascended community where exchange mirrors natural law is the way of the future and the only way in which all the pieces and aspects of the original Receiver can merge back with Source.

Chapter 12

Love, Intimacy, and Sexuality

Among men, sex sometimes results in intimacy;
among women, intimacy sometimes results in sex.

– Barbara Cartland

Our entire Universe and everything in it were created by a simple, self-sustained, and powerful geometry: a torsion field. It is shaped in the form of a doughnut around which energy rotates in perpetuity on the surface of the doughnut. Everything—including subatomic particles, elements, objects, planets, suns, and biological life forms—emits a magnetic energy signature that is shaped like a torus. It is everywhere, and it can be weak, strong, minuscule, or vast, depending on your current state of being. It is the building block that creates and manifests everything. In humanity, that energy signature is most prevalent and expansive during these three activities: at death, while meditating, and during a lovemaking and bonding experience. Notice that I did not say during sex. It has to be a bonding and merging experience; otherwise, instead of an amplifying experience, it deflates the energy grids of everyone involved. A lovemaking experience inflates and expands the torsion field and takes the lovers into a spiritual state of resonance with Universal creative principles, whereas casual sexual encounters often deflate, separate, and break down the torsion field. And since the Universe is not a vacuum, implants, parasites, and devices can penetrate the boundaries of the weakened torsion field and host therein. Furthermore, every fear-based experience breaks down and reduces the torus, while every loving, blending, and merging activity causes the torsion field to grow. Lovemaking, meditation, and dying are about letting go and allowing the unifying force that permeates our Universe—love—to expand our consciousness and by extension inflate our torsion field.

Finding Love

To say that the lovemaking experience is a rare occurrence is an understatement. Some may spend a lifetime and never experience it. But the entire planet is obsessed with finding the ideal partner who will lead to this ecstatic communion and bonding experience. There are so many books written about how to find your soul mate or twin flame. Additionally, there are so many relationship experts who are promising to help you find the ideal partner by taking their workshops, coaching sessions, or channeled guidance. So many promises made, raising such high expectations, yet so little fulfillment and actual lifelong connections resulting from these sessions.

Personally, if I had spent the same amount of time, effort, and energy toward fulfilling my purpose that I had spent looking for the ideal partner, I would have ascended and my work here would have been done. As an intuitive who has been blessed with remembering my purpose and is moving to fulfill it, I now realize that I did not come to earth to experience the relationship thing. I came here to do group work, share a body of knowledge, and initiate a collective rescue mission. The relationship pursuit is secondary. I am open to it, but my purpose comes first. Besides, as I looked deep into my soul, I realized that the obsession to find a partner was externally driven.

External Influences Driving Our Desires to Find Love

Make sure that you are not pursuing something that is not authentic to your core and purpose. Be true to who you are. This obsessive search is often triggered by your peers, family, and a biological clock, if you are a woman, which may be telling you that you are approaching the end of your child-bearing years. In truth, what everyone is really seeking is to end the illusion of separation and fragmentation by bonding and merging with another soul. All loving relationships provide the training wheels for the ultimate bonding experience: merger with God.

Love as a One-to-Many Experience

I have now realized that I did not come to earth to have a one-on-one experience, but a one-to-many. I am not poly-amorous; I have always been monogamous in my past relationships. I mean to say that my capacity to unconditionally love is so great that it cannot be limited to one person. When I used to work in an office setting, there were days when the unconditional love that was busting out of my heart was so great that I would walk out of my office and give a long hug to everyone on the floor. I would pour my love into one person after another, for if I did not share this great love exploding inside of me, I would probably become sick. It was always well received, for it was nonsexual. It was my divinity blessing their divinity and telling them how much God and the Universe loved and appreciated them.

That capacity to love is so great that when it was directed at one person or a partner, it was always perceived as being too intense. Furthermore, the collective that I am one incarnated aspect of has been sentient for several billion years. Not having a one-on-one bonding relationship for the 80 years comprising the average life span of a human being is not even a drop in the ocean for a being who is consciously immortal. Spending 80 years on this plane to fulfill promises made long ago and not bonding with one person but sharing unconditional love with many is exactly what I came to do. Moreover, I am not missing anything. When I have these bonding, loving, and hugging moments with multiple people, my torsion field expands several blocks wide, something that cannot be done in a one-on-one sharing experience.

What Is a Collective?

It may help to explain what a collective is. We were originally created as a singularity that is called a Monad. At every step of our descent into dimensional existence, we fragmented into a multiple of 12. These secondary 12 branches are called Oversouls. At the next step of the descent, the 12 Oversouls each fragmented into another 12 to yield a collective of 144 Soul Extensions. You and I are Soul Extensions that belong to a collective of 144.

Your role as a Soul Extension is to experience life, remove the bread of shame, and become self-realized. This will initiate the ascent back to the Oversoul level at which the Christ Initiation occurs, and then the Monadic level, which is the integrated planetary ascension level. Past this level, the process continues on a solar, galactic, Universal level, and beyond. Your planetary-level Monad is the Soul Extension into another Monadic family at the solar level, and so on, all the way back to Source.

Fulfilling the Purpose of the Soul Extensions vs. Finding a Loving Relationship

Now, when you happen to meet other Soul Extensions of your Monad, there is a very powerful attraction, for you are meeting another aspect of you. This may explain the concept of soul mates, but let me be very clear: it is not one soul mate that you have, but a vast multitude of everyone who belongs to the same collective. Moreover, when you meet members of your collective, it does not automatically mean that you are going to have an intimate and life-bonding relationship with them. Each fragment is here to learn something that the Monad needs to assimilate, and the purpose of that specific fragment of you may separate you from one another for the time being.

Most of these encounters are not sexual in nature. They are often filial. In this embodiment, I have met a member of my galactic self. We are not in an intimate or sexual relationship. It was never a consideration. We are very different from each other. I am more about bigger pictures and ideas while she is about details and minutia. Yet when we speak, it is a type of communication that I don't have with anyone else on the planet. I just have to start speaking, and she begins to see a vignette of what I am trying to say. The reverse is also true. She begins to speak, and I perceive a 3-D download of what she is telling me.

Surrogate Partnerships vs. Soul Mates

To all who are looking for a soul mate or twin flame, understand what you are asking from the Universe. You are calling back to you an aspect of yourself, and the relationship may not be sexual. Moreover, if the relationship does not work out because you each have to assimilate different lessons for the Monad, stop the devastation, panic, and mourning. There are at least another 142 soul extensions on the planetary level to whom you can connect. Granted, they may not all be in physical incarnation or otherwise appropriate as a life partner, but chances are there are a few members of your collective in embodiment. Short of finding this illusive soul mate, you may end up in intimate relationships with souls with whom you have contracted to be life partners and surrogates for the purpose of balancing karma and removing the bread of shame.

These experiences can be just as soul fulfilling as those of soul mates. Intimacy is a beautiful thing. It is great to have someone with whom you can open up, be vulnerable, and share your dreams. We are all part of the same original being. The fragmentation of the original Receiver released countless cosmic Monads that descended the dimensional ladder to incarnate as humans. We are all cells of the same body. Yes, it will be easier for us to communicate and bond with the members of our Monad, but in truth, everyone is part of the same family.

Balancing the Masculine and the Feminine

No one can maintain a loving relationship without balancing the masculine and feminine within themselves. Every man must blend his inner feminine. Every woman must blend her inner masculine. This is the mythical alchemical marriage of the medieval alchemist. Without this, you are not whole, and you will project unrealistic expectations on the relationship. If you are interacting in the relationship solely from the wiring of your gender, you are going to have problems.

Men are quick at making decisions and resolving conflicts. Women assess differently. They sense and analyze all the possibilities and then make a decision that takes into account the entire picture. In order for you to have a successful partnership, you have to understand how your beloved functions. You have to anticipate his/her needs and wants. Since men behave and think differently from women, you have to step out of your gender and learn how he/she feels. This is a process and not an event. It may take a lifetime for you to understand, for example, that when she is telling you about a problem she is facing, she is not asking for quick solutions. She simply wants to be heard. Acknowledge her issue and mirror it back to her. She simply wants to know that you are listening. Give her the respect and time to come up with her own conclusions. A man does not understand hints. They could be small, medium, large, or billboard size hints. Save yourself a lot of time and headaches; just tell them what you mean. There are a myriad of situations similar to these that represent the differences in wiring between a man and a woman. Because of the love and care that you have for your partner, over the years, you will assimilate the thinking, knowing, and consciousness of your partner's gender and by association marry and blend with your own inner gender opposite.

Loving: Giving and Receiving

The process of loving is in two acts: giving and receiving. Remember that the original Receiver fragmented as a means to remove the bread of shame by learning to give and receive from his fragmented aspects. These acts of giving and receiving should not fixed roles that genders play, but rather an alternating flux of possible acts and states of activity and receptivity needed for a couple to remove the bread of shame. If the roles are fixed and the man is the giver and the woman is the receiver, then the bread of shame is not being removed. Remember that the original bread of shame program came into being because the Desire to Receive was not capable of either earning the gifts or giving back to the Desire to Give for the bounty it was receiving. Any fixed role will perpetuate this pattern and intensify the bread of shame program.

No torsion field can be enlarged and maintained in this dynamic. The giver has to allow the receiver to give back and vice versa. It is a four-way infinity loop that actually makes the energetic flow of a relationship a lot more interesting. Additionally, when these exchanges are taking place, one has to be present. You have to be in the moment, fully aware of what you are doing, and own your part in the flow of energy. So many people are not present during a lovemaking act. They are somewhere else, thinking about work, what they need to do, or another person or body parts. You need to be fully engaged in the present act of energetic flow that is going on. Otherwise this will create a back flow, break down the torsion field, and cause possible energetic attachments to come into this sacred union.

Loving in Same-Sex Partnerships

God does not care about the gender of your partner; as long as love, caring, and merger are being exchanged, the Universe will respond and the Heavens will sing. Like straight couples, same-sex couples giving and receiving in a balanced manner will create a similar geometry that will resonate with the frequency that created the Universe. It is the merger and blending of souls with self-awareness that intensify the torsion field and not their genders. All those who feel threatened and disturbed by same-sex love are revealing insecurities about their own gender identification. If you are secure in your gender, no alternate sexual orientation should bother you. If you are perceiving an external threat or fear, it is often a mirror about some internal process that you have not addressed yet.

Besides, in the higher dimensions, gender does not exist. Polarities are simply switched at will from activity to receptivity, according to the nature of the exchange. If you are removing the bread of shame program and you are a same-sex couple, God approves of you. God cares not about who you love; how this loving energy flows is of great importance. Your gender identification is not a factor in the ascension process. However, loving and not allowing the receiver to give back to you will derail the creation of the torsion field like a lead balloon.

Mastering a Sexual Energy

Short of a bonding, intimate, and loving experience, we all have sex. The corruptions of this energy are the unhealthy programs that we collectively associate with sexual experiences. If you are living in the West, take a look around you. Every newsstand is selling magazines with models showing body parts. The vast majority of music videos have scantily dressed dancers and models gyrating. Madison Avenue has long realized that the sexual energy can easily be associated with a brand and can sell products. In fact, sex sells. Yet with another breath, the culture is telling us that we should be chaste and pure.

Our puritanical and repressed religious culture is a suppressor of sexual liberation. In fact most holy books are telling us that sex is only for the purpose of procreation. In other words, if we enjoy sex, we sin. It is like saying we eat food to live, and if you enjoy eating, you are a sinner. There is incredible shame attached to what should be a normal and enjoyable activity between consenting adults trying to eliminate the illusion of separation and experience ecstatic union. In cultures where you do not learn about sex in the locker room but from the classroom, the myths are busted, and the population can now focus on the healthy pursuit of a satisfying connection with other beings.

Gender Physiology

Let us now speak frankly. Men are polygamists by nature. The male ejaculation has enough sperm in it to populate a small village. This is part of the exuberance and over-propensity of the masculine nature. It is profuse, abundant and gives to overflowing. Women are monogamous by nature. The feminine womb has one to two ova ready for fertilization per month. This is part of the selectivity and restriction of the female nature.

This is not to say that men cannot have monogamous relationships or that women cannot be polygamous. It is a statement of physiology and of how genders are wired. What it does mean is that women will take time to select a mate before becoming sexual while men can be sexual without a lot of thought about a selection process. In the animal kingdom, this is why the males do a courtship dance for the female, which then selects the right partner based on the nuance of the dance. Understand this and save yourself a lot of time in arguments as a couple.

Although we can and should overcome our physiology and merge our inner masculine and inner feminine and become spiritually androgynous, certain characteristics will remain. Men are going to look around. They are visually motivated and are easily distracted. However, it does not mean that they are going to be sexual with everyone they look at. Women: Stop reacting about something you cannot change if you are being honored and celebrated when you are with him. Be happy for the blessings. If he is engaged in sexual pursuits and gathering phone numbers, then you have a problem.

If you are a straight couple, the natural polygamous wiring of the male will be balanced by the monogamy of the female. If you are a lesbian couple, the bonding, coupling, and monogamy will come easier to you. If you are a gay couple, monogamy will be a challenge. This is not to say that gay couples cannot be monogamous. I have gay friends and clients who have been in monogamous relationships for 19 to 25 years. I recently asked a gay couple how they do it. The answer was revelatory: "I made a promise and commitment to be in this relationship, and this is a choice that I reaffirm every day. Besides, there is no one else in the world with whom I want to spend the rest of my life but my partner." Men: Choice is everything. The biggest sex organ is not between your legs. It is in your head. Make a choice and commitment, and your wiring will follow.

The Sexualization of Our Culture

Since our youth are influenced by what they see in advertising and TV, let us take a look at how America's youth are dressed to go to school to gauge the effectiveness of the media campaigns. The girls look like streetwalkers, and the guys are wearing hoodies with pants falling down below their buttocks and onto the floor. I often wonder if the caregivers of these young men and women really look at them before they leave their home. Walk on any street in the Western world and sexual charge and tension is in the air. It is particularly visible in the warm months. You want to be comfortable for the warm weather, but many take this as an excuse to expose what should be covered. This is not being prudish. I am simply stating a fact that we can all witness.

Since this eye candy is everywhere, the natural tendency is to become over sexually stimulated. Now your head is on a swivel, and you are hunting and looking at every opportunity to be sexual. This is the same look that a lion hunting for gazelles on the savanna gives his prey. The fight and flight hormonal releases are at full peak, and this is on a continual basis. Do this for an extended period and you end up having adrenal fatigue that will lead to kidney failure. The adrenal hormones are too powerful to be maintained on a continual basis; they eventually will damage the body.

On an energetic level, what you are doing is blending your energy grid with other sentient life forms without consent. These are acts of energetic aggression and a form of rape. Men are generally guilty of this. It takes a lot of mental mastery for the average man to walk down the street and not sexualize every encounter. I can tell you that it can be done. I have done it, and I have shown others how to do it.

While walking down the street, repeat the short version of the Ho' opon-opono to everything and everyone at which you look, like an endless mantra: *"Please forgive me. I love you and I let go."* Do this for several days and you will end up having Holy encounters with other sentient life instead of sexual and predatory exchanges. Every predatory thought and intent will be neutralized by the forgiveness of the Ho' oponopono and bring you into stillness.

The sexual over-stimulation of our world can cause one to do the exact opposite. Since going to the grocery store should not be a sexual experience, many shut themselves down and become numb and frigid to the over sexual stimulation. While this may sound like a good thing, the consequences of doing this over time are that muscle memory takes over; the subconscious mind will do this continuously and loop what is now a program in perpetuity. Now in order to overcome these programs and become sexual, you have to be stimulated in a different manner, for the typical manner has been shut down. The plain vanilla stuff will no longer do. Your sexual repertoire has to expand into the more advanced and unusual to get an arousal out of you. Again, this is a sexual malfunction that is the result of a society that is sexualized and puritanical at the same time.

Sex is everywhere: on the media, TV, posters, billboards, etc. The consequence is that our youth are coming to sexual maturity as early as 10 years of age. I know this is shocking, but it is not an exaggeration. It was a shock to me when I became aware of this in my coaching practice. At that age in the development of a child there is no way for them to understand the complex physical and emotional experience associated with a sexual act. What they really need at this stage of their development is unconditional love and acceptance and not performances of sexual favors. Since the sexual stimulation feels good to the body, they therefore begin to associate love with performance of a sexual act. Conditional love becomes a program, and that malfunction will now rule them. If by the age of 10 you are sexually active, what will stimulate you by the age of 30 or 40? You will end up requiring more and more advanced methods of stimulation to pleasure yourself. Anyone who is sexually active that early has inner child issues that need to be addressed.

Finding Intimacy

Put that aside for a minute and consider this reality of today's society. If you look at the porn industry as a reflection of what our society is sexually seeking, it is all performance driven. The scenes look like something that a circus performer, acrobat, or gymnast would do. It is not something that the average person could do, however it is the expectation in the bedroom. Nowhere are bonding, sharing, and intimacy being addressed. Where is the chemistry, caring, tenderness, passion, and, dare I say, love being displayed?

None of these actors or talents look like they care for and love each other. They appear to be matched for the scene and are mechanically good at what they do. It is a job, no more and no less. For a society consuming this, we are talking about people trying to have mechanically flawless sexual performances without chemistry, caring, tenderness, and passion. To my mind this is bad sex. I would rather not have it at all. If indeed you are at a sexual phase and you are seeking this out, make sure that it is an exploratory, caring, sharing, and tender experience and not just a performance that leads to a sexual release moment. In other words, are you giving and receiving on a physical and emotional level throughout the experience? If not, you are being cheated out of an opportunity to have a pleasant experience. Additionally, performance-based, mechanical sexual acts attract negative attachments that will host on you because your torsion field becomes open and undone during an uncaring coital act.

Sexual Magic

Some misguided lightworkers, glamorized by sexual energy, look toward ancient grimoires of sex rituals and sex magic as a means to gather power. As if normal sexual acts were not generally complicated enough, now introduce the invocation of disembodied beings and principalities to focus sexual energy for the fulfillment of an ego-driven purpose. Often this is done not only by a couple, but by a group. The more individuals introduced into the circle, the greater the chances for contamination. This is a formula for easy attachments by the disembodied beings who will now drive group members to fulfill their dark purposes. If you look at the lives of those who are participating in these rituals, you will see chaos. It is true enough that a lovemaking experience creates a torsion field that will resonate and attune with the very pulse of the Universe. This in turn will reach the highest level of divinity. These individuals are not making love, they are performing. This is ritualized sexual theater. Therefore their torsion fields are being undone, and the invoked beings are implanting within them a dark magic. I strongly recommend that you stay away from this.

Merging a Group through Meditation

Now this is a corruption of an ancient knowledge: there is no separation and, given the right frequency, we can merge back together. This is done by allowing our torsion fields to expand to maximum capacity. Lovemaking is not the only way that the torsion field is enlarged in humans. This also occurs during meditation. I have off-planet memories of a council that would gather and intensify their torsion fields through meditation by allowing Universal resonance to drop into their souls. This act would harmonize them with the pulse of the Universe. Like tuning forks of the same pitch, they would begin to reverberate and amplify a power far greater than the sum of the parts. They would collectively blend their torsion fields and ask Spirit for assistance toward an ascended purpose, like the rescue of a world. This was a complete and total blending of multiple souls into a unity-mind. It was an absolute, intimate sharing and sacrifice of self and its personal agenda with others for a higher cause. This reassembly is the key to Universal salvation. This can also be done on Earth, and it is in fact the only way that the planet can be redeemed. This would require a great amount of work, with the potential participants in this circle spending years working on their negative ego in order to arrive at the level of clarity and purity where this could be done.

Eliminating Sexual Abuse from Your Spiritual Practice

Under no circumstances are you to engage in any romantic or sexual relations with anyone who is in your spiritual care. It is a violation and abuse of the highest kind. I know that this topic is taboo in the lightworker community, and no one dares to speak about it. It is time to remove another skeleton from the closet. Anyone that you are healing, coaching, teaching, and mentoring is off-limits to you as a current sexual partner. If you were already romantically or sexually involved with them before they became your student, that is a different story. Your spiritual charges are in a weaker position and are looking to you for a lifeline and support.

Sexualizing this sacred trust is the highest of sins. Doing this will damage them and muddle your relationship with any Ascended Guides and Light Beings who are overseeing your work. Do this and all the Ascended and Holy Hosts will withdraw their overlighting presence and support from you, and since the Universe is not a vacuum, other imposters and shape-shifting beings will surface, pretending to be the Masters that departed. The Ascended are not just pictures on a wall or statues on a table. They are as real as you and I and are very sensitive to the kind of energy that we are broadcasting. If they sense that some fundamental law has been violated, they will not be congruent with you anymore and will cut off all connection to you. The people who are in your spiritual care are your spiritual children. To have a romantic or sexual relationship with them is incest. The karma and payback for this will be severe.

Sexual Abuse and Leadership

There is a fundamental psychological reason why so many fall into this trap. All you have to do is open the newspapers and you read about the sex scandals committed by priests, rabbis, ministers, teachers, etc. A little knowledge goes a long way to identify and help master what could otherwise be a blind spot. Healing of any kind is an act of unconditional love. Your clients are often feeling unconditional love and support for the first time. They will naturally project into it romantic and sexual feelings, for this is the model they know. This is called transference.

But the healer is not immune to this dynamic. It is not a one-way street, but rather a two-way lane. The healer is going to feel the now-romanticized and sexualized energy from the client and may reciprocate the feeling. This is counter-transference. Sometimes the healer actually initiates the romantic and sexual flow of energy, and then the client reciprocates. This dynamic frequently becomes the Achilles heel for all healers, teachers, coaches, and beings in positions of leadership. Be vigilant; identify and address any transference and counter-transference.

In truth, it is not just about a projection of romantic love unto a healing setting, but often about the abuse of authority and power. A lot of abusers have power issues with which they are not dealing. Their positions as leaders give them the false sense that they can do anything they want without consequences. This is a mistaken sense of invisibility, omnipotence, and power. If you have identified these threats in yourself, you need help. Seek the help of a qualified professional.

I have been asked out by both my male and female clients and students on numerous occasions. All you need to do is acknowledge the feeling and tell them something like this: "I am very flattered. I acknowledge that there is a powerful feeling moving between us, but it is not romantic or sexual. Let's keep it in the heart space." This usually suffices for the transference to be redrawn. However, on occasion, I had to sever relationships, for the lustful and longing looks were getting too uncomfortable for me to continue my work with objectivity. I simply had follow-up conversations to say that this behavior had to stop, or I would end the relationship. And

165

if it continued, I would then ask the client/student not to come anymore.

Light community, you have been warned. Let not the mistakes of the priests, clergies, and authority figures be your failing. You are called to be masters. Exercise your will and master your desire body. Besides, why would you want to sleep with your students? Find an equal. There are 7 billion people on the planet. It should not be hard for you to have fun with another consenting adult who is not in your spiritual care.

Chapter 13

Authenticity

*What people in the world think of you
is really none of your business.*

– Martha Graham

T o the initiates of the Ancient Temple in Luxor, Egypt, the inquiry into higher truth was filled with tests and challenges. From the time they arrived in the outer temple, they had to continually prove themselves worthy by overcoming personal and spiritual tests. Only then would they qualify to enter the inner temple where they would see written on the walls: "Man, know thyself ... and thou shalt know the gods."

Who we really are is a mystery that sages have been pondering for centuries. Our perception of ourselves defines who and what we become and is the driving force that operates at the core of our identity. But these perceptions may not be authentic to our nature. So many outside forces and influences conspire to tell us who and what we should be. If we believe them, we may end up allowing false identities into our core and live an inauthentic life. The emptiness and shallow existence that we may be experiencing are probably the results of false identities operating in our core.

What is in our authentic core and how do we follow the path to fulfill that purpose? How do we go about separating the wheat from the chaff? How do we become true to ourselves? If we have the courage to look within and dig, we may find surprising answers that may solve years of internal conflicts and bring us to a state of internal peace and personal fulfillment.

Repetitions and the Splintering of the Subconscious Mind

From the time we are born, we are being told by the environment what we should be. The family is busy forcing upon us roles and identities that pre-exist in the égrégore or group body. We are reared to be good sons, daughters, brothers, sisters, husbands, wives, mothers, fathers, and family members. The school system, the church, society, the nation, and humanity at large are all coercing us into accepting pre-existing identities as our own. If you are doing cold-call marketing, you are trained to repeat your sales pitch at least five times, for even if the potential customer says no, by the fifth repetition they are likely to give your product a try. If you follow this idea further, anything that gets repeated continuously for 21 days drops down the threshold of consciousness and into the muscle memory of the subconscious mind. At that point, it becomes a splinter psyche operating by the rules and regulations connected to the behavior or repetition. The subconscious mind now connects to the vast network of the collective unconscious of humanity to prove the behavior or belief to be true. In effect, it seeks outside circumstances to confirm the validity of the program that was dropped into it during the 21-day period.

Over time, so many programs are running that you have no idea what is authentic and what is false. You are simply on autopilot, and the subconscious mind is happy to endlessly bring to the threshold of awareness as many programs as you have allowed to be created for their fifteen minutes in the sun. It is like being in a room with 1,000 people all speaking at the same time and trying to get your attention. In this case, self-awareness is nothing more than a stage upon which these programs battle, display, and re-affirm their validity. This means that your will center is weak and that you are not in your personal power.

The Mask: Subpersonality Modules

Let us be clear. A subconscious program is a habitual behavior that after 21 days drops down into the subconscious mind. An addiction is a habit that evolves a chemical dependency and therefore a physical component to it. A false identity is a false axis or center that creates an inauthentic lens or filter through which we experience reality. It is not simply a program related to a set of circumstances, events, or individuals. It is not just a set of behaviors that overtakes us given the right circumstances, leaving us surprised by our reactions when the program is finished running. Rather, this is a complete persona. It is a highly sophisticated, complex, and evolved pattern of behaviors that serves as a buffer between us and the outside world. It is a subpersonality module that involves highly complex programming and intelligent preconceived behaviors and responses given specific external triggers and events. It is initiated in such a smooth manner that no one on the outside can notice that it is not the real self. It is initially created as a means to bridge our core and authentic nature with the outside world in order to protect the vulnerability that we feel in our core from the world. It is not by any means who we are. It is a mask, persona, or role that we play like an actor in a drama. It can operate for hours, days, months, and years.

The problem is the same as described in previous chapters: everything that you repeat for too long allows muscle memory to take over, and pretty soon, self-awareness does not remember that we are playing a role. We begin to believe that the role or character is who we are. What makes matters worse is that we can create multiples of these false identities. Certainly the expected behaviors at work, school, home, or the locker room are not the all the same. Each requires a different persona, mask, or subpersonality module. If we are a skilled actor and we are consciously accessing these characters for the purpose of protecting our core, job well done. But in reality, we unconsciously tap into these false identities to allow us to protect the fragility of our core. It is an automatic and sub-conscious phenomenon. Over time, there are so many false axes that the roles consume us and all of our psychic energy by siphoning vital life force and energy from our true center, causing us to abandon and even forget our authentic core and purpose. This visually looks like a central axis or core with multiple satellite axes and secondary cores surround it. At times there are so many of these false axes that the authentic core shrivels and becomes malnourished and atrophied. A lifetime of these roles will choke our authentic nature.

The Need to Be Accepted

Our desire to be accepted by the group with which we identify ourselves is one of the powerful forces fueling this sophisticated buffer mechanism. We all want to belong, to be accepted and loved by our family, friends, peers, community, and nation. No one wants to be ostracized or perceived as being weird or freaky. As we grow up, we learn subtle and subconscious clues from our environment about what behaviors are acceptable or reprehensible to the group, and we quickly incorporate the acceptable behaviors into the creation of the subpersonality modules or false identities. But since we are making assumptions about what we think the group wants from us, we may be incorporating within these false identities what is only our interpretation or reading of what the group wants from us, not the actual.

Additionally, because each one of us is created with a unique key vibratory signature, we instinctively know that our unique core will not fit into the collective group. Our early childhood is spent learning to do, what is good and acceptable to the group. Individual expression does not fare well in the group dynamic. The environment has certainly reminded us often that we are to comply, and as we get domesticated, we hide and bury our core and authentic nature deep inside.

Our core is a vulnerable and fragile essence that everyone on the planet is driven to protect, for we fear rejection by the group. So initially, these personas serve us. They are the shields or filters that keep the world away from the most intimate and cherished part of our nature. As long as we are in charge of this process and are creating and activating these filters at will, we have the upper hand and mastery. For most on the planet, this is not the case. We are unconsciously reacting and interacting with the outside world from subpersonality module to subpersonality module while the desires and needs of our core are ignored. With time, we no longer remember that there is a core. What it looks like or feels like is alien to us.

Many on the planet are living what appears on paper to be a good life. They may have a great job, good family and friends, and be socially responsible, yet they are dead inside. The subpersonality modules are so convincing that they are now fooling self-awareness into believing that they are true to their nature. However, deep inside exists emptiness, and it is a void that we cannot rationalize away. It is not something that we can put into words or explain to anyone. It is an inner knowing that what we are doing is a lie. No true or sustainable happiness can be found outside our core. By now we may not remember or are blind to what resides in our core. But with every outward success and achievement, the sense of internal discontent is increasing, along with the ever-blatant realization that we are frauds. The most damaging lies are the ones that we tell ourselves.

The Vulnerability of Our Center

For those of us who cannot stand this any longer and have mustered the courage to venture within and explore the territory of our core and authentic self, we have discovered the vulnerability of our center. I remember well when this awareness came to me. I was meditating and focusing my awareness into my heart space. It was part of a spiritual practice, a desire to find my core and central frequency. I spent several days noticing multiple false centers and axes that I simply acknowledged as inauthentic and pushed them aside while continuing my search. There were so many of these false axes that the thought of never finding my true center crossed my mind. One day, I perceived a vision of a nearly extinguished fire, with smoke slowly rising from the burned logs. This vision sent my entire being into panic. I instinctively wanted to fan or blow on the logs to rekindle the fire. My core was being extinguished, and I had to do something to bring life back into this center and revive it to full vitality. I also felt extremely vulnerable and exposed, as if I were seeing something so intimate that my perception violated the sanctity of a sacred and holy space. I sensed that my core was a precious, sensitive, fragile, and breakable point that even the slightest movement could destroy.

The Courage to Be Authentic

Authenticity is the bravery to uncloak this precious space and reveal it to yourself by aligning your life to that truth. It is about you being true to what makes your heart sing. In the process of doing this, you are going to unveil to the world a part of you to which no one in your life has been privy. For you to do this, you will have to ignore all the subconscious fears of being ridiculed, laughed at, and perceived as being crazy. It takes tremendous courage to do this, and even after the fact, you will continue to battle the voices in your head and outside of self that are saying you have ruined your future. This may sound counterintuitive, but if you do not reveal to the world this unique core fragility, you will never be fulfilled. More importantly, when you do this, you give permission to others to find their own center and core and to express themselves unapologetically to the world. Your act of bravery breaks the cycle of lies and falsehoods and gives others the permission to do the same.

Many of us spend our entire lives moving from one subpersonality module to the next without ever allowing our authenticity to come through. The performances are so well done that they are Oscar worthy. In fact in time, we even believe them ourselves.

Work and Emotional Relationships

Most men identify themselves with what they do: I am an attorney, a carpenter, a fireman, or a doctor. After years of training to learn the skill of the profession, a subpersonality module is created that is now the buffer mechanism that smoothly interacts with the world. Give it enough time and we begin to believe that this mask or professional persona is who we are. Ask any man who he is, and he will tell you what he does for a living. It is however a false identity. What you do to put food on the table is not who you are. If they happen to lose their jobs, they become lost; and in fact, the depression and suicide rate among unemployed males is a high number. Most women identify themselves with their emotional relationships: I am a mother of two, a wife, a sister, or a caregiver. What role you emotionally play in your life can quickly evolve to become a subpersonality module. All the subtle nuances of what others expect of them are learned and developed into a full-blown persona that fulfills the expectations of the world, but not the core and essence of who they really are. It is easy to lose sight of your inner life when you feel that so many are depending on you. You are not just the caregiver, provider, mother, sister, and wife. Although you play these roles, you are much more than that. You are a unique expression of the Divine Matrix.

Gender Identity

Many people identify so strongly with their gender that it begins to define who they are and what they do. Gender identity can be a powerful way that we align ourselves with a collective. If your biological makeup resembles that of a collective, it is natural to identify yourself with the group and read the nuances and mimic the behaviors of the group. This in turn creates a subpersonality module that gives you full admittance into the collective ethos of your gender. But gender identity is not limited to your biological makeup or what is between your legs; rather it is how you perceive yourself in your core. You can be one gender biologically and internally identify yourself with the opposite gender. Gender identity exists within. If you happen to be transgender, your entire biological existence is a sham and a lie that does not reflect how you see yourself in your core. Therefore, your outer gender is a false belief.

Moreover, your sexual orientation can derail your identification with your gender. If you happen to be bisexual, gay, or lesbian, then the subpersonality, mask, or persona, which by all appearances tells the world that you belong to your gender, may indeed be true; however, the logical conclusion of sexual attraction to the opposite gender is not valid. The rules that operate the ethos of your gender are not who you are. You are more than that. Many gays and lesbians who come out of the closet feel the experience to be so freeing that they identify themselves as being gay or lesbian with total abandonment. Some go so far as taking their sexual orientation and identification to the level of defining everything about them. They are gay or lesbian first, and everything else is secondary. This also is a false identity. You are more than the gender you sleep with.

If you allow your gender identification and your sexual orientation to define you, you are limiting your connection to your core. What you are internally is something that cannot be limited by biology or sexual orientation. Your essence is freer and more elusive than that. To find that freedom you have to let go of those false identities.

Lineage and Ancestry

Your family, ethnic origin, and bloodline can create an identity that binds you. This is a powerful égrégore, for you carry within your DNA the epigenetic memories, strengths, and weaknesses of your ancestors. It is not just an unrelated collective to which you belong by association. It is a biological and ancestral connection that makes you predisposed to repeat some of the same behaviors, mistakes, and achievements. You will inherit the genetic adaptation of your bloodline. Some of your ancestors may have had an aptitude for art or science, and this may pass on to you. You may also have had a genetic predisposition for specific diseases based on your ancestry. Yet this does not mean that you will develop those health conditions. Many studies have been done to figure out what is inherited and what is environmental. In one such study where the genetic marker for cancer existed, researchers found that adopted family members developed cancer as well, by the same percentage as that of blood relatives. If your existence boiled down to the totality of your ancestral lineage, then we would be defined and limited by our genetic inheritance. Although our bloodline and genetics have a great influence on how we perceive ourselves, it is not the entire picture.

In primordial and shamanistic cultures, your bloodline will determine which ancestral spirits are protecting you. Just by birth, you are included in the group that the spirits of the ancestors will guard and protect. To a great degree, this has defined individuals who belong to this collective and has restricted them in terms of moving forward or choosing a different path. In such ancestral traditions, you don't have a choice but to serve the spirits of the ancestors. If you choose not to, it is believed that great misfortunes, disasters, and chaos will befall you. Yet many have successfully evolved past such beliefs and cultural taboos and restrictions.

The power of the bloodline is not just an exotic cultural idea; it is at the foundation of Christianity. According to Christian doctrine, one cannot be saved without the blood of Christ, for he died for our sins and his blood washes them away. In the Catholic Church, this is ritualized as the communion where you symbolically ingest the body and blood of Christ. Participation in this sacrament gives you admittance into the rank of the saved and the protection of the group body. A more arcane Christian knowledge is the concept of the Sangreal or "real blood" or "Holy Blood."

This is the resurrected bloodline with the reconstructed DNA of the world Savior that washes away all sins and imperfections. This is based on the power of the restored or saved blood lineage of Christ: the real blood. Since Jesus had brothers and sisters and given the possibility that he was married or had children, his progeny and bloodline may exist today and would be the true members of the Christian égrégore. This would invalidate the authority and power of the Church that claims it can grant admittance to that collective ritualistically.

The concept of the power of the bloodline is ancient, for there were 16 other world saviors before Jesus the Christ in recorded history. Moreover, no church can be consecrated unless it has the relic of a Saint under the altar. This is generally a bone fragment or body part of a dead Saint. The restored DNA of this Saint sanctifies and gives spiritual authority to the church. Below the altar at Saint Peter's Basilica in the Vatican is the relic of Saint Peter's body encased in glass for everyone to see. There is a morbid connection to the dead DNA of a Saint that is glaringly present in Church ritual, belief, doctrine, and ritualistic authority and sanctification of a Church that no one talks about or questions.

We cannot alter the family and bloodline to which we find ourselves embodied. The genetic memory of our bloodline has great influence, but it does not limit or define us. Jesus Christ said it: "Follow me." He was an example that we all need to follow, and if you do what he did—become authentic and allow the Christ within to blossom—you will restore and entrain your bloodline and salvage everyone with whom you share a genetic connection. According to Christian Church doctrine, the admission into the restored bloodline can only happen through its sacraments. This is not part of the ministry of Jesus the Christ. He wanted you to follow him and restore your own bloodline to Sangreal by ascending as he did. You cannot be saved or ascend through osmosis by having a relic or "being washed by the blood"; you have to do the work.

Bloodline and genetic memories may be a starting point, but they are not the end point. You are not limited, restricted, or confined by your roots. You can soar as high as you want. The sky is the limit. To hold your consciousness prisoner to your ancestry is to clip your own wings. This is another mask, persona, or false belief that is inauthentic to our core.

Racial Identity

My racial characteristics place me by default into a collective. By my look, skin tone, hair, or facial characteristics, I am linked to a collective. Whether I am White, Black, Hispanic, Asian, Native American, or East

Indian should not define and limit me. It is true that the world will project stereotypical expectations and behaviors onto me in common with my racial characteristics. I can very easily read these projections and create a false identity to respond in a manner that will allow me to belong to the collective and society at large. With all the past and present racial inequities and social injustices between races, I would be quick to identify myself with the struggles or privileges of my race. Although the examples enumerated below are broad and in some ways stereotypical, they allow us to understand how someone can create a racial identity that is a response to these broad strokes.

If you are White, there is an entitlement mentality that pervades the ethos of the race. The White race has dominated the world stage now for several thousand years. Therefore, they are privileged and expect the entitlement that comes with this status.

If you are Black, you have to work twice as hard as a White person to get the same recognition. After four hundred years of slavery, the emancipation of slaves in America and the Civil Rights movement have managed to provide the Black race with the same legal rights as White. But racism lives, and the struggle for equality continues. Bonds of kinship that are created in the trenches of battle and struggle with others experiencing a similar hardship are strong and will create a powerful identity.

If you are Hispanic, you may identify with a sense of family that may extend beyond the borders of the nuclear family setting. This will create a specific persona that will connect you to your extended family in a different way from other races.

If you are Asian, your relationship to work and achievement status will be guided by a sense of value that is different from other races. The Asian culture does not believe in debt. Families would rather endure lower economic standards and save money until there is enough cash to acquire the next item or symbolic achievement on the socioeconomic climb. This will create an identity that will drive you differently than other races.

If you are Native American, your sense of victimization, gentrification, and deep connection to the land may color your view toward the outside world.

If you are East Indian, your relationship to parental approval may be different from that of other races. The dominant cultural practice of arranged marriages subjects you to the will and control of your parents. Your assimilation of class status is different than other cultures. For in the East Indian culture, no one transcends their physical class.

Yet none of these racial identities are authentic to who you are inside. You are something unique and more subtle, sophisticated, and refined than any group, race, or peer projection. You are not limited by your inclusion in any race. This is only the vessel that contains you. What is inside is far more precious. Let not the outside define what exists within.

Health Condition as an Identity

Depending of the state your health, you may easily identify with your health conditions. In modern society, many who are struggling with chronic pain, devastating illness, and recurring health scares identify themselves with their pain. They spend so long battling and struggling to remain healthy that the pain and discomfort become a familiar landscape or point of reference. After a time, the pain becomes an identity. A lightworker friend of mine who is a nurse told me about patients who keep coming back to the doctor's office seeking refills on their pain medications. It is always the same moaning litany: "Doctor, I have this pain." She and the other nurses have nicknamed these patients the "frequent flyers." These patients describe themselves, imagine a future, or dream of a tomorrow with pain in place. They are busy clipping their own wings. My great-grandmother used to say to me: "Pierre, never dream of skinny goats, only dream of fat cows." If you cannot conceive or even dream of yourself without the pain or illness, you will never be free of it. And even if you are born with a crippling disease or illness, do not let that stop you from doing what you want to do. Many let a wheelchair or a physical handicap stop them from achieving their life-long dreams, while others soar, like theoretical physicist Stephen Hawking, who is a quadriplegic and yet has become one of the greatest minds of the 21st century. He has contributed more to the advancement of his field than any able-bodied physicist.

The fact that the Universe may have dealt you a card that might include a congenital illness should not define the rest of your life. This is not the totality of who you are. You can become whatever you dream and put you mind to. After all, Beethoven composed his last and greatest symphony while he was deaf.

Let not your pain or health condition define you. You are larger and bigger than that. Reach for your dreams and let no physical boundaries stop you from being all you can be.

Fear as an Identity

As aspects of the fragmented Receiver in exile from infinity consciousness, our separation from Source has created individual personalities and

176

a clear demarcation as to where we end and where the outside begins. But the outside may have intentions that are hostile to self; therefore, self must be guarded about everything that exists outside and fear the external, unknown and unfamiliar. It is the basic operating system of our Universe. Yet, if we fear and perceive a threat in everything, we will be paralyzed and will not expand our consciousness and allow the removal of the bread of shame program. Some level of fear is needed for our own survival. If there is a physical threat around you, by all means do your best to survive. The problem is that, most of time, the threat is perceived, but is not real. As long as we exist in dimensional reality, we will perceive fears of all kinds.

The level of fear and threat that you allow to take root in your consciousness will determine your level of ascension. Given the programs that we are running, we can perceive the world and the people around us as attackers. We begin to react to defend and protect our personal agenda and self-interest, or we can see them as supporting a collective agenda and work with them to a common goal.

However, the 3-D environment in which we all exist is constantly reinforcing fear. This begins the moment we wake up. As we get ready for our day, every news and media outlet is broadcasting fears by repeating one bad news report after another. If you stay in front of a television long enough, the same video clip of the day is repeated every hour from 5:00 a.m. until 9:00 a.m. Whether it is a burning building, a car crash, or a hostage situation, seeing this footage four times or more in four hours allows it to drop down into the subconscious mind and trigger fear within you. We can analyze any one-hour news broadcast and find not even 15 minutes of good news. Brothers and Sisters, you are not blind. The world is not that dark. There are acts of kindness, compassion, and love happening all around us. It is simply not sexy for consumption and does not elevate ratings. Fear does.

When you go to church, most pastors give an interpretation of the Bible that is filled with perceptions of fear: the devil and his minions are out to deceive you and lead you into perdition. No disrespect meant, but if you just read the story of the Old Testament, you will meet a vengeful, jealous, egomaniacal, and unforgiving God. Add to that the pastors who are using fire and brimstone to motivate parishioners, and you have a perfect formula for the ignition and propagation of fear programs.

Additionally, our politicians and government officials are also using fear as a means to gather votes, support, and further a political agenda. The spinning of any event into a national threat can help polarize the base and rally everyone to a political and tactical win. It is not about what is right. It is not about what is good for the country or the planet. It is about manipulating the masses with fear as a means to gain political advantage over the opponent.

Fear as a motivating tool is far more visceral and reactionary than love. So at every level of modern society, it is being used to agitate or paralyze us. No wonder we need antidepressants. Fear is extremely familiar to us, for it reinforces the basic operating system that governs this Universe, but it is not who you are. You have the power within you to transcend this basic operating system. You are a being of unimaginable power. In your core exists something else than fear.

God Concepts as Identities

The great sages and mystics of ancient time never dreamt of creating religions, but as their lives, journeys, and teachings were written down, the texts became holy books. At first, these were great acts of historical preservations that kept records of these great beings for prosperity. This would also help seekers follow in the footsteps of the Masters. However, something curious happens within the second or third generation after the ascendance of the Master. The writings become immutable laws or dogmas. Orthodoxy arises among the followers to hold everyone account- able to the letter of the holy books. Any other spiritual idea, explora- tion, and journey outside of the scriptures are now considered heresy. And there are only two ways for you to deal with heresy: you convert everyone to your belief, or you physically destroy other beliefs by suppressing any attempt to seek alternate ideas or interpretations. Every major religion in the world has followed this unfortunate pattern.

True enough, the Master's life is an example for seekers to follow. In fact in many cases, these mystics are "chariots" that have blazed a trail for others to follow. For a novice entering the path, this trail and the protocols left by the Master are invaluable. I don't believe that any of the Masters intended their teachings to be the sole and only way to reach the heavens. They are most often meant as guides for the seekers to follow. Moreover, once the seeker reaches a certain level of mastery, he is to continue forward and blaze his own trail into even higher truth and consciousness.

The god concept that you hold will determine the level of truth to which you evolve. If you are holding the god concept of your grandfather, your spiritual journey will be limited to the same level of growth he had achieved. It will become a false identity that will stun your ongoing growth. This is probably one of the most difficult subpersonality modules to release, because often there is so much fear, fire, and brimstone attached to any spiritual exploration outside of the box. I am not suggesting that you reject the belief of your ancestors. I am simply saying that you should use this as a departure point and remain open to the possibility that there are higher truths and more transcendental knowledge that can further your spiritual evolution. Twenty year from now, if my readers are still holding the same god concept of this book, then they are holding a false identity that they must remove to allow themselves to further evolve. Your god concept should always be expanding. God is infinite and infinity has no end point. No static concept can ever encompass a consciousness that is "becoming." If you are going to mirror God, you need to enter a state of "becoming" by allowing your god concepts and consciousness to ever grow and expand.

The External Implantation of False identities

We were originally created with 12 strands of DNA. As of today, the majority of the planet's population has only two strands of DNA. According to cosmic records, about 500 million years ago a subset of the angelic race attempted to hijack Creation and usurp the purpose of the created Universe. To do this, they altered our DNA and dumbed us down to remove any memories of the path of return back to God. This was a violation and rape of the highest kind, but it happened so long ago and the memory of the violation is buried so deep that we don't remember. However the path of return is not entirely removed. The etheric or shadow strands of the 10 dismantled DNA strands exist and are accessible given the proper conditions.

Now the status quo does not want you to know that you have the power to liberate yourself and begin the process of regrowth of your 12 strands of DNA. For this reason, they have inserted DNA codes and "fear pockets" in our 2 strands of DNA to trigger major and customized fear events that will stop us from initiating the regrowth protocol. Because it is a customized code, I can only say that the fear event will be major and will cause you to experience your greatest fear in an attempt to stop you from beginning the regrowth process.

Truth be told, the moment you realize that it is code designed to stop you from evolving back, the fear stops, and you can resume the process. All you have to do to initiate the process is to listen on a daily basis to the DNA Reconstruction recording from the 2008 Wesak Celebration, available on my website—www.iammonad.com—and the process will be initiated.

Additionally, anyone who has grown up in a shamanistic culture will be familiar with "remote influencing and implantation." The process involves a shaman going into your dreams while your defenses are down and implanting ideas, thoughts, and even identities that are not authentic to you. Because you are vulnerable in the dream state, over time, these foreign and inauthentic thoughts take root and begin to change and define us in favor of the implant. When I saw the Hollywood movie *Inception*, I was terrified, for I was seeing a glamorized version of my early childhood in the Caribbean. For a while, the U.S. government ran a program called "The Stargate Project," where psychic spies where trained to conduct remote viewing and influencing. This program was defunded and now exists covertly under other agencies in the government. Imagine that in your sleep, ideas and concepts that may be contrary to your nature are being implanted in your subconscious mind without your approval and consent. This is a sneaky and cowardly violation of one's personal power.

The only way to stop this from happening is to be in your personal power and to have impeccable boundaries. This will cause you to become lucid in your dreams and stop the inappropriate behavior and invasion while it is taking place. Once you are lucid, you have two choices: You awake from the dream and break the psychic connection, or you take control by changing the dream and push the invasion out. The first scenario is probably the most common way to deal with this type of invasion. The second, which is taking control over your dream, requires a certain level of sophistication on the part of the dreamer. If your boundaries are strong enough, you will be able to do this effortlessly.

How Do I Find My Authentic Nature?

Given the multiple false beliefs, identities, and subpersonality modules that exist within us and the ease and facility that we use to move from one subpersonality module to the next, we begin to forget our authentic core. How do we find our authentic nature? What we are seeking is an internal truth and frequency that is preordained. It descended from the heavens long ago when the Universe was young, and it is not created in our minds, by our thoughts, imaginations, or the dictates of the environment. It is the unique vibratory signature with which we descended. It has no duplicate, and it is our vibratory fingerprint.

Our Universe is one of many that exists in a field of uncreated energy called Source or hyperspace. Source is a field or state from which everything emanates and to which everything converges. In Source there is no individuality, only collective awareness. It is zero point. In that field, there exists what are called the 24 Elders in Front of the Throne of Grace. This is not 24 elderly men. Here, we are using language to describe and state that which transcends the limitation of words. They are what we could term God Seeds. Just the same way that an apple or orange has seeds, there exists in that field seeds that will become Source if placed in fertile ground. Everything that descended into dimensional reality, including us, came from one of these God Seeds. The vestiges of these God Seeds exist in us as 24 cranial nerves that bring energy and vitality to our body. At the descent from the uncreated Source energy into dimensional reality, the God Seed begins to fragment into 12 aspects. At the next level down, each of the original 12 aspects fragments further into multiples of 12 lower aspects, resulting now in 144 pieces. This process of fragmentation into multiples of 12 continues down the dimensional scale until we find ourselves in the 3-D density.

What was undifferentiated in Source evolved into individuality, self-awareness, and ego, making choices as they descended the dimensional ladder. At every stage of the descent and fragmentation into dimensional reality, the 12 aspects further separated, and each piece individualized while making free choices. Given our unique and individual path of descent from Source and the choices that we have made, our authentic nature and original core frequency with which we were created is further enhanced by our unique trajectory throughout the Universe. Therefore, my core frequency and that of any one member of my collective are not the same.

My authentic nature at its root is made up of the vibratory signature with which I was created when I dropped down from Source. It happened so long ago that most of us do not have any conscious remembrance of it. Yet in our prana seed, the memory of that moment and unique key frequency exists. Try the following meditation every day for 60 days to help you remember.

Meditation on Finding your Authentic Nature

Close your eyes and take a deep breath. As you inhale and exhale very slowly, allow the Universal life force that permeates everything to enter into your lungs. Keep breathing in and out. Now let your awareness and head drop into the middle of your chest. You are now perceiving the world from that point in your body. Breathe in and out slowly, and notice what you notice. Realize that you can perceive energies all around you.

Become aware of your physical body, and locate in your physical body points or areas where there are false identities and subpersonality modules. Notice what you notice. Breathe deeply, and repeat to yourself: "Please forgive me. I love you, and I let go."

Breathe deeply and allow the light of Source to descend into those areas and dissolve them.

Now, become aware of your emotional body, and locate in your emotional body points or areas where there may exist false identities and subpersonality modules. Notice what you notice. Breathe deeply, and repeat to yourself: "Please forgive me. I love you, and I let go." Breathe deeply and allow the light of Source to descend into those areas and dissolve them.

Become aware of your mental body, and locate in your mental body points or areas where there may exist false identities and subpersonality modules. Notice what you notice. Breathe deeply, and repeat to yourself: "Please forgive me. I love you, and I let go." Breathe deeply and allow the light of Source to descend into those areas and dissolve them.

Become aware of your spiritual body, and locate in your spiritual body points or areas where there may exist false identities and subpersonality modules. Notice what you notice. Breathe deeply, and repeat to yourself: "Please forgive me. I love you, and I let go." Breathe deeply and allow the light of Source to descend into the areas and dissolve them.

Now, become aware of your skeletal system, and locate in your skeletal system points or areas where there may exist false identities and subpersonality modules. Notice what you notice. Breathe deeply, and repeat to yourself: "Please forgive me. I love you, and I let go." Breathe deeply and allow the light of Source to descend into those areas and dissolve them.

Become aware of your muscular system, and locate in your muscular system points or areas where there may exist false identities and subpersonality modules. Notice what you notice. Breathe deeply, and repeat to yourself: "Please forgive me. I love you, and I let go." Breathe deeply and allow the light of Source to descend into those areas and dissolve them.

Become aware of your circulatory system, and locate in your circulatory system points or areas where there may exist false identities and subpersonality modules. Notice what you notice. Breathe deeply, and repeat to yourself: "Please forgive me. I love you, and I let go." Breathe deeply and allow the light of Source to descend into those areas and dissolve them.

Become aware of your respiratory system, and locate in your respiratory system points or areas where there may exist false identities and subpersonality modules. Notice what you notice. Breathe deeply, and repeat to yourself: "Please forgive me. I love you, and I let go." Breathe deeply and allow the light of Source to descend into those areas and dissolve them.

Become aware of your autoimmune system, and locate in your autoimmune system points or areas where there may exist false identities and subpersonality modules. Notice what you notice. Breathe deeply, and repeat to yourself: "Please forgive me. I love you, and I let go." Breathe deeply and allow the light of Source to descend into those areas and dissolve them.

Become aware of your nervous system, and locate in your nervous system points or areas where there may exist false identities and subpersonality modules. Notice what you notice. Breathe deeply, and repeat to yourself: "Please forgive me. I love you, and I let go." Breathe deeply and allow the light of Source to descend into those areas and dissolve them.

Let your awareness drop back into your heart space in the middle of your chest, and find your original and core frequency. Find your unique vibratory signature with which you were created. Find your unique key and vibratory fingerprint. If you perceive any false axes and identities, just move them behind you, and keep looking for your authentic nature. This part of the process should take at least five minutes.

Take a deep breath, and when you feel, ready open your eyes.

Chapter 14

Neutrality

Conflict is inevitable, but combat is optional.

– Max Lucado

Before there were time and space, there existed no polarity. Although there did exist a duo of forces, the condition in which they cohabited was unique. They were complementary to each other. There was an infinite Desire to Give, who was equally matched by an infinite Desire to Receive. The Giver was fulfilling every need of the Receiver instantaneously. It was the perfect balancing of the yin and the yang. But over time, the Receiver began to feel great shame for the gifts and blessings that it was receiving from the Giver without any ability to give back or earn the gifts. This became such a problem that the Receiver said "no" to all the gifts coming from the Giver. Instantaneously, the Receiver shrank from being infinite to being finite and as small as the head of a pencil. The change was so abrupt and jarring that it precipitated the perception that self-awareness was fragmented, small, and separated from infinity; moreover, that infinity, now outside of self-perception, might have good or bad intentions toward the Receiver. This in turn created fear of the outside. The perfect balance was now broken, and the Universe had to find a way to restore harmony. The singularity created by the fear-filled awareness of the Receiver was a major contrast to what preceded.

The Giver knew that it could fulfill every desire that the Receiver had, except that it could not remove the shame, for their roles were fixed and the Giver could not receive. It therefore shattered the Receiver further so that it would learn to give and receive from its fragmented aspects and thereby remove the shame, thus restoring harmony. With that move came time, space, and the physical and dimensional reality in which we exist as an arena for this exchange and salvation plan to occur. Singularity was broken into duality and then into multiplicity as a means to allow the various fragments to remove the shame and earn their way back to this infinite and blessed field over time.

Each aspect of the fragmented Receiver had self-awareness and free will. This self-awareness was concluding what the original Receiver perceived: the outside might have good or bad intentions toward it, and since it could not discern which, it needed to be on guard. And because this perception was backed up by free will—the ability to chart its own course and make its own decisions—multiplicity began to move against itself. Yet all the fragmented and separated forces that were then opposing each other were part of the original Receiver. Although the suspicion of what existed outside of self-created fear, it is important to remember that everything that existed was (and is) part of the body of the original Receiver.

The problem is that self-awareness separates us from unity consciousness and consequently generates fear, inducing paranoia and causing us to act from a defensive and negative ego standpoint.

On one side of the spectrum, unity consciousness makes you realize that all aspects of the Receiver are part of the same body. On the other side, all aspects of the Receiver perceive all others as potential foes. One side brings you back to a total merger with the Giver; the other represents the aspects of the Receiver in exile, trying to remove the shame and the illusion of separation. This elimination will lead to a merging experience back into Source. One side is ascension; the other is separation.

As incarnated aspects of the Receiver, the degree of separation that we perceive is directly proportional to our level of ascension. One can perceive enemies everywhere and move to control and dominate others, or one can begin to realize the ultimate truth: that separation is an illusion and that everyone around us is an aspect of self. It requires a high level of soul maturity and spiritual evolution to attain and remember this truth.

Laws of Our Physical Universe

In our 3-D dimensional Universe, opposites and polarities exist: Light vs.

Dark, night vs. day, good vs. bad, proton vs. electron, positive vs. negative, etc. Every polarized energy system, force, or condition that exists has an opposite polarity that is separated from it by space. The Universe seeks out balance and equilibrium and will create the conditions for this to occur. When opposite forces are brought together in the same space, there is an explosion and they annihilate each other. This phenomenon is at the root of the fundamental laws of physics that operate in our Universe.

However, the opposite and polarized states are not the only things that exist in the Universe. There are zero point and neutrality. At an atomic level you have protons that are positively charged and electrons that are negatively charged, but you also have neutrons with zero charge. Neutrality is alive and well in nature.

The Trappings of Battle

A cursory look at human history will tell you that we are far from the goal of removing the bread of shame. There have been examples of great souls who have blazed a path in that direction, but the vast majority on the planet are far from this goal. We have perceived threats from family members, friends, neighbors, coworkers, political leaders, corporations, other nations, religions, races, or groups of people. We have therefore been polarized into taking a visceral, emotionally charged position against the threats we register. We have been doing this individually and collectively since we have been the sentient life-form on this planet. No matter how justified or enlightened our reaction, if it is polarized, it is maintaining one aspect of a toxic relationship. It is therefore unsustainable. This is only one extreme of a pendulum swing that will eventually move to the other side in a reverse direction with an equal amount of velocity and energy. This is the Universe seeking balance and equilibrium. Put differently, as long as you are lifting your sword, someone or something will block it.

In some ways, it matters not if you serve the good or the bad, the Light or the Dark; as long as you are battling, you are maintaining a toxic relationship that will keep you tied to the wheel of karma for future repairs and corrections. Many of us have done some unspeakable things, have committed some ghastly acts in the name of the Light or the Dark, which we are now repairing and which we will reconcile sometime in the future.

Spiritual Battles in the Heavens

The spiritual battles between the Light and the Dark began long before anyone can remember. It is so old that humanity does not recall when or why it got started. However, the Akashic Record states that this polarization started 500 million years ago when subsets of the Elohim Cloister decided that they favored the descent of the Uncreated into dimensional reality but not the reverse path of ascension. Instead of the original two-way path of descent and ascent, they moved to change the course of our created Universe by altering themselves and creating progeny with their altered DNA in an attempt to usurp the purpose of creation.

Now it is perfectly fine for any aspects of the Receiver to choose to allow only the path of descent to be activated. Free choice is the foundation of our Universe. It is however something entirely different to create a 3-D lineage with similar DNA sequencing, deliberately crossbreed them with the originally created aspects of the Receiver, and by so doing, dilute the originally created aspects of DNA and the path of return back to Source. It was a coup or attempt to usurp the original purpose of creation by removing the bread of shame. If there is no path of return, the bread of shame, fear, and separation will remain in perpetuity, and the Receiver will be trapped in this 3-D density forever.

All Spiritual Beings of the Light of God, including but not limited to the Elohim, Archangels, and Angels, came together to stop this aberration and began a campaign to oppose this cancerous growth and restore God's original purpose. It started with all good intentions, and it was such a noble cause. First there were attempts to reason with the fallen beings, engage in conversation, and influence them until eventually all-out war broke out. For 500 million years, many battles and wars have been fought. Campaigns have been won and lost. But to date the battles continue. The pendulum will continue to swing back and forth. Unless something different occurs, one can predict that the battling will continue for another 500 million years with no resolution to the conflict.

This may be a shock to all lightworkers who are actively participating in this battle and see themselves as foot soldiers in the armies of God. They are polarized into thinking that the Light will eventually vanquish the Dark. This is a fallacy. This battle has no exit strategy. Pushing the Light or the Dark is equally unsustainable. Both the Light and the Dark exist in a seesaw relationship, and in that dynamic, no side is ever the winner. The only way to get off the hamster wheel is to embrace the path of neutrality.

Neutrality as Accelerated Conflict Resolution

Every time I say this, people believe that I am proposing a disconnection from the injustices of the world. I am not betraying the Light. I am proposing a path of reconciliation for the Light and the Dark back to Source, a way out of these endless battles and conflicts. Neutrality is accelerated conflict resolution. When oppositely charged particles come together in the same space, they annihilate each other. When separated by the safety of space, duality is an endless exchange between opposite, but equally charged, positions that would eventually lead us to resolution. This is time consuming, may take multiple lifetimes, and will certainly take a great deal of maturity and understanding to change one's visceral reaction into an evolved and reconciliatory position. However, if either opposite enters into neutrality, the scalar invert data and information that is needed to bring it to zero charge is given. If the polarized object or entity now in zero point is willing to accept this information, it becomes neutral.

Neutrality or zero point brings to you an infinite number of possibilities and solution sets. In duality there are typically two sides and two choices. This perception is so limiting. Source is infinite and has an endless number of ways and lenses through which one can view any situation. In a neutral space, you connect to the field of infinite possibilities.

Being neutral is not disengagement from the problems of the world. It simply disconnects you from the emotional charge that was viscerally polarizing you and gives you multiple other possibilities and courses of action. You become, in fact, better armed to create positive changes; if you are neutral, you are not blinded by rancor and vengeance. You simply choose the path that will reconcile you in the most efficient and ascended manner to the situation with which you are dealing. If things do not turn out the way you had imagined, you are not crushed. You have preferences, but no attachments to the outcome.

Now I have created that field of neutrality around students and clients to allow them to resolve conflicts. Some of these conflicts were resolved within 20 minutes while others have taken as long as three years to resolve. It is encouraging to know that even in neutrality your free choice is not removed. The data and information to understand your visceral position under different lenses may be presented to you, but you still have the choice to accept it or not. In some cases that choice is instantaneous, and in others, it takes a while to let go of the rancor, vengeance, and tit-for-tat mentality. Three years of experiencing this blessed field before one can accept the gift of liberation and neutrality may seem like a long time, but it is all relative. Three years is better than three lifetimes of attempting to do the same thing.

An Evolved Understanding of Forgiveness

At the foundation of accepting the neutral path is the acceptance of responsibility, the owning of our co-creation in the polarized dynamics that exist in time and space. It is the realization that no one is a victim. In over 500 million years of combats, battles, and struggles, we have all attacked, offended, and hurt others. None of us are simply victims. We may not remember the time frame or details of the offense, but the situations, events, and individuals that are causing us to feel victimized are actually those we have somehow offended in the past. Any current tormentor, we have tormented in the past. This is often a difficult concept for people to accept. Plenty of individuals see themselves as spotless and innocent. "I have never hurt anyone in my life." Even if that were so for this lifetime, are you sure of this about previous lifetimes? We have to be man enough to accept the possibility that we may have offended our tormentors in a past that we may not remember right at this moment.

The Christian tradition asks us to forgive those who have hurt and offended us. This is all well and good, but what we are really saying is this: "You have offended and hurt me. I am going to be the bigger person and forgive you for what you did." But deep down inside, you are still identifying yourself as the victim. More congruent with the concept of neutrality is the understanding of forgiveness put forward by the Kahunas of Hawaii, called the Ho' oponopono. Please see the section on Reconciliation in Chapter 6: "Psychic Self-Defense" for the full Ho' oponopono Liturgy. This powerful and deceivingly simple prayer of reconciliation asks you to consider that since the beginning of time until now, you and your ancestors may have offended your tormentors or their ancestors by thoughts, deeds, words, actions, and inactions. The following prayer can effectively end the cycle of toxic connections, to disconnect the cords and halt the energetic ping-pong role that karma plays: "Please forgive for my offense. I love you. I let go and thank you."

Whenever you encounter a person or situation that is causing you to feel agitated, uneasy, or charged, you are holding an energetically toxic relationship with them. Even if I feel that I am a victim, there is a cord connecting my tormentor to me. This cord is held at two points, and I share equal responsibility in the perpetuation of this dynamic across many lifetimes. Half of the responsibility is mine, and the only way to end the tension and the toxic relationship, is to ask for forgiveness for my co-creation. Then, I send unconditional love and I let go of the cord. If you do this with sincerity, a palpable release will occur. Behind this is a sense of freedom, peace, and liberation. You need not do this in person or aloud; it can be done silently and energetically. The result is the same. Keep repeating this request over and over again. Stop doing this when you think of your tormentor and feel no negatively charged response.

When you arrive at a point at which you feel no emotional charge, you are neutral and have completely let go of the cord. Once this happens, there is a great sense of freedom and liberation, and the energy dynamic is forever changed. The cord has been severed and released; so it does not matter whether the opposite force is in agreement with this. Just keep doing your part to release the toxicity, and the cord will be removed.

Think of all the people in our family, jobs, friendships, and past love relationships with whom we have these toxic cords. Think of all the people with whom we have contentious relationships. Think of all the groups, collectives, and institutions that we feel have wronged us. Think of a soul-stream that has lived for the multiple billions of years we have been in existence, and we will get a picture of the work that we need to do to completely reconcile and blend back with Source. As daunting as this task may be, we must start with what is in front of us today. Once we are neutral to this situation, we keep moving to the next person or issue that comes into our awareness.

Toxic Energy Cord Split

The relationship between you and your toxic opposite is not always one to one; it is often one to many. Let me explain. Suppose in one lifetime you perceived a threat from someone and moved to offend or hurt them. This offense now connects you to this being for later reconciliation. But now imagine they were the head of a household or a village leader. Your offense did not just affect one person, but an entire family or village. The cord exiting from you is now split into the entire family or village. In a future time, you have to reconcile with all of them. This split configuration is common. For all healers who have psychic perception, it is often seen in a client's energy grid as a negative energy cord that looks like a fan or a spider web.

Since we gather as a family, group, village, and nation, we create an égrégore or group body that is a living psychic entity made up of the sum of the parts. The group body is much more powerful than its parts but is susceptible to the same failings of any typical human. It has higher and lower aspects. If the group body perceives a threat or fear, it can move to attack another group body. This pattern has been repeated many times in human history. A perfect example of this would be what the Nazi Germany group body did to the Jewish group body. Granted, the German collective was manipulated by charismatic and deceitful leaders. But there are sins of commission and sins of omission. Inaction is also an offense. Perceiving a wrong and not doing anything about it because you don't want to go against the grain is just as toxic as participating in the active offense. So the German people have had to reconcile and become neutral with the Jews. In contrast, the Germans who protected and hid the Jews, risking their own lives, demonstrated, by acting against the collective belief of the group body, how a group body evolves over time. It is through the actions of individuals who disagree with the collective belief that the living psychic energy of the group body matures and grows. Often we perceive a collective wrong and cannot figure out how we can resolve it. Act according to your conscience and take actions to the level that you can. In your small way you are affecting and evolving the group body.

Let's look at another example of how group evolution occurs: the 400 years of the African slave trade. The White race as an égrégore must reconcile and become neutral to the offenses of the 400 years of slavery. Now even if you are the progeny and later descendants, the ancestral memory of the acts exist in cellular memory. You must become neutral to all these ancient and historical acts that are keeping you bound to past offenses. All Whites who participated in the Underground Railroad acted to resolve the wrong, evolve the group body, and reconcile the cellular debts. Certainly, President Abraham Lincoln made a great stride toward that by the Emancipation Proclamation, initiating the end of slavery in this country.

The Mechanics of Combat vs. Neutrality

There exists in the Universe a basic magnetic geometry that is at the root and foundation of all expressions of the fragmented Receiver. It is the torsion field. As aspects of the Receiver, we are comprised of this geometric resonance. When we are in our heart space, this geometry expands and radiates from us in the shape of a doughnut. The torsion field is a neutral space. It broadcasts zero point energy. This is in fact a control room with a vertical axis in the center that connects heaven and earth through us. When you stand authentically with your nature and align with your central axis, you become a pathway, tunnel, or doorway between the finite and the infinite. At this level of realization, you are a co-creator with God. Any thought that you hold in your torsion field manifests. Notice the verb tense. I did not say "will manifest," but "manifests." I will explain below why, in 3-D reality, we have problems manifesting. Every direction radiating from the center of the torsion field coupled with a thought will have an effect. If your awareness is in the central axis, the multitude of directions that surround you is endless.

The human brain is a highly complex device. It is capable of extraordinary computation. The average person on earth has not even begun to access his or her full potential. As vast at this may be, it is finite. It cannot contain infinity. When we are in our heart space and torsion field, we can access infinity. Let me show you:

> *Close your eyes for a moment and think of what you had for breakfast this morning. Locate in space around you where this memory exists. Now, think of your mother. Locate in space around you where she is. Think of a challenging relationship. Locate in space around you where it is. Think of Source. Locate in space around you where He/She is. You may open your eyes.*

All these experiences are being held in various directions in your torsion field. Often when new information comes in during meditation, you will notice, if you pay attention, that it comes from a special location around you. Even if the link to the message is broken because you have stopped meditating, you can reconnect at a later time by focusing on that direction and by holding the thought on the already received message. More information will follow.

If we hold a loving, positive, and empowering thought, we experience merger and the realization that everything outside of us is an overtone amplification of who we are. At this point, the edge of our torsion field begins to resonate at a frequency that allows the overlapping and blending of the edges of the torsion fields of everything around us to our center. We experience merger and the realization that separation is an illusion. Through this expansive experience, we understand that all aspects of the Receiver are one. This is a blending and unification of parts.

Our inclusion into an égrégore or group body functions in a similar manner: the edge of our torsion field blends with the center of the congruent neighboring axis and torsion field, thus creating a gigantic spiritual and intelligent collective that includes the sum of the parts.

When we perceive a threat and experience fear, we are in dissonance. Instead of experiencing the interlocking torsion fields, we contract and solidify our boundaries against the perceived threat. The torsion field shrinks down and emits a specific pitch that creates a magnetic tunnel between itself and the perceived threat. It is a destructive act and an attempt to disrupt the sovereignty of another. This tunnel remains in place as a cord that connects our torsion field to the threat. Since this is an attack, the outside threat will typically respond by defending itself or counter attacking. Either way, it is a response pitch and frequency. And so begins a dynamic that may last many lifetimes. In the process, the direction in which the center of this tunnel exists is now using a vast amount of psychic resources to keep the dynamic in place. Energy is being diverted from our core and central axis within the torsion field to maintain a false axis.

After many perceived threats and lifetime after lifetime of this combat and attack behavior, our psychic resources are being diverted to maintain a vast number of false axes and identities. Keep in mind that most of us are billions of years old. If we could psychically perceive our torsion field, we would realize the number of false axes that are keeping us in energetic bondage and obligation to people, places, and things.

This is the reason why in our current state we cannot manifest. Our psychic energies are being syphoned off to maintain the lie of separation. The only way to solve this problem is to engage in the path of neutrality: one by one, bring accelerated conflict resolution to these false axes. Every time you become neutral to about 8.3% of the total number of the false axes that exist within you, you are regaining control over your ability as co-creator with God. Do enough of this work, and you will get to a point where thoughts that you place in the torsion field do manifest. You will regain the ability to move your awareness into this control room that is the torsion field and be a force for good.

Kindness to Self

When we begin to be truly honest with self and entertain the possibility that we may have wronged others in the past, the knowledge from cellular and visceral memories will come back to us. Add to this the tangled web of toxic connections of the one to many and expand this over our many past lifetimes on earth and off planet, and you begin to realize the scope of the work. The number of beings to whom we must become neutral is staggering.

In this process, let not the memories turn into guilt and shame while inflaming any lack of self-worth or negative ego programs. So many fall into this trap by simply feeling overwhelming shame over past actions that they cannot change. Some plunge into a deep depression over this real-ization. Everyone is redeemable. Even Hitler is capable of ascending if he were to do the work and become neutral to those he hurt. God loves you unconditionally, and that love is a constant that never fluctuates. God may not like your behavior at this instant, but God's love is ever present. Do not beat yourself up over the past; this is completely counterproductive. No one is born a saint. We have all offended and hurt others. Be kind to self, and act to resolve your past by becoming neutral to all toxic relationships.

The Indian saint Paramahansa Yogananda once said: "A saint is a sinner that never gave up."

In Sanskrit, karma means "to do or to make." The word karma implies action, work, and deed. This is not a passive state in which we are subjected to our past actions and choices. Rather, it is about acknowledging the past in order to create a different future. It is an active state. We can choose to wallow in guilt and shame over the past or take action to transform our consciousness and change our future.

The Courage of Neutrality

The choice of neutrality is not for everyone. I will be the first to admit that, in order to proceed down this path, there is a certain level of soul maturity, honesty, and courage that many lack. When the Guardian Alliance of Light first presented me with the idea of neutrality, I thought: "Great. I will simply declare that I am neutral." I have evolved and grown in depth and height light years away from where I began. My understanding of neutrality is continually evolving. The one thing that has been constant throughout this journey is that I am teachable. However, there are souls on earth that are so steeped in anger, vengeance, rancor, and tit for tat that the concept of neutrality and conflict resolution is beyond their understanding. They have been battling for so long that they glamorize combat. In fact some are addicted to it and will not give it up under any circumstances. Moreover, they believe that they have earned at great cost any gain made during combat and deserve to keep it.

I have met many young Indigo souls incarnated now, who are holding these kinds of convictions for what they think are noble purposes. They often gather in groups to do battle and grid activations by dropping Light codes in specific geographical locations for "the Light." No matter how eloquently I explain neutrality to them, they are not going to get it, at least not in this lifetime. They are the paradigm destroyers, and their soul contracts are to combat and battle in order to remove the old grid. Save yourself a lot of time and walk away. Although anyone can renegotiate their soul contract at any point if they so choose, most will not. They will simply follow the path that they chose off planet.

For my part, I expose them to the idea of neutrality and let the seed be planted. How quickly it will take root is not up to me. I have had multiple encounters with these young souls. They keep coming to me, asking me to alleviate the retaliatory consequences of their battle. Remember that the pendulum will swing back and forth. Every time they return, I explain to them that while I hold a frequency of neutrality, I don't have fairy dust;

I cannot blow on them and make their problems go away. Neutrality is a choice, and on their part, it requires putting down the sword and releasing all conquests and battle trophies. This is the path of reconciliation and accelerated conflict resolution. It is neither giving up, nor allowing the Dark to win. It is an act of great courage to realize that you have to do something different in order to exit the hamster wheel. I keep explaining, and they keep hoping that I will wave a magic wand and make their problems go away.

Shamanism, Battling, and Neutrality

Most of these souls are attracted to a version of shamanism that has been spun in the past five years to look like ascension. I am not making disparaging remarks about shamanism. After all, it is part of my heritage. I grew up in Haiti and lived in a shamanistic culture during the early part of my life. I honor what this experience has given me, and I would not be the person that I am today without it. However, clarity is a powerful thing. The shamanistic tradition is thousands of years old, and shamans are not ascending. They are increasing their energy body to serve a specific personal agenda: they are seeking power. This could be for negative ego purposes or for more selfless reasons. Some are trying to find love, power, fame, knowledge, or fortune. Others, and I have met a few, are seeking wisdom. The latter are great sages and beings of profound insights whom I hold in great esteem. If the reader wants to understand the true environment of the shamanistic tradition, he should read the book by Carlos Castaneda, *The Teachings of Don Juan: A Yaqui Way of Knowledge.* It is a culture steeped in fear, paranoia, battle, and combat.

For reasons that I cannot explain, shamanism has now been recast as ascension. On the one hand, shamanistic tools for gathering power and battling are being used, yet on the other hand, it is being cloaked as an ascension mechanism. I don't understand the reason for this deception. What is wrong with being honest and calling things what they really are? No ascended master battles or has power animals. To ascend, one has to sacrifice and transcend all personal agendas. One has to tame the negative ego and allow selfless motives; service becomes the driving force.

I suppose that this version of shamanism is a perfect fit for these indigo souls who are not ready to accept neutrality but who want to think of themselves as pushing the agenda of the Light. So these young urban shamans are gathering their power animals, doing shamanistic extractions, and participating in ayahuasca ceremonies while claiming that they are ascending. Whether or not they are aware of this difference is not clear to me. It is not factual. It could be that they are being deceived by teachers and leaders who are looking to capitalize on their naivety and need for an adrenaline-charged experience. Keep in mind that whatever forces you attack, you establish an energy cord with them, and they will know how to reciprocate in kind and with malice. That cord will not be released or cut even after death. It will follow you lifetime after lifetime. The only thing that can cut it is for you to become neutral and ask this energy system for forgiveness for this offense.

Even if you are going into battle for the Light, you are holding one end of the duality that imbalances the Universe. I suppose that all souls move through various stages of maturity and spiritual realization. So get the battling out of the way, and you will arrive at a point at which you will be burned out and want to exit the combat zone. This is when you begin your journey into neutrality and begin to release these toxic cords, thus gaining back your freedom and restoring energy back to your authentic nature.

Meditation on Releasing Toxic Cords

Close your eyes and take a deep breath. As you inhale and exhale very slowly, allow the Universal life force that permeates everything to enter into your lungs. Keep breathing in and out. Now let your awareness and head drop into the middle of your chest. You are now perceiving the world from that point in your body. Breathe in and out slowly, and notice what you notice. Realize that you can perceive energies all around you.

Become aware of your physical body, and locate in your physical body points or areas where there are toxic cords and battle traumas. Notice what you notice. Breathe deeply, and repeat to yourself: "Please forgive me. I love you, and I let go." Breathe deeply and allow the Light of Source and Neutrality to descend into those areas and dissolve them.

Now, become aware of your emotional body, and locate in your emotional body points or areas where there may exist toxic cords and battle traumas. Notice what you notice. Breathe deeply, and repeat to yourself: "Please forgive me. I love you, and I let go." Breathe deeply and allow the Light of Source and Neutrality to descend into those areas and dissolve them.

Become aware of your mental body, and locate in your mental body points or areas where there may exist toxic cords and battle traumas. Notice what you notice. Breathe deeply, and repeat to yourself: "Please forgive me. I love you, and I let go." Breathe deeply and allow the Light of Source and Neutrality to descend into those areas and dissolve them.

Become aware of your spiritual body, and locate in your spiritual body points or areas where there may exist toxic cords and battle traumas. Notice what you notice. Breathe deeply, and repeat to yourself: "Please forgive me. I love you, and I let go." Breathe deeply and allow the Light of Source and Neutrality to descend into those areas and dissolve them.

Become aware of your Atmic body, and locate in your Atmic body points or areas where there may exist toxic cords and battle traumas. Notice what you notice. Breathe deeply, and repeat to yourself: "Please forgive me. I love you, and I let go." Breathe deeply and allow the Light of Source and Neutrality to descend into those areas and dissolve them.

Become aware of your Buddhic body, and locate in your Buddhic body points or areas where there may exist toxic cords and battle traumas. Notice what you notice. Breathe deeply, and repeat to yourself: "Please forgive me. I love you, and I let go." Breathe deeply and allow the Light of Source and Neutrality to descend into those areas and dissolve them.

Become aware of your Glorified Body of Light. Now let your awareness drop into the center of your chest. Take a deep breath and find your authentic nature, your original core frequency, your key vibratory signature. Keep breathing deeply and slowly and notice what you notice. "Please forgive me. I love you, and I let go." Let all false axes and beliefs, battle scars and traumas, and toxic cords be released. It is not your burden to do or fix anything. Just release and let go. "Please forgive me. I love you, and I let go."

Let the Light of Neutrality give you freedom, liberation, and autonomy and release you from bondage. Now allow your authentic core frequency to be broadcast from your core and radiate to everyone in your circle of influence.

Take a deep breath, and when you feel ready, open your eyes.

⤚◍⤙

Chapter 15

The Work

Before enlightenment, chop wood and carry water.
After enlightenment, chop wood and carry water.

– Lord Buddha

Knowledge without application is perverse. Much has been shared with you in the previous chapters on how to initiate your ascension process. Each chapter is a zip file from which a dedicated soul will know how to extract a full-blown spiritual practice leading to the first level of ascension. I cannot do the work for you. It is your job. You have to find the discipline, put in the time and effort, stalk self, and reorganize your consciousness into that of an ascended and spiritually illumined being. As you reprogram your negative ego, slowly but surely, the situations and people that used to trigger you will bother you no more. As you become more and more neutral to people, places, and things, you will increase your Light Quotient, which will allow the remembrance, fueling, and nurturing of your authentic nature.

The Test

Since you are approaching ascension in a safe manner by doing the negative ego work that is needed to reorganize your consciousness, there is a test at the threshold of the first stage of ascension that will simply be an annoyance to you. It is called many things, but most commonly it is referred to as "The Dweller on the Threshold." As you are about to break this evolutionary glass ceiling and move into a higher level of existence, a series of beings will attempt to derail your efforts. They are called the archons, genies, or djinns. They are highly intelligent beings that exist at the threshold of ascension. They are incapable of creating anything new, however; they are geniuses at corrupting what is in existence by amplifying and capitalizing on your weakest point. Their test is custom-made and tailored to match the weaknesses of the subject.

The great historical example of this event is in the Bible. After Jesus fasted in the desert for 40 days and nights, a demon appeared to him and brought him to the edge of a cliff, promising to give him all the food and riches of the world. Jesus replied: "It is written, Man shall not live by bread alone, but by every word of God" Matt. 4:1-11. Please be aware that Master Jesus did the work and approached ascension in a safe manner, therefore he was able to see this being for who he was. He passed the test and so will you as long as you are doing the work. Those who are not doing the negative ego work, but are focused on the Light and energetic work only, will be corrupted by the archons. They are the principalities that are using the untamed fears of your subconscious mind as a trap to hold you from ascending. If you fall into the trap, they become your puppet master, and you serve them. So many candidates for ascension are lost, for few are willing to do the grunt work needed to slowly and safely approach ascension. If you do the negative ego work, you will easily see through them and through the amplification of your own fears, and you will be able to march on free and autonomous.

Power Increase

At first, this elevation in consciousness begins with shots of ecstatic bliss exploding in your head, à la Kundalini-rising. It began for me during meditation as shots of bliss and overwhelming joy coming from the base of my spinal cord and exploding in my head. Soon, these moments were not limited to meditation. They were happening throughout the day while I was doing my normal routine. This bliss expanded into larger and larger segments of the day. Soon pain and suffering were banished from my consciousness, and the perception of my day-to-day reality dramatically changed.

Heal and rescue yourself first, and once this is done, a profound peace will descend upon you; you will know in every cell of your body that you are not the person you used to be, for you have now ascended into a higher level of awareness. I would be neglectful if I did not share with you that at this stage, in remembrance of your original estate, you will perceive your entire spiritual body. The infinitude and expanse of who you really are will be in front of you. The experience is accompanied by a powerful desire to let go of the imprisonment of the physical vessel and merge back to the vastness that composes your spiritual body. Some may leave the body, for the pull to go back is intoxicating. In my case, I was reminded that I was not done with the work I came to earth to accomplish, and I reconnected to the earth grid. Let me just say here that the profound peace and perception of the spiritual body did not happen all at once. Profound peace and serenity settled in first and were in place for several months before I experienced the expanse of my spiritual body.

Sharing Your Peace and Love

Everything is now changed. It is not that life challenges disappear, but they don't affect you the same way. You see them for what they are: opportunities to grow and expand in consciousness. Moreover, the peace and serenity with which you handle everything are now blessings that you want to share with others. In fact with their permission, you can banish their pain and suffering. It is hard to write about this or explain it. It is done simply by an act of great care and compassion, a wish, and a desire to pass your light, peace, and serenity to another. It is not complicated. It is as simple as blinking your eyes. This comes from a complete understanding that everyone outside of you is a disempowered aspect of you. At this stage, this is not just intellectual mumbo jumbo; it is as real and solid as the ground on which you are standing. It is something you know through and through. You just know this in your core. I am reminded of the words of the Oracle, in the first *Matrix* movie, talking to Neo about being the One: "Being the One is like falling in love. You either are in love or you are not. You have the gift, but it looks like you are waiting for something."

Let us be clear that this is not the elimination of karma. You drop these individuals into the neutral field, and you let go and allow light of neutrality do the rest. You simply help them get into a neutral state where zero point energy brings them the scalar invert of their conflict so they can accelerate its resolution. How quickly the solution set gets assimilated is not up to you. It is not your burden to do or fix anything. Some may experience immediate, miraculous, and permanent transformation. Others will experience reprieve and amelioration. Everyone walks away changed in some significant way by this act of compassion.

With this expanded understanding, your heart space opens up to incorporate everyone in your circle of influence and humanity at large. At that moment, you begin to sense merger and unity consciousness to all life forms. You become vastly understanding and tolerant of the shortcomings of others. You are compassionate for the pain and suffering of others. You desire to share your peace and serenity, not just by removing the problems for them, but by teaching them how to do it for themselves. "Don't just give them fish, but teach them how to fish."

The Evolution of Wisdom

With this open and compassionate heart comes a deeper and penetrating understanding of human suffering. The more you truly care for someone the greater your empathy and ability to know and understand their pain and suffering, and the reasons for their stumbling blocks. Expanded knowledge is attached to this stage of ascension. You are now privy to penetrating insight into the lives, psychology, and emotional wellbeing of those who are in your care. Moreover, your insight is information to which they are blinded. What you do with that understanding and knowledge will determine the path of your further evolution.

Knowledge is not power. It is responsibility. The more you know about the people in your care the more gingerly you must act. You cannot reveal this penetrating understanding and knowledge to them, for you may damage them in a profound way if the information is brought to them too soon. If you have the psychic knowledge that someone may have been victimized in the past, just because you perceive it is not a reason to reveal it. If they are blocking the information, your disclosure of it is a careless and unethical act. There are reasons why their psyche is blocking the information. The maturity and sophistication that are needed to process the issue has not coalesced yet. In time, this will happen and till that moment you can only present to them information that matches their current frequency level and assimilation. Even if they ask you to reveal the whole truth to them, you are not to tell them if you realize they are not ready to hear the entire truth. Do not keep silent, but reveal a version of the truth that they are capable of processing. Ask yourself if this revelation is in their best interests, and if the answer is no, present a version of the truth that they can understand. Master Jesus did this many times with his parables to the young children.

The Ascended Masters of the Spiritual Hierarchy with their expanded knowledge and understanding will reveal to us only what we need to know so that we can evolve and mature according to our own timing. They will give us the "bread crumbs" that we need to find our own way. Revealing too much may cheat us out of our opportunity to grow. I have crossed that barrier before with the Spiritual Hierarchy when it appeared that they were silent on a topic about which I was inquiring. When I pushed further for an answer, their response was: "This is on a need to know basis, and right now, you don't need to know." It is very humbling. I know that they are not withholding information from me. They are simply concerned that I don't have the maturity level yet to understand the answer to my inquiry. They are in fact trying to protect me from hurting myself and causing a fracture of my psyche. If you keep asking the Ascended for an answer and you are not receiving a response, it is simply that you are not psychologically prepared to know the answer.

With the people in your spiritual care, timing is everything. You eventually evolve a sense of when say what you need to say. It is not your timing, but their timing that rules.

Ascension and the Necessity for Group Work

Ascension always involves a natural evolution into planetary world-service work. The time to go to the mountaintop—meditating, ascending, and leaving the planet—has past. The seeker, initiate, and Ascended need to spiritualize the planet. No one can ascend in a vacuum. Besides, the solitary path only gets you across the threshold. It will not lead you into the Promised Land. Ascension is only the beginning. Past ascension, it is your responsibility to share, teach, mentor, broadcast, organize, and do the group work that is needed to manifest the ascended living here on earth. The ultimate goal is to co-create heaven on earth. Indeed, this is the "work" to which all traditions have cryptically referred.

In Chapter One, I described the various paths that the newly ascended can follow beyond ascension. Depending on our penchant, authentic core frequency, and pre-life agreement, the choice will be clear. Yet all these paths involve group work. We are all connected to each other by past collective efforts, filial and energetic obligations, and by agreements. As we ascend, we begin to blaze a path that the individuals in our circle of influence can see and follow—if and when they are ready. Ascension leads you naturally into a planetary leader.

Think of a giant jigsaw puzzle where each piece plays a unique but key role. No two pieces are alike, and each plays a critical and vital role in the creation of the whole picture. Some pieces are directly connected to your piece while others are further away, and still some are in the outer perimeter. If you look at the pile of disconnected pieces individually, you cannot see the overall image. In fact, the average onlooker will only see a multitude of forms, shapes, and fragmented images that make no sense at all. Moreover, no other piece in the pile can recognize its connection to its neighbors. In this state, it would take a long time for the original image to be reconstructed.

Now, imagine for a moment that there was a process by which a piece of the puzzle could become aware of its own image, role, position, and purpose, a way by which a piece could see where it belongs. With that awareness, this piece could seek and attract adjacent and fitting neighbors, thus allowing an accelerated re-creation of the picture.

This giant jigsaw puzzle contains the fragmented pieces of the original Receiver. They are members of humanity, and you are called to ascend so that you will know where you belong in the greater scheme. When you ascend, an added dimension comes in. You see and know your puzzle piece. It is like you were in a flat land and you suddenly evolved into 3-D perception. You now understand what role you need to play to attract and magnetize your neighboring pieces or members of your circle of influence. Each piece must have the same understanding that you now have. Everyone must stand shoulder to shoulder. You now need to do what is necessary to help awaken the members of your circle of influence from their slumber.

The Challenge

This is easier said than done. As aspects of the Receiver, we have to give and receive from each other in a balanced manner. By karma and prior agreements, we are connected to family members, friends, communities, institutions, nations, and various égrégore or group bodies to which we have to reconcile and become neutral. The issue is that, due to the glamour of the powerful negative ego and the emotional and psychic cords of karma, the Universe will present us multiple opportunities to restore balance and harmony. Individuals and situations will be re-created lifetime after lifetime, with all participants playing different roles. In one lifetime, you are the victim and in another you are the perpetrator.

It is sad to say that for most on the planet, these opportunities are not epiphanies or lightbulb moments. They simply repeat the past. The perception of fear, threat, and fragmentation is a powerful and persuasive illusion. Added to this is the group body component, where most members of the group want to be accepted and not make waves. They will go along with the lowest common denominator. But in order for us to balance the wheel of karma and remove the bread of shame, we have to first become neutral to the individual to whom we are connected. Second, we have to initiate a change within the group body by opposing and challenging the majority in our small way. Since the group body is the collective intent of every member, the internal opposition to the collective perception of fear has enormous consequences.

As an ascended being doing group work with individuals with whom you may have toxic cords, you will find these relationships challenging, though bearing a hidden reward if the lessons are learned. I have faced multiple moments in which I discovered that I had offended and hurt individuals in the past who were in my spiritual care. These relationships were difficult from the beginning, and after this revelation, I approached the individuals and made full disclosure. I asked them for forgiveness for my offenses, explained the past roles, and invited them to bury the hatchets for the greater good and the evolution of the work. In some instances, this was all that was needed to repair and mend the relationship. In others, I became neutral to the toxic cord while the other parties continued to re-live the past with displays of poisonous and destructive behaviors.

In such a case, you have to let them go and walk away, for they are too mired in revenge and retaliation. Their proximity to you will sabotage the work that you are trying to accomplish. They are not ready for conflict resolution and the acceptance of a higher and harmonious relationship. It may take them another lifetime to get there, and in the meantime, you have a purpose to fulfill. Keep moving forward to the best of your ability.

In the chapter on neutrality, I described how every perception of a threat creates an energy cord or tunnel in our torsion field, which connects us to the subject of our fear. This initiates an energy dynamic that transcends time and space. These cords survive death and will haunt us in future lives. We are bound to these individuals, institutions, and communities, and we will reincarnate around them until the energy dynamic becomes neutral. We need to remove the fear, anger, victimization, acrimony, attack, and battling and replace them with forgiveness and love.

Our consciousness is not in our brain. It exists around us in a morphogenic or torsion field, which is a magnetic projection all around us. It is in this field that perceptions of past threats create false identities and axes. Our authentic core is typically a vertical frequency and energy column. Every perception of threat splinters a filament from this core axis and places it in a diagonal or horizontal relationship to your center. Given the multiple lifetimes and all the contentious relationships we have held in the past, our torsion field looks like a porcupine with filament after filament draining resources from your core and central axis. These filaments are locked into an energy dynamic of battle with the subject of the perceived threat, lifetime after lifetime, until we achieve neutrality. At this point, the horizontal filament goes back to becoming vertical.

Let me also state that we do not just have negative energy cords with others. There exist positive ones, although the geometry of the relationship is different. When we are in resonance with our core and allow unconditional love, unity consciousness, and merging, we amplify the torsion field. Since the torus is the geometry that creates everything in the Universe, we join together with other separated fragments, the central axis of one joined to the edge of a neighboring torsion field. Our consciousness fluctuates between the porcupine fear base and the locked torus-to-torus geometries, depending on where our consciousness is.

As you become more and more neutral to the diagonal and horizontal false axes of fear, you strengthen the energy, light, and illumination of your core. This in turn will give you the power that is needed to be true to the broadcast of your core and authentic nature. This will then cause you to spend more and more time in the locked torus-to-torus geometry, accelerating your ascension and bringing you into a state of effortlessness.

Deus Ex Machina

Deus ex machina in Latin means: "god from the machine," and it was a device used in Greek tragedies to solve impossible and convoluted plot situations by having a Greek God appear on stage and resolve the plot melee with a happy ending. It literally referred to the fact that the actor playing the god was lowered onto the stage by pulley or crane, thus a machine or machina. In some ways, the evolutionary path of our planet and its inhabitants is receiving outside help to solve the karmic enmeshment problem.

Although the experiment we call life and the descent of the Receiver into the 3-D density is allowed to progress within the framework of free will and the law of noninterference, it is not unchecked. Given the fact that our DNA strands were altered and manipulated by higher, but misguided fallen beings about half a billion years ago, the path of return back to Source has since been corralled by Galactic Beings who oversee the governance of the Milky Way Galaxy. At specific times, the Galactic governance checks on the evolutionary progress of our world. They are called the Galactic Regent Council, and they are a regency of 12 Galactic Elders who watch over the evolutionary path of the 200 billion solar systems that compose our Galaxy. If the evolutionary path is not in alignment with expectation, they orchestrate a correction by creating cosmic events that foster a leap forward. They cannot act directly, but they can externally influence, and with great effectiveness.

About every 31 million years, our planet and the solar system align with the Galactic center. The Mayan Elders predicted that such an event would happen in our lifetime. Although the precise moment of this event is not certain, the claim is that when the earth aligns directly with the "galactic magnetic equator," the planet will go through three days of darkness, for the sun will disappear. From a human point of view it will appear as a cataclysmic event, and many will die from fear, but on the third day, the sun will return. Since the Mayan Elders were so accurate about many astronomical details, we should pay attention to what they are saying.

As of a mid-2013, telescopes around the world are observing a rare astronomical event: we are receiving light and radiation from the Galactic core without any stellar body blocking the way. At the Galactic center is a massive black hole that is 4 million times the density of our sun. It is located in Sagittarius A. Since 2004, a giant plasma cloud has been feeding this black hole, causing the "inner horizon" or internal core of the black hole to eject deep-space radio waves and gamma and cosmic radiation in the general direction of our planet. It is a light show the likes of which scientists have not seen before. Be aware that gamma and cosmic waves cause DNA and genetic mutation. Additionally, radio waves at 150-megahertz frequencies cause the human brain to produce DMT (dimethyltryptamine), a psychotropic chemical called "the spirit molecule" by Rick Strassman, which induces an involuntary altered state of awareness.

It is not just the Galactic Core effects with which we have to contend. Closer to us, our sun has been extremely active in this solar cycle, releasing flurries of solar flares and magnetic storms, which are colliding with the earth's own magnetic field, causing it to shake, vibrate, and deform. To put this in perspective, in 2009 there were 269 days without solar flares. Since 2012, there have been solar flares every day. Not all solar flares are earth directed, but the ones that are, are responsible for the Magnetic North of the planet to move toward the equator. In 2012 the rate of motion was 40 miles per year. In the first six months of 2013, it has moved 261 miles toward Siberia. These movements in the earth's magnetic axis are causing rotations and adjustments in the earth's iron core, moving the tectonic plate and generating earthquakes. Furthermore, the planet is full of powerful subtle energies—such as telluric energy, ley lines, magnetic and electrical currents all of which are moving—causing instability and disturbances in the fabric of the ether and atmosphere and creating storms and strange weather phenomena.

This is not just a random act from a stellar body, rather it is an orchestrated means to dismantle the collective false belief of lack and fear that 7 billion people are holding in place. The égrégore and group body of the planet is projected and held in place in the magnetosphere of the earth. The sun is destroying these false beliefs and axes. There is great intelligence, care, and benevolence in these emissions from the sun no matter what circumstantial evidence may prove. The sun is not trying to destroy the earth. It has been the source of life for several billion years and will continue to be the source of life and energy for us now on a higher octave. The current 3-D paradigm of lack and fear is being replaced by a grid of truth, authenticity, and transparency. Therefore all that is hidden on earth right now will be revealed.

These solar magnetic storms are not just affecting the planet. As it happens, like the earth, we are electromagnetic by nature, and these bombardments have a direct effect on our physiology and evolutionary trajectory. Our brain is populated by magnetite. These magnetic particles are highly sensitive to the magnetic radiation coming from the sun. The following symptoms have been reported by lightworkers during solar flare activities: migraine headaches, sleep pattern disruptions, loss of balance, nausea, panic attacks, heart beat irregularities, sensations of an external buzzing, sensations that something is moving or crawling on your skin, hallucinations, and even temporary blindness.

When the brain senses such disturbance and imbalance, the pineal gland begins to produce DMT (dimethyltryptamine). Please note that this is not a voluntary intake of DMT. Humanity is completely unaware of this, and suddenly it finds itself fully immersed in a psychotropic experience. The result is often registered as fear and panic.

Our personal fears, false beliefs, and identities are also being destroyed. To help accelerate the process, do the following meditation:

> *Close your eyes and take a deep breath. Allow the Universal life force that permeates everything to enter into your lungs. Keep breathing deeply and slowly. Now, let your awareness and head drop into the middle of your chest. Ask Galactic Master Vywamus to give you sight with the Universal Light. Notice what you notice. Become aware of all false beliefs and identities that you may be holding in your core and outside of your body. Keep breathing deeply and slowly. Ask the sun and the solar flares to blend with you and dismantle all false axes, beliefs, and identities that you*

are holding. Take a deep breath and allow the sun to do its work. Just surrender, allow, and let go.

Studies done with participants voluntarily taking DMT have reported a disconnection to the 3-D reality, a travel through a spatial kaleidoscope, entrance into blinding light, and a conversation with Higher Beings or God about the meaning of life. What if the Galactic core releases and the solar storms were the preparation for a mass planetary DMT experience? This would be a means by which the Galactic Regent Council could reach all of humanity, push the delete button on the 3-D personal agenda, and create a collective remembrance of its authentic nature. Moreover, gamma and cosmic rays are capable of causing genetic mutation, altering our DNA. It is possible that we could be upgraded from the outside. Is this the end of time as we know it, as predicted by the Mayan elders?

But not all DMT experiences are blissful. Many who participated in aya-huasca ceremonies can attest to this. DMT, the active ingredient in aya-huasca, has caused many to experience their worst fears. If such an event is in our future, many will not find this pleasant. Imagine for a moment that you are going about your daily activities and, without warning, you enter into a DMT experience without initiating anything. Most would be in panic or fear, or think that they are going insane.

Understand that when the forces of nature are acting they are impersonal. They have an intelligence that is heart centered and nonlinear. Therefore they exist in a torsion field, and if you are in fear and in dissonance to that geometry, they cannot see or communicate with you. These forces have a purpose and a role to play, and they will do that without taking into consideration a population that is invisible to them.

The majority of the planet's population is experiencing fear. The fear geometry is not something to which the sun's magnetic radiation and the Galactic core emissions are attuned. These forces will initiate the changes that are needed, impersonally, without taking into consideration the people factor.

But this issue was also foreseen, and a collective of volunteers have agreed to be the transformers that will maintain an open line of communication between our 3-D world, its inhabitants, and the higher dimensional realities to come. They are the eyes through which the Galactic Masters can perceive humanity. Without these volunteers, beacons, and wayshowers, this transition would be a difficult and rough passage. They play a critical role in the grounding of the future earth.

The Volunteers

If we have to wait for every human to ascend before ascended living can be made manifest on earth, we will have to wait a long time. A cursory look at human existence will prove that the majority of the planet is far from ready to do the work necessary for this to happen. For 7 billion people to get to this Promised Land, a different plan was initiated by the Galactic Masters. They realized around 1945 after the detonation of the first nuclear bomb in Hiroshima that humanity was so mired in vengeance, rancor, and retaliation that even if the Ascended were to forewarn them, they would not stop. Furthermore, humanity was so blinded by the bonds of karma and the reciprocal dynamics that polarity creates that they could not see the forest for the trees. Because of the law of noninterference, The Galactic Masters cannot interfere in human affairs from their elevated state.

A plan was devised. They asked for Galactic, starseed, and Angelic volunteers to descend the dimensional scale, incarnate as human, and go on a group rescue mission. A collective of 144,000-plus beings began to incarnate as human at specific geographical locations on earth. At a pre-appointed time, they will begin to ascend and become columns of light or gateways through which the rest of humanity would follow. The idea was that this collective would become the critical mass to initiate the 100th monkey effect, thus allowing the rest of humanity to ascend by osmosis. These beings are on their first, second, or third incarnation on earth. This gives them a great advantage over the rest of humanity, for they are not enmeshed into the webs and complicated energetic dynamics that karma and negative ego create.

They are descending by choice, and in the process, they shed and fragment their powers, abilities, and knowledge of who and what they are. No matter what dimension they are coming from to get to the 3-D density, they fragment into multiples of 12 at every step of the descent. For example, if they are originally from 5-D, they will fragment into 12 to descend into 4-D. Each of the 12 fragments will again break into an additional 12 pieces to get to 3-D, giving a total of 144 pieces. Understand that in the process of descending and planning for this mission, they hide their powers and aspects of themselves into objects, trees, people who agree to be surrogates, and locations around the earth. They cannot descend and physically manifest or embody their full powers for this would make them stand out before they are ready.

As humans, they are subject to the same frailties as the rest of us. They have negative egos that need to be tamed, but they have fewer distractions, negative energy cords, and karmic reconciliations to forge that would otherwise keep the average human busy for many lifetimes. Given the right environment and support, these beings will ascend faster than the rest of humanity and will blaze paths, doorways, and gates for others to follow. They will remember quickly the promises and oaths taken and will begin to retrieve the fragments of themselves that they shed on their descent to earth.

These starseed souls may have forgotten a lot about their former selves, but they are born with an inner knowing. Something that they cannot describe or communicate to others: that they are here to save the world. This is not some foolish messianic complex, but an inner understanding and drive that they are here for a noble and important purpose. They are blind to what that looks like and how to accomplish it, but the knowing is clear. For these reasons, they will have a difficult time relating to the rest of humanity. They are not motivated by the needs and desires that polarize the rest of the world. They tend to be loners and have a hard time understanding and assimilating the reasons behind cruelty, abuse, personal gain, and need for conquest that the rest of the planet shares. Fears and perceptions of threats are foreign to them.

Imagine that one moment you are an 8-D dimensional being and next you are on earth watching man's inhumanity to its own kind and the hording of the planet's precious resources for personal gain. No matter how much you prepare for the descent, the actuality of 3-D is a shock to the system. Many become so depressed that they become suicidal. They want to exit this place for they feel that they do not belong here. Looking at a cross section of humanity, you can easily spot them for they often look lost. They look puzzled, like they are trying to figure out humanity. The only thing holding them to this grid is the promise made long ago to help rescue his world.

At pre-appointed times, they will be attracted to certain objects, locations, and people in which aspects of themselves are held. The retrieval process of the fragmented pieces requires care. They have to be careful not to bring back to their energy bodies any pieces that have not been cleansed and purified. From the time of the placement of the fragmented pieces until their retrieval, there may have been contamination. Placing the fragments back into the energy bodies of the starseeds without purification would cause them to become ill. They would then need to cleanse the toxicity out of their systems. The more pieces and aspects of themselves that they retrieve, the more memories and understanding will return, revealing who they are and why they are here.

Once embarked on their ascension process, they will rise quickly. They still have negative ego with which to contend, but they will know what to do. If they follow what I have described in this volume, they will remember who they are in record time. They must first rescue self and then attempt to save the world.

The Rescue Plan

Our beautiful world, planet earth, is alive. It has a form of intelligence and consciousness that is unlike us. It is an inclusionary intelligence that interconnects every eco system and every life form on the planet, combining them into a giant collective awareness called Gaia. Like all living things, Gaia has an energy body, and that body has special points, centers, or chakras. The earth has 156 chakra locations, and Robert Coon in his book *Earth Chakras* describes them in copious details. Each earth chakra radiates a specific frequency that adds value to the general theme of the current age and planetary evolutionary path. Let us be clear, this is not humanity's evolutionary path, but that of Gaia, the collective awareness to which humanity belongs.

At the start of every age or eon, which is a period of about 2,000 years, the theme for evolution of the planet shifts and evolves. Through a sequential order, the broadcast and radiation emanating from each earth chakra is reset to reflect the new theme for the upcoming age. Planetary chakras have a broadcast range that is about 777 miles wide.

The commitment, promise, and oath taken by all starseeds on their descent are not made to the people of the earth. They are made to Gaia. This is an important detail, for it obligates the rescuers to a higher calling, suitably guiding their actions and behaviors. They are not doing this for humanity's sake, but for the salvation of the entire planet. Although humanity stands to benefit the most, the mission is about the totality of the planet. Humanity is just one life form living on earth, but equally important are millions of other species residing on her. All starseeds have to assimilate this truth and the grounding and commitment to the specific earth chakra locations in which they are posted.

The Galactic Regent Council and the magnetic radiation coming from the sun cannot see beings that are not in the torsion field geometry. Therefore, when they push the reset button of the evolution of the planet, humanity has to be visible to them. They cannot protect or include what they cannot see. Every life form on the planet exists in a torsion field except for mankind. If these forces cannot communicate or see us, they may harm us without meaning to. Many erroneously think of saving the planet by adopting a sustainable lifestyle. Gaia and all other species will live. It is humanity that needs to be concerned about survival.

The reason for this blindness is that humanity is disconnected most of the time from the Universal geometry in which every sentient life form and particle exists: the torsion field. It is the basic geometry that makes everything: atoms, molecules, planets, suns, galaxies, superclusters of galaxies, black holes, and the Universe. Although it is the default setting that humanity experiences at death, during lovemaking, and while meditating, the rest of the human experience is lived outside this geometry. When human consciousness perceives a threat from the outside and moves into fear, that geometry breaks down. The collective 3-D grid that 7 billion people are sharing and that is encoded in the magnetosphere of the planet is made up of lack and fear. For the most part, humanity is in dissonance to this geometry and therefore is not visible to the natural and spiritual forces.

It stands to reason that the starseed volunteers would incarnate as humans so that they might become the bridges and connections that would allow the powerful natural and spiritual forces to perceive and help shepherd humanity. Without them and their sacrifice, our species would not survive the shift. So it is up to these starseed volunteers to keep informing the solar storms, gamma ray emissions, flood waters, hurricanes, tornados, and wild fires about the individuals who happen to live in the 777-mile radius of the chakra location in which the starseeds happen to be posted. They are the 2-way transformers that will help humanity survive the changes that are upon us.

It is necessary for us to talk about the way this is done. I have seen many groups of lightworker forums attempting planetary group healing work concerning the recent hurricanes or natural disasters. They were all trying to stop the hurricanes or natural disasters. The arrogance of this position is beyond words. These forces are sentient and serve a very specific and often elevated purpose to which the lightworkers are blinded. No one can go against them. It is the wrong approach. Instead, follow this protocol:

> Go into your heart space and create your torsion field. Ask the natural force (hurricane, etc.) for permission to blend and communicate. If there is no response, you may have to repeat this step a few times until you get an answer. You may sense or hear "yes" or feel a let-go or release. Once you have permission, drop your heart into the center of the phenomenon and communicate information about the people factor to the intelligence or force of nature. Just

ask it to consider that there are many individuals in its path. Say
thank you for this opportunity to blend and let go.

During the communication, you may have visions or precognitive perceptions of what is going to happen. In some instances, you may have to do
nothing. In others, you and the people in your care may have to move out
of the way.

As the starseeds and lightworkers ascend, they are becoming beacons of
light that will entrain everyone in their circle of influence into the higher
frequencies. As their DNA is restored, they are broadcasting the regen-
eration codes and path of return to everyone with whom they transact,
something that is not normally accessible to humanity. I have recently
realized that my purpose is not to be famous, find love, make money, or be
adored. All I came here to do is to be a conscious tunnel of light that allows
an ascent and descent of information between the core of the planet and
Source. This is my job. When I wake up, I key in that awareness, and if I
have spent most of my day in that consciousness, I have had a great day
at work.

Suppose that at your earth chakra location 12 or more starseeds stand up
and hold that same awareness. A sizable tunnel of light would be bored
into the heavens from that location. When 12 or more stand holding one
intention, an exponential gate or doorway will be opened and all beings
and species of that geographical location will find sanctuary. Here is what
Lord Melchizedek had said about this in January of 2011:

> *It is indeed with joy and happiness that I take this opportunity*
> *to welcome and support you in this ascension effort. You are re-*
> *sponding to the call of Spirit, and you are fulfilling promises that*
> *you made long ago. It is in a group ascension effort that the salva-*
> *tion of the earth is assured. One individual ascending will not be*
> *able to transform this planet to the next dimension, but where 12*
> *stand, a decisive difference can be made. You are called to create*
> *a gateway, doorway, or bridge allowing others to follow. Under-*
> *stand that you are architects and engineers fabricating a vertical*
> *tunnel toward the heavens. You are to become the armature and*
> *structure that will hold this piece of architecture toward heaven.*
> *In collectively refining your consciousness and re-programming*
> *your negative ego, you are creating a doorway, opening, and gate*
> *through which others will follow. The entire heavenly hierarchy is*
> *supporting this effort, for this gateway is to connect to a similar*
> *structure at the ascended planetary level, which then connects to*

a part of this system at a solar level, and this in turns connects to a similar structure at a galactic level and so on all the way back to Source. You are creating a means by which all life forms in your geographical area will find a sizable pathway where light can ascend to and descend from heaven and bless everyone in your earth chakra location.

We are here to support you. We are here to guide you, and I and the entire hierarchy want to make sure that this work happens in the simplest and easiest manner, with love and peace. We say unto you, sparks of Divinity: we are proud to watch our own essences and aspects of ourselves generating a motion back to the beginning. This is as it should be and is very encouraging to us. The vortex and ascension column that you are creating will be so big that it will be a means by which many others will connect heaven and earth. You are not ascending for yourselves. You are ascending so that the planet will move into the Light, Love, and Peace of the Divine. This work cannot be done by one individual. It is to be done by a team that will assemble at every earth chakra location. There need to stand a minimum of 12 at these locations to become the main beams, armature, and structure that will create this network and open the gates of heaven.

In conclusion, we bless you and say unto you that this is nothing more than the first wave. There will be additional waves coming through the chariot-pathway and trail that you will leave behind.

I am Lord Melchizedek, the soul that animates this Universe. Blessings, my children. And may the Love of the Divine be always with you. And thank you for this opportunity to share.

Having rescued a geographical area, creating a 777-mile-wide safety zone and ascended bubble, a higher dimension will be grounded. Now suppose that another group of 12 or more starseeds will have done the same at the earth chakra north of your location. A second higher-dimensional safety zone of 777 miles wide will come into manifestation, and the two safety zones will interlock from each central axis to the neighbor's perimeter field. In succession, the same will occur at the earth chakra locations to the south, east, and west, all interlocking their central axes to the neighboring perimeter fields. When all 156 chakra locations around the planet have volunteers standing up and embodying the purposes of their descent to this blue planet, the entire earth will become the living flower of life, as 156 tunnels of Light allow open communication of the earth with Source.

At this instant, the prana seed of the earth will be reset and will explode out in a spiritual detonation, causing the bio-regenesis of all life forms on earth to be initiated. The golden age will be here.

Marching toward the Future Earth

For this ascended future to happen, we have to plan and create a better, sustainable, intentional, and ideal living environment now. The future earth will not drop into our laps just by doing lightwork and broadcasting it. The lightwork is important, but equally important are the concrete steps and daily acts taken by illumined consciousness leading to this golden future. It is about organizing and taking actions today so that we can walk into this future.

So while we are working on our ascension, we should be involved in socially minded, progressive, and sustainable groups, projects, and communities. We have to demonstrate on earth the mastery of our illumined consciousness. In fact, no one can really ascend without doing group work. Our higher and expanded awareness must be demonstrated in the 3-D density for true mastery to occur, and for that to happen, we have to play well with others. No one can ascend by going to the mountaintop away from the world in the hope of reaching nirvana. That time has passed. We must now bring heaven to earth. We have to spiritualize the planet.

In the fall of 2007, while doing a spiritual practice in the Catskills Mountains of New York, I received a vision from Gaia about an ascended community. This was a significant download that activated me, transformed my consciousness, and made me understand that this was one of my puzzle pieces: the creation of a place of healing and dwelling, where 350 families live in a village based on the spiritual principles I have described in the previous chapters; a template that will show that this ascended blueprint is achievable; and an open source effort that can be repeated anywhere on the planet.

I and a small group of founding collaborators are moving to create such a place, called Gaiaville®. This is not only a green, sustainable, and zero carbon-footprint community, but it is a place where the wellness and health care system is integrative, bringing together modern medicine and herbal, naturopathic, and energy medicine for the accelerated and preventive healing of all. In addition, it embraces an educational system that teaches not only core subjects, but also the principles of interdependence, the expansion of human consciousness, and respect for all life forms. Also included is a green and sustainable farming and food production system. And finally, a commerce and economic system based on the principle of equal exchange by giving and receiving in a balanced manner. (For more information, visit **www.gaiaville.org**.)

Ideal communities have been attempted before and the measure of their successes and failures are directly connected to the people factor. If the members of the community are not working on their negative ego and the expansion of their awareness, the community will eventually unravel.

Source, as the infinite potential for manifestation, can only become self realized through the descent of the Receiver. As fragmented aspects of the Receiver, the moment we begin our ascension, a cell in God's body is reflected back to Source. Cell by cell and individual by individual, God will eventually become self-realized. When this process is completed, the bread of shame will cease to be, and the physical Universe will deflate and be re-absorbed into Source, the field of endless potential. This describes the in- and out-breath of God.

Ascension is a natural, incremental, and evolutionary process. Every cell in God's body will eventually get there, fulfilling the promise of redemption for all. However, this may take an endless time frame to happen. Given the perilous state of man's evolution, the survival of our species now rests on a knife-edge. A proactive and accelerated ascension path must be followed.

To the best of my ability, I have shared with you how to accomplish this task. I cannot do it for you. I can only communicate the urgency and the importance of the work. Your motivation and the speed with which you respond are your responsibility. It is my hope that you will remember your oaths and stand up to fulfill your purpose. This is a collective rescue mission. If one person fails, the rescue is in jeopardy. The entire collective of volunteers must awaken to this awareness and act as one body. You need to factor this into your final decision. I pray that all the volunteers will hear my call.

Epilogue

Dear Seeker, I have so far shared with you enough information to initiate a forward motion toward your ascension. The topics discussed above are not the only issues with which you will have to contend. However, the mastery of the previous information will give you sufficient knowledge and ease to traverse the unmentioned territories with grace. The skeletal framework to achieve a safe and accelerated ascension is within these pages. It is my hope that you will put in the time and effort that are needed to attain mastery. The fulfillment of your destiny is in the balance; keep focusing on the end goal and everything else will fall into place.

The task is in front of you, and you have been blessed with the mechanism with which to accomplish it. I cannot do it for you. God, Spirit, the Angels, and the Masters cannot ascend for you. This is your responsibility. Start by rescuing self, and the means to save our world will come to you. As the saying goes: "Jump and the net will appear." You signed up for this. Fulfill your Divine purpose.

The path toward illumination is a solo act, but it is not a lonely road. Along the way, you will meet many other travelers who are seeking the same goal. For a while, you can travel together and focus your common interests and desires toward a greater good and even planetary ascendance. Many on the path find this extremely beneficial. In fact, the rescue of our "blue world" hinges on this type of group work.

On a weekly basis, I hold ascension classes to support the continual evolutionary process and group interactions that are necessary for planetary ascension to become a reality. Where two or more are gathered together, a force greater than the sum of the parts is created. If you feel inclined to join us and add your light to ours, you can go to **www.iammonad.com** for more details.

It is my hope that you will remember your oath and fulfill your purpose. This remembrance is key, for the moment it happened for me, it changed the direction of my life and moved me rapidly toward ascension. I have great hope for you as well.

Pierre Richard Dubois

Glossary of Terms

Angels: They are choirs of the Angelic race that are further down the line in the chain of manifestation of the Will of God. They are below the Archangels and in the construction analogy are the sub-contractors that work on the creation of God's plan. They have specific areas of expertise.

Archangels: They are mighty generals in God's army who respond to the feeling energies of God. They each have specific talents, expertise, and roles that they play in manifesting God's Kingdom. To continue the construction analogy, they are the general contractors who take the blueprints made by the Elohim and initiate manifestation.

Ascended Masters: They are beings who have evolved to the next step in the evolutionary ladder. They are no longer obligated to return to the earthly plane, since they have balanced their karma. They can choose to remain behind to help the rest of humanity or continue up the evolutionary scale.

Atmic Body: It is a higher and subtle body that connects you to the essence of undifferentiated awareness. There is no individual or group Identification, but there is a connection with the essence of life itself. It gives you clear mindedness, uncanny focus, and extreme and profound peace.

Bird People: They are an extra-terrestrial race of sentient bird-shaped beings who are one of the many species created originally in the Lyra constellation of space. They have since migrated to other quadrants in our Universe.

Buddhic Body: It is a higher and subtle body that eliminates separation and allows one to experience the gradual overlap of the individual consciousness with that of others. This will continue until complete merger is experienced.

Djwhal Khul: He is a member of the Spiritual Hierarchy who ascended from Tibet around 1900. He works closely in the Second Ray with Master Kuthumi. He leads the Synthesis Ashram and is one of the most accessible Ascended Masters.

Dracos: They are an extra-terrestrial race of dragon-like beings with wings who populate the Draco constellation of space. Although originally created in an ascended form with an abundance of First Ray energy of Will and Power, many have manifested the lower aspect of this energy, seeking control, domination, power, and the imposition of their will on others. To date, the latter are the biggest bullies in our Universe.

Dr. Lorphan and the Twelve Galactic Healers: Around the Star of Sirius B exists a great Galactic School. Dr. Lorphan is a Master Healer and Teacher in that facility. He operates with 12 other Galactic Healers to restore harmony and balance to all of our bodies.

El Morya: He is an Ascended Master and member of the Spiritual Hierarchy. He is the lens through which humanity experiences the First Ray of Will and Power. This energy embodies singleness of purpose, dynamic power, leadership ability, and the gift to lead self and others. He is a strict and disciplined teacher.

Elohim: They are a choir of mighty beings who respond to the Fiat Lux of the Lord God to create worlds: "Let there be Light." They act to help manifest the thoughts of God. They are often referred to as "the creator gods." It is through them that all manifestation happens. They are the blueprint makers similar to architects and engineers. They create patterns for manifestation.

Extraterrestrial: Considering that the Milky Way Galaxy contains more than one trillion planets and that our universe has more than 100 billion galaxies, there is a high probability that other inhabited planets exist in our universe. All life-forms that are not from earth—whether organic, inorganic, energetic, or dimensional—are extraterrestrial by nature. Therefore, extra-terrestrial means life-forms that are not from earth.

Galactic Mathematicians: They are a collective of Galactic Elders who are masters of time and space. Their purpose is to restore balance and harmony to everything in the Universe, from sub-atomic particles to planets, and emotional, psychological, and spiritual imbalances. They can restore harmony to all. They are precise and accurate.

Galactic Regent Council: This is a collective of 12 Galactic Elders that compose the spiritual governance of the Milky Way Galaxy. They oversee the evolution and growth of the 200 billion suns that make up our galaxy. Our sun and planet, which are located in the Great Bear constellation, are under the regency of Lord Melchior.

Glorified Body of Light: It is a higher and subtle body that connects you to your already-ascended self. Since there is no time or space, you can shift your awareness to connect with your ascended body and bring, although temporarily, the wisdom, love, and peace of ascended consciousness into physical reality.

God: It is the highest spiritual being, truth, or organizing force of which a man can conceive to explain the world around him. Since it is a manmade concept, it is limited to the level of evolution of the mind that created it. Therefore, God concepts are relative and are not absolute truth. They may not resemble or match the actuality of the governing principle that exists in the Universe.

Guardian Alliance of Light: They are a specialized collective of guardians and protectors created 500 million years ago at the beginning of the Angelic wars. They are composed of many races and species, including humanoid extra-terrestrials of great abilities and powers. Their mission is to protect and ensure that all species discover and fulfill their genetic plan of bio-regenesis. They want to insure that the return path to Source is accessible to all. They exist in neutrality.

Indigo Souls: This term was first coined by Kryon, channeled by Lee Carroll. It refers to a collective of souls who started incarnating on earth with a specific indigo color to their aura. They are warrior spirits who came to earth to help break down the existing stagnant paradigm.

Insectoids: They are an extra-terrestrial race of insect-shaped beings who are sentient. Although they have individual intent and personality, they interact and are motivated by a collective consciousness. They do what is best for the collective and not the individual.

Kuthumi: He is an Ascended Master and member of the Spiritual Hierarchy. He is the lens through which humanity experiences the Second Ray of Love and Wisdom. This energy embodies radiance, attraction, compassion, universal love, and the process of ascension. He is known in the Hierarchy as the Planetary Teacher.

Lightworker: This term generally refers to all human beings who are working for the enlightenment and evolution of the planet. More specifically, it refers to the beings who are energetically working on grounding Light and transformation in the world.

Lord Maitreya: A member of the Spiritual Hierarchy, Lord Maitreya is the Buddha of the future and has held the position of the "Office of the Christ" for the past 2,000 years. He overlit Master Jesus when He was incarnated on earth, fulfilling his mission as the Avatar of the Piscean Age.

Lord Melchizedek: The Melchizedek Order is one of the many collectives and orders that support and watch over the development and growth of Universes. The Melchizedek Order is concerned with the evolution and growth of consciousness. In our Universe, Lord Melchizedek is the soul and consciousness that animates everything that exists.

Mahatma: It is a term that means "great souls." This is a giant collective of beings composed of every life-form, human or not, that has ascended in our Universe. This collective exists at the foot of the Throne of Grace, and it is a blessing to know that we have access to the help that it provides.

Metatron: He is a Mighty Archangel who resides at the Throne of Grace. To the Archangelic race, Metatron is their Archangel. He is a powerful cosmic ally, who connects us to the highest realm of divine energy.

Monad: In the beginning, the Receiver was fragmented into a number of aspects, each called "Monad" or "one." As each Monad began to descend the dimensional scale, they further separated into 12 pieces, each called "Oversoul," like a hand with 12 fingers. At the next dimensional descent, each of these 12 Oversouls fragmented again into 12 "Soul Extensions." Thus each Monad has 144 Soul Extensions within it. In the three dimensional worlds, we are each a Soul Extension belonging to a specific Oversoul and Monad.

Pleiadians: They are extra-terrestrial inhabitants of the planets that rotate around the suns of the Pleiades.

Source: Outside of time and space, there exists an endless field of potential for manifestation. Source is the center of this field. It is a point from which everything emanates and to which everything converges. It is the "nothing" that created "everything." It is a form of existence that is unlike anything we know and is at the root of everything.

Spiritual Hierarchy: They are Ascended Masters who take various offices and positions in the planetary hierarchy or governance of the planet to help shine the Light of God to humankind. As the clear Light of God moves from Source, it diffracts into various rays or colors that become attributes or aspects of God's personality. These Masters are the conduits through which all these rays shine onto the planet.

Starseed Souls: This refers to a collective of souls who started to incarnate on earth around 1945. They are from the stars, from higher dimensional existence, and have very little experience on earth. They are not enmeshed by the obligations of planetary karma like the rest of humanity.

Vywamus: He is a galactic being formerly known as "Sanat Kumara," the Logos of planet earth. He has left that post since the Harmonic Convergence in 1987 to assume a position in the spiritual governance of the Milky Way Galaxy as a member of the Galactic Regent Council.

About the Author

PIERRE R. DUBOIS is a registered architect in the state of New York, with two advanced degrees from Columbia University and 25 years of experience, focusing primarily on nonprofit affordable housing. He owns a successful private architectural practice and held instrumental positions within the NYC Department of Housing Preservation & Development and the NYC Housing Partnership Development Corporation. In 2010, Pierre also founded Gaiaville®, the first sustainable intentional community of its kind, which seeks to teach humanity how to live in balance and harmony with all resources on planet earth.

Pierre's journey toward ascension started at the age of 11 and has been an essential component of his daily life ever since. He grew up on the Caribbean island of Haiti and was raised by a single, middle-class mother who instilled in him a great thirst for knowledge. He applied himself and excelled in the curriculum of the Platonic model of education common in Western countries but found that this knowledge often conflicted with the religious beliefs of the island's indigenous culture to which he was exposed. As a result, Pierre developed a keen talent to explain with science the "magic" of the spiritual and supernatural.

A gifted healer, spiritual teacher, and counselor, Pierre is also a certified life coach and hypnotist, regression therapist, channel, and a non-denominational ordained minister. He was initiated in the mystery schools and studied all world religions, belief systems, and spiritual movements. Throughout his extensive studies and worldwide travels, he discovered that no matter how we choose to express them, we all have the same desires: to find love, fulfill our purpose, leave a positive footprint behind, and ultimately experience merger back to God. From this realization was born his passion and dedication to teach about ascension.

Because of his genuine, non-judgmental observation of the human condition, Pierre has acquired a reputation as an insightful listener and counselor, and has successfully helped many on their journey of healing, expansion, and ascension. He deeply aspires to share with others the serenity, purposefulness, and peace of mind he has acquired and warn against all the pitfalls to avoid in order to accelerate one's ascension process. Since "one can only keep what one is willing to give away," he is willing to give his all so that others can accomplish their all.

For decades, he has opened the door of his own home in New York City to teach ascension classes weekly and frequently offers lectures and workshops throughout the country on topics such as "The Power of Forgiveness," "Claiming your Personal Power," "Psychic Self-Defense," "Remembering Past Lives," or "Searching for a Soul Mate." Although he specializes in healing the healers, his private sessions are for all truth seekers and are completely tailored to one's specific needs, from healing, clearing, and activation, to dream interpretation, and DNA reconstruction. With Pierre's support and guidance, there are very few blocks on one's journey toward self-realization that are left undiscovered.

To learn more about his programs, feel free to visit **www.iammonad.com** or contact Pierre directly at **pierre@iammonad.com**.